The
van Arteveldes
of Ghent

BOOKS BY DAVID NICHOLAS

Town and Countryside: Social, Economic and Political Tensions in Fourteenth-Century Flanders

The Domestic Life of a Medieval City: Women, Children, and the Family in Fourteenth-Century Ghent

The Metamorphosis of a Medieval City: Ghent in the Age of the Arteveldes, 1302–1390

The van Arteveldes of Ghent: The Varieties of Vendetta and the Hero in History

The
van Arteveldes
of Ghent

THE VARIETIES OF
VENDETTA AND THE HERO
IN HISTORY

David Nicholas

Cornell University Press
Ithaca, New York

Library of Congress Cataloging-in-Publication Data
Nicholas, David, 1939–
    The van Arteveldes of Ghent.

    Bibliography: p.
    Includes index.
    1. Ghent (Belgium)—History. 2. Van Artevelde family.
3. Artevelde, Jacob van, 1290?–1345. 4. Artevelde,
Philip van. I. Title.
DH811.G46N54 1988   949.3′1   88-3858
ISBN 0-8014-2149-7 (alk. paper)

Copyright © 1988 by Cornell University

First published 1988 by Cornell University Press.

Printed in the United States of America

The paper in this book is acid-free and meets the guidelines for permanence and durability of the Committee on Production Guidelines for Book Longevity of the Council on Library Resources.

Contents

Maps, Figures,
and Illustrations

Preface

The career of James van Artevelde, the captain of Ghent who led his city and indeed the entire county of Flanders into an English alliance at the beginning of the Hundred Years War, has inspired the imaginations of many historians but the critical faculties of few. He evidently came to power in 1338 as an ally of the powerful weavers. Although the dean of the weavers' guild was to engineer his assassination in 1345, the van Artevelde name was irrevocably associated with the revolutionary weaver party by 1382, when James's youngest son, Philip, for ten months assumed the captaincy that his father had occupied for seven years. So powerful was the impression made by the two captains that seventy years later, in 1451, as Ghent was about to undertake a futile war against the Burgundian count of Flanders, pamphlets were distributed near the town hall calling for "a new van Artevelde."

But James van Artevelde was not a hero to the substantial pro-French party among the wealthy upper orders of Ghent. Even as the commoners were evoking his name as a war cry in the fifteenth century, for one aristocrat to call another "van Artevelde" was an insult legally actionable in the courts. The great Belgian historian Henri Pirenne attributed the van Artevelde legend in large measure to the literary excellence and popularity of Jean Froissart's Chronicle, in which both van Arteveldes figure prominently, and realized that van Artevelde, far from being the resplendent hero favored by the Flemish popular press, was actually a wealthy broker whose career fell within the framework of the political traditions and economic interests of the narrow elite that had governed Ghent during the thirteenth century.[1]

The incident of 1451 highlights an extremely important aspect of the historiographical problem surrounding the van Artevelde family. Serious Belgian historians now seem inclined to minimize James van Artevelde's role in the great social and economic changes of the fourteenth century. The standard modern biography, that of the late Hans van Werveke, which has been followed closely by a more recent treatment in English by Patricia Carson, concentrated on van Artevelde's political career and particularly on his dealings with the Flemish count and Ghent's English allies. Van Werveke in particular seemed reluctant to venture into the treacherous domains of historical heroism.[2] James van Artevelde is scarcely mentioned in the second edition of the *Algemene Geschiedenis der Nederlanden* (General History of the Low Countries). But more popular writers, including some with historical training, have argued that his struggle on behalf of Ghent against the Francophile Flemish counts presaged the Flemish national struggle for equality with the Walloons in Belgium in the nineteenth and twentieth centuries. They have thus claimed both van Arteveldes, particularly James, as "democrats." Only in the nineteenth century did a perfervid Flemish nationalism manage to divorce James van Artevelde totally from the context of his time and enshrine his name in a mythical folk consciousness. His and his son's careers

---

1. Henri Pirenne, *Histoire de Belgique*, 3d ed., vol. 2 (Brussels, 1922), particularly pp. 111–13.
2. Hans van Werveke, *Jacques van Artevelde* (Brussels, 1942); Dutch translation *Jacob van Artevelde* (The Hague, 1963); Patricia Carson, *James van Artevelde: The Man from Ghent* (Ghent, 1980).

became episodes, albeit crucial and colorful episodes, in the medieval proletariat's quest for the holy grail of democracy.[3] "Democracy" to an English or American mind suggests an attitude on behalf of the "working classes" toward society's rulers. Neither James nor Philip van Artevelde was ever a democrat in that sense. American writers unfamiliar with scholarly literature in Flemish have tended uncritically to combine Pirenne's thesis of class struggle in the Flemish cities during the fourteenth century with the Flemish nationalists' claim that the van Arteveldes were democrats, thus perpetuating a grossly ahistorical legend. Yet even some Marxists outside Belgium seem uncomfortable assigning the role of social revolutionary to the aristocratic James van Artevelde, for many of his actions suggest less a desire to end the power of the city patriciate as a group than a cynical use of mass hysteria to end the lives of certain patricians.[4] A judicious modern treatment calls James van Artevelde "the opposite of a people's man, . . . although raised to power by an insurrection."[5]

In view of the immensity of the literature, any new study of James van Artevelde requires justification. This book had its

3. The historical literature on the van Arteveldes is immense, and much of it is pure fantasy. In addition to van Werveke and Carson, see D. Nicholas, *Town and Countryside: Social, Economic, and Political Tensions in Fourteenth-Century Flanders* (Bruges, 1971), 173–202. Of crucial importance is Henry S. Lucas, *The Low Countries and the Hundred Years War, 1326–1347* (Ann Arbor, Mich., 1929). For the van Artevelde legend, see J. Vermeulen, "De groei en de bloei van de Arteveldefiguur in de Vlaamsche volksziel," *Oostvlaamsche Zanten* 13 (1938): 101–208. For James van Artevelde the democrat and Flemish nationalist, see Paul Rogghé, *Vlaanderen en het zevenjarig beleid van Jacob van Artevelde,* 2 vols., 2d ed. (Eeklo, 1963); and Rogghé's articles, notably: "De Democraat Jacob van Artevelde," *Appeltjes van het Meetjesland* 14 (1963): 56–68; "Gemeente ende Vrient: Nationale Omwentelingen in de XIVe eeuw," *Annales de la Société d'Emulation de Bruges* 89 (1952): 101–35; and "Het Gentsche Stadsbestuur van 1302 tot 1345. En een en ander betreffende het Gentsche stadspatriciaat," *HMGOG,* n.s. 1 (1944): 135–63. There has been scarcely any work done on Philip van Artevelde apart from the studies of his father.
4. Yves Barel, *La Ville médiévale. Système social. Système urbain* (Grenoble, 1977), p. 91.
5. Michel Mollat and Philippe Wolff, *The Popular Revolutions of the Late Middle Ages,* trans. by A. L. Lytton-Sells (London, 1973), p. 61.

genesis in 1971, when I was asked to write a biographical sketch
of him for the Flemish *Nationaal Biografisch Woordenboek* (Dictionary of National Biography).[6] Although my portrayal of the
Flemish hero was far from being uniformly critical, its tone was
evidently less adulatory than was desired, for the translator
modified some passages over my strenuous objections. I realized even then that the commonly held view of van Artevelde
was at variance with the facts, and I set myself the job at some
ill-defined time in the future of setting things right. A few years
later, while studying the polder village of Weert in northeastern
Flanders, I stumbled onto documentation showing that James
van Artevelde had owned and diked a large block of land there
and in neighboring Bornem, and that people living at Weert or
related to persons who did had assassinated James van Artevelde
the younger in 1370.[7] Subsequent research showed that the killing of James the younger was closely tied to the development of
family factions in Ghent.

Yet this book is not intended to be primarily a political biography of James and Philip van Artevelde. All previous work,
including my own, has focused on their political careers, particularly that of James, the more successful and certainly the longer-lived of the two men of this family who held extraordinary
power in Ghent. Although his struggle against the French was
determined less by the missionary's zeal for a holy war against
the Walloons than by the realist's comprehension of Ghent's
dependence on an uninterrupted supply of wool from England,
his ability to continue in power for seven years against overwhelming odds made him appear larger than life. But my other
studies of the ruling orders of fourteenth-century Ghent led me
into a tangled skein of family relationships that made it apparent
to me that the careers of James's sons were not only significant
in themselves but also held the keys to some important aspects
of their father's career.

The two generations of van Arteveldes are inextricably and

6. D. Nicholas, "Artevelde, Jacob van, kapitein van Gent," *Nationaal Biografisch Woordenboek* 5 (1972): cols. 22–35.
7. D. Nicholas, "Weert: A Scheldt Polder Village in the Fourteenth Century," *Journal of Medieval History* 2 (1976): 239–68.

tragically linked in a pattern of family feuds that had only tangential bearing on their public careers. This book not only adds new material and a decidedly revisionist interpretation of the career of James van Artevelde but also provides the first scholarly evaluation in any language of Philip van Artevelde, who appears not as a flawed savior of the masses but as an avenging angel of the apocalypse. More fundamentally, as its title indicates, this is intended to be a study not of the politics and institutions of later medieval Ghent but rather of the activities and strategies of a prominent fourteenth-century lineage. In contrast to earlier studies of the van Arteveldes, this book is thus much more a family history than a political history.

My previous work had shown me that this book would be unlikely to add building blocks to the hagiographical edifice constructed for James van Artevelde by Belgian historians and antiquarians. Still, I must confess that I was utterly unprepared for the level of calculated, homicidal villainy perpetrated by these men, particularly Philip van Artevelde. Not all the van Arteveldes' contemporaries thought of them as heroes. There was bitter opposition to them even among the working classes of Ghent, the group they are most often portrayed as having championed. Most contemporary chroniclers were partisans of the Flemish counts and disliked the van Arteveldes. Modern scholars, as a result, have understandably tended to dismiss their sometimes lurid stories of the Flemish leaders as politically inspired smears. A central thesis of this book is that the chroniclers' tales have often been taken out of context and thus misunderstood. When their allegations can be compared to official records, notably in the case of Philip van Artevelde, their essential accuracy and sense of responsibility seem beyond dispute.

The fact that so little is known of James van Artevelde's intentions and policy has made him a good subject for propagandists, who have used him as they saw fit and excused his failings on grounds of broad visions and *Zeitgeist*. In 1920 the Belgian historian and genealogist Napoléon de Pauw published most of the extant documents directly naming James van Artevelde and his children in his *Cartulaire historique et généalogique des Artevelde*.

De Pauw's collection has been indispensable to me, but there are gaps; material in the city records not mentioning the van Arteveldes by name has important implications for their public careers, and other documents in the municipal archives, some of which de Pauw evidently knew but misunderstood, are also useful. De Pauw also omitted considerable chronicle evidence bearing on Philip van Artevelde's career. He included material on van Arteveldes who were not related to James's clan, and his work was further vitiated by his attempt to forge a genealogical link between his own family and the van Arteveldes.

In 1933 Henry S. Lucas surveyed the sources in a classic article that is particularly valuable for its inclusion of chronicle and other narrative evidence from the fourteenth and fifteenth centuries.[8] The evidence of these sources can be supplemented by the manuscript material available in such abundance in the archives of Ghent. Unpublished evidence is particularly important, for it shows the van Arteveldes' ties of amity and enmity with the other leading lineages of the city. In addition to scattered pieces of information such as guild lists and rent books, the most important series are the transactions of the two benches of aldermen, the Law Aldermen (aldermen of the *Keure*) and the Estate Aldermen (aldermen of *gedele*), and the "Atonement Books" kept by the Estate Aldermen in their capacity as justices of the peace.

Truth is never stranger than fiction, which by its very nature involves either a distortion of the truth or a speculative flight from the secure grounding of the factual into the stratosphere of the imagination. I would be more comfortable with the message of this book if it were a historical novel or drama. But it is not. My disquieting task has been to establish, to the best of my ability, the actual setting of a historical morality play worthy of the great tragedians.

D. N.

8. Henry S. Lucas, "The Sources and Literature on Jacob van Artevelde," *Speculum* 8 (1933): 101–35.

Abbreviations

AJC	Archive of Church of St. James, Ghent
ARA	Algemeen Rijksarchief (General Archives of the Realm), Brussels
BB	Boek van den Blivene
BR	Baljuwsrekening (Bailiff's Account)
CA	Napoléon de Pauw, ed., *Cartulaire historique et généalogique des Artevelde* (Brussels: Librairie Kiessling, 1920)
EP	G. Espinas and H. Pirenne, eds., *Recueil de documents relatifs à l'histoire de l'industrie drapière en Flandre*, 4 vols. (Brussels: Commission Royale d'Histoire, 1906–24)
G	Registers of aldermen of *gedele*
GB	Groenen Briel
HMGOG	*Handelingen der Maatschappij voor Geschied- en Oudheidkunde te Gent*
K	Registers of aldermen of the *Keure*
RAG	Rijksarchief te Gent (State Archive of Ghent)
Rek. Gent 1280–1336	Julius Vuylsteke, ed., *Gentsche Stads- en Baljuwsrekeningen, 1280–1336* (Ghent: F. Meyer-Van Loo, 1900)
Rek. Gent 1336–1349	Napoléon de Pauw and Julius Vuylsteke, eds., *De Rekeningen der stad Gent. Tijdvak*

	van Jacob van Artevelde, 1336–1349, 3 vols. (Ghent: H. Hoste, 1874–85)
Rek. Gent 1351–1364	Alfons Van Werveke, ed., *Gentse Stads- en Baljuwsrekeningen (1351–1364)* (Brussels: Commission Royale d'Histoire, 1970)
Rek. Gent 1376–1389	Julius Vuylsteke, ed., *De Rekeningen der stad Gent. Tijdvak van Philips van Artevelde, 1376–1389* (Ghent: A. Hoste, 1893)
SAG	Stadsarchief te Gent (Municipal Archive of Ghent)
SM	Church of St. Michael, Ghent
SN	Church of Saint Nicholas, Ghent
WD	Wijsdommen der dekenen (SAG, ser. 156, no. 1)
Z	*Zoendincboeken*

Dramatis Personae

Ackerman, Francis: captain of Ghent; leader of city after death of Philip van Artevelde, 1382

Aper, Joseph: fuller; captain of Ghent, 1345

Bette, Simon, in the Ameede: first Law Alderman, 1381; killed by Peter van den Bossche or Philip van Artevelde, January 1382

Beys, John: pursemaker; also a fishmonger of this name

Borluut, John: alderman 1341; implicated in plot against James van Artevelde, 1343

Bornaige, Zeger: knight; second husband of James van Artevelde's widow

Damman, Peter: father-in-law and ally of John van Steenbeke; leader of plot against James van Artevelde, 1343

de Backere, Matthew: goldsmith; married Wijvin de Roede, granddaughter of James van Artevelde

de Bake, John: fuller and alderman; captain, 1338–42

de Coster, Catherine: second wife of James van Artevelde

de Grutere, Gilbert the son of Baldwin: brewer, landowner, and alderman of Ghent, late 1379

de Grutere, Gilbert the son of Gilbert: brewer, landowner, alderman of Ghent, August 1379, dean of small guilds, 1381; murdered by Philip van Artevelde, January 1382 de Hert, John: captain, 1382; probably shipper, perhaps weaver

de Kortrijzaan, Zeger: commander of militia of Ghent, executed, 1338

de Maech family: prominent weavers, allies of van Arteveldes

de Mey, Walter: principal killer of James van Artevelde the younger; kin of van Merlaers

Denijs, Gerard: dean of weavers, 1343–46; leader of plot to assassinate James van Artevelde

de Roede, Godfrey: husband of James van Artevelde's daughter

de Roemere, Nicholas: pursemaker

de Scepene, William: probably baker; exiled, 1379

de Schachtmaker, Philip: baker on Kalandenberg; father-in-law of John de Mey

de Scoteleere, John: husband of Catherine van Artevelde, James's daughter

de Scouteete, John: carpenter, captain 1345–46, killed by John van Artevelde, 1361

de Westerlinc, Paul and Simon: relatives of de Meys and van Merlaers

de Winter, Peter: probably dyer; Ghent captain at Bruges, 1382

Diederic, Peter: shipwright; second husband of Yolante van den Brouke, widow of Philip van Artevelde

Guy of Dampierre: count of Flanders, 1280–1305

Heinmans, John and James: tanners; overseers of property of de Scoteleere grandchildren of James van Artevelde

Herman, John: weaver; captain, 1382

Louis of Male: count of Flanders, 1346–84

Louis of Nevers: count of Flanders, 1323–46

Mabenzoon, Pieter: dean of weavers; van Artevelde ally

Panneberch, John: resident of Weert and Ghent; implicated in assassination of James van Artevelde the younger

Parijs, Simon: dyer; dean of the small guilds, 1345

Parneele, John: probably tailor; leader of White Hoods, exiled, 1379

Pauwels, John: relative of van Merlaers and de Meys

Rijnvisch, Giles: hosteler; opponent of van Arteveldes

Rijnvisch, James, father and son, in the Drabstraat: allies of Parijs and van Merlaer families, van Artevelde enemies

Rijnvisch, Lievin: moneychanger; perhaps opponent of van Arteveldes

Robert of Béthune: count of Flanders, 1305–22

Ser Sanders, Jordan: creditor of John de Scoteleere, son-in-law of James van Artevelde; the Ser Sanders family eventually bought the van Artevelde family complex on the Kalandenberg

Sloeve, Francis: alderman, 1345; son John left Ghent, 1381

Soyssone, James: dean of butchers; murdered, 1382

uten Dale, Zeger: alderman, 1344; son Nicholas killed 1382

uten Rosen, Fulk: partisan of Count Louis of Nevers, killed by James van Artevelde

van Artevelde, Catherine and Margaret: daughters of James van Artevelde

van Artevelde, James: captain of Ghent 1338–45

van Artevelde, John and James the younger: sons of James van Artevelde

van Artevelde, Philip: son of James van Artevelde; captain of Ghent, 1382

van Artevelde, William the elder and the younger: father and brother of James van Artevelde

van Bost, John: alderman, 1344; son Daniel left Ghent, 1381

van Coudenhove, Peter: weaver and alderman, 1340s

van den Bossche, Peter: captain of Ghent, leader of White Hoods, chief ally of Philip van Artevelde, 1382

van den Brouke, Yolante (Lente): wife of Philip van Artevelde, probably illegitimate daughter of shipwright Peter van den Brouke; her brothers were John and Peter

van den Hovene, Peter: fuller; captain, 1338–42

van den Voerde, Raes: landowner; captain, 1382

van der Pale, Baldwin and Giles: kinsmen and neighbors of van Arteveldes on Kalandenberg

van der Vloet, John: weaver; alderman, 1344

van Erpe, Walter: husband of Margaret van Artevelde, James's daughter; their son was Martin van Erpe

van Haelwijn, Daniel: knight; husband of Catherine, daughter of John van Artevelde

van Huusse, William: weaver; captain, 1338–42, alderman, 1342, 1345

van Lens, Gelnoot: weaver and captain, 1338–45; closest ally of James van Artevelde

van Loevelde, James: city clerk, period of James van Artevelde the elder

van Lovendegem: noble family of Ghent, allied with de Meys

van Meeren, John: cheesemonger; ally of van Arteveldes

van Merlaer, Andrew: kinsman of de Meys and of Walter van Merlaer, killer of James van Artevelde the younger

van Merlaer, Walter: kinsman of de Meys; killer of James van Artevelde the younger

van Steenbeke, John: landowner and dean of weavers; led plot against James van Artevelde, January 1343

van Vaernewijc, Alexander: landowner; captain, 1382

van Vaernewijc, Simon: landowner; alderman of Ghent, 1381, exiled, early 1382

van Vaernewijc, William: landowner; captain of Ghent, 1338–46

van Wackine, John: dean of weavers, 1340s

van Waes, Lievin: weaver-draper; alderman, 1344; son and namesake left Ghent briefly, 1382

van Zinghem, Francis: city clerk, 1340s

Wederic, Nicholas: baker on Kalandenberg and landholder at Tielrode; killed by John van Meeren of van Artevelde party

Zoetaerd, Peter: furrier, dean of small guilds; ally of James van Artevelde the elder

Wool, Grain, and Blood: Ghent and James van Artevelde on the Eve of the Hundred Years War

The county of Flanders was the most densely urbanized region of Europe north of the Alps during the central Middle Ages. As early as the twelfth century its five greatest cities—Ghent, Bruges, Ypres, Lille, and Douai—had developed a prosperous trade based on importing high grade English wool and manufacturing it into luxury textiles for export. During the thirteenth century, the "five good cities"—a number reduced to three by the loss of Lille and Douai to France in 1305—limited the power of the counts of Flanders to govern without their participation. Indeed, long before James van Artevelde took power in Ghent in 1338, the cities had acquired some rights of administration and jurisdiction over the rural communities in their environs. Although the Flemish counts were powerful enough to prevent the cities from assuming as much power beyond their walls as the great communes of contemporary Tuscany and Lombardy and the Free Cities of Germany, the extent to which Ghent was able to dominate Flanders, if not the extent to which James van Artevelde was able to control Ghent, can be understood only against the background of the domination of Flanders by its cities and particularly Ghent, the largest of them.

The counts held southern Flanders as a fief of the French crown. While north and east of the Scheldt river lay "imperial Flanders," dependent on the Holy Roman Empire, the political conflicts of the fourteenth century revolved around the French allegiance of the Flemish counts, who were unable to reconcile their loyalties as French vassals and their Francophile personal inclinations with the by then crippling dependence of Ghent, Bruges, and Ypres on English wool. Even as they imported vast quantities of this wool, the aristocratic rulers of the Flemish cities during the thirteenth century shared the French culture of their count, while the lower orders, consisting largely of textile workers in the thirteenth and early fourteenth centuries, came to view their Flemish ethnic heritage as both a cultural and a political identity.

Hence, as conflicts between the English and French crowns intensified from the 1290s, and particularly during the 1330s, the Flemings were caught in the middle. Adding to the problem was the fact that by the fourteenth century Flanders was being fed chiefly by grain imported from northern France. Nowhere in Flanders was French grain more important than at Ghent. Indeed, by 1357 the shippers of Ghent were making an immense profit on the grain staple, the offices in the port of Ghent where all cargoes coming downstream on the Leie and Scheldt rivers had to be recharged before being sent on to more distant destinations.

Thus the famous "Battle of the Golden Spurs" outside Courtrai in 1302, where the artisans of Bruges were joined by smaller contingents from Ghent to inflict a crushing defeat on the French army, was simply a momentary setback for French influence in Flanders. Although the narrow merchant oligarchies of the thirteenth century were gone, many of their members returned after a few years and reentered the governments of all the major Flemish cities. In 1305 the French forced the Flemings to accept the humiliating peace of Athis, which entailed the payment of an enormous indemnity and the cession of the Walloon castellanies of Lille, Douai, and Orchies by Flanders to the French crown. The assessment and collection of this payment was to cause untold problems for the counts of Flanders during the fourteenth century.

The governance of Ghent during the fourteenth century is illustrated on figure 1. The city had been governed in the thirteenth century by the infamously cooptative "Thirty-Nine," perhaps the most exclusive urban merchant oligarchy of the medieval Low Countries. This clique was displaced in 1297 in favor of two boards of thirteen aldermen whose membership was rotated every 15 August. These two councils were selected by electors chosen in equal numbers by the count and the outgoing aldermen. They had clearly defined and separate functions during periods of peace, or what passed for it. Each board had a "first alderman," and the first Law Alderman [alderman of the *Keure*] was the official head of the city government. But the importance of both van Arteveldes lies in the fact that they bypassed the aldermen through an extraordinary regime, the captaincy. Between 1320 and 1329, and again between 1338 and 1349 and between 1379 and 1385, the five parishes of the city chose captains. These men controlled policy in fact, although technically only the aldermen could bind the city to a course of action. But no single captain before James van Artevelde, and none after Philip, was able so totally to dominate the city and its organs of ordinary administration. James and Philip van Artevelde also used to great advantage occasional meetings of the general assembly of citizens and the Collacie, the meeting of the guild deans and ten representatives of the persons who owned land inside the originally settled part of the city (it was possible for one person to own the land while another owned the buildings on it). These aristocrats, called *poorters*, were recognized collectively as a separate estate.

Sources of conflict in Ghent on the eve of the Hundred Years War thus included disagreements over the proper role of the Flemish counts and their French lords in the city's affairs, which tended to pit the wealthy wholesalers and rentiers, who preferred the French language and culture, against the Flemish-speaking middle and lower social orders. This rivalry, however, transcended social "class" lines, since some guilds with a large

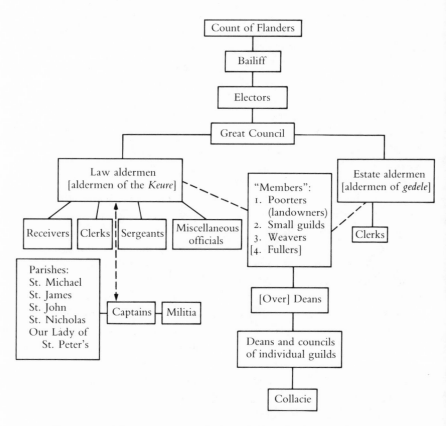

FIGURE 1. The governance of Ghent during the fourteenth century

unskilled labor force, notably the shippers, derived their liveli-
hood from dealing with France.

In addition to the ethnopolitical conflicts, guild rivalries constituted a tinderbox of hostility. The politically privileged
groups of Ghent were probably divided into "members" before
James van Artevelde came to power in 1338, although the term
is first used in the municipal account of 1339 to mean the
weavers, fullers, and the "small guilds" (the various locally
based service and industrial occupations, the shippers, and some
of the smaller textile trades). There was a pronounced tendency
for embassies outside the city in James van Artevelde's period to
consist of equal numbers of persons from each member. But
though the revolutions of 1302 had resulted in the admission of
guildsmen to the boards of aldermen, the practice of reserving
seats for particular guilds and groups of guilds began only in the
1360s. Although some historians have seen the captains as representatives of members, the basis of their selection was always
the parish organizations. The small guilds are first mentioned
collectively in a text of 1317 and had an overdean by 1325, but
the number of trades became fixed at sixty-three by 1332 and
fifty-nine by 1357. The weavers, until 1360 the fullers, and each
of the individual small guilds chose deans as their chief officers,
and the deans were assisted by guild councils.[1]

The landowners (*poorters*) were also extremely powerful.
Most landowners were also brokers, moneylenders, hostelers,
or textile entrepreneurs, but during James van Artevelde's ascendancy they were also part of the member of the small
guilds.[2] Representatives of the landowners and/or the small

1. See arguments by D. Nicholas, *The Metamorphosis of a Medieval City:
Ghent in the Age of the Arteveldes, 1302–1390* (Lincoln and Leiden, 1987), chap.
1, based on *Rek. Gent 1280–1336*, 121, 117, 426, 339, 389, 536, 538, 540, 544;
Rek. Gent 1336–1349 1:27–33, 365; 2:45–46; *Rek. Gent 1351–1364*, 296–97. A
later chronicle claims that James van Artevelde initiated this division of the
small guilds, but the municipal accounts show clearly that it dates from shortly
before he assumed power; see P. C. van der Meersch, ed., *Memorieboek der stad
Gent*, 4 vols. (Ghent, 1852–61), 1:54.

2. See the equation of the two groups in text of 19 May 1338, *Rek. Gent
1336–1349* 1:184–85; the editors of the printed accounts insert a comma, imply-
ing a distinction, where there is none in the original.

guilds were found in every government formed in Ghent in the fourteenth century. The weavers and fullers were the two largest textile occupations, but the period of James van Artevelde's rule was the only time during the fourteenth century when they shared power. During the 1320s a fuller-dominated regime supported by the Flemish count excluded the weavers and levied a fine on them; one of the collectors of that payment in the parish of St. John in 1326 was none other than James van Artevelde. The weavers were readmitted to the magistracy at his instigation in 1338. Although the weavers quashed a fuller rebellion over wages in 1345, an event that may be linked to van Artevelde's assassination, some fullers continued to serve in the government until Ghent submitted to Count Louis of Male in early 1349. The count then installed a regime that excluded the weavers. Beginning in 1358, some weavers returned to the government, and they had ejected the fullers permanently by early 1361. By Philip van Artevelde's time, the three members were the landowners, the weavers, and the small guilds.[3]

Indeed, there is reason to think that the antagonism between the weavers and fullers in the 1340s was a comparatively recent development, perhaps brought on by the overall decline of the clothmaking industry. Neither group had political rights or corporate organizations before 1302. Although some weavers were simple handworkers, their guild, in common with all trade organizations, was ruled by a wealthy elite. It was these drapers who entered the city government in 1338, shortly after James van Artevelde became captain. It was they who sold fine cloth on foreign markets and to the city administration, and it was they who employed the fullers and paid their wages. Below the drapers were the master weavers, who were still working cloth but had privileges in the guild that could, with limitations, be passed from father to son; and below the masters were the journeymen.[4] The fullers, as the less prosperous group, tended to

3. See D. Nicholas, "The Governance of Fourteenth-Century Ghent: Potentiality of Rule and Actuality of Control," forthcoming.

4. See calculations of the wealth of weavers and fullers, and a discussion of the generally but not invariably applicable identity of draper and weaver, in Nicholas, *Metamorphosis*, chap. 5. See also Rogghé, "Gemeente ende Vrient,"

look for protection to the counts of Flanders, while the weavers, although substantially wealthier per capita, were a more revolutionary element. There was considerable mobility among trades within the textile industry; the son of the fullers' dean John de Bake, James, became a cloth wholesaler on the Friday Market (*Map 1, G–H 6–7*).[5] In addition to the social, cultural, ethnic, and occupational rivalries that racked fourteenth-century Flanders, family feuds that had no discernible tie to the ideological or economic struggles, and indeed crossed the more obvious party lines, were an important and hitherto neglected aspect of social life in Ghent. The municipal aristocrats maintained gangs of liveried retainers. Extended families were expected to support and defend their members, and their senior males had a solemn obligation to avenge deaths and injuries, either by arranging the payment of a blood price, or by assassinating the offending party, or both. There was no notion whatsoever that homicide is immoral. Though murder was a violation of the laws of the Flemish counts, the city had no statutes forbidding it. Since the magistrates of Ghent were concerned chiefly with limiting the competence of the count's bailiff in the city, and only the count's court could exercise blood justice, most violent deeds never went to trial. The city government maintained a police force, but it was totally inadequate to contain the pervasive violence. The aldermen arranged truces and attempted to bring warring clans to the conference table, but they imposed no penalties unless a sworn truce was broken. The career of Philip van Artevelde is a classic demonstration of the family father's solemn, God-imposed duty to avenge all slights, if possible without invoking the assistance of the legally constituted authorities.[6]

112; Hans van Werveke, *De Koopman-ondernemer en de ondernemer in de Vlaamsche lakennijverheid van de Middeleeuwen* (Antwerp, 1946).

5. SAG, G 1, 2, fol. 14r, compared with K 12, fol. 32r, and lists of cloth wholesalers, SAG, K, behind books of 1377 and 1379.

6. D. Nicholas, "Crime and Punishment in Fourteenth-Century Ghent," *Revue Belge de Philologie et d'Histoire* 48 (1970): 289–334, 1141–76; Nicholas, *The Domestic Life of a Medieval City: Women, Children, and the Family in Fourteenth-Century Ghent* (Lincoln, Neb., 1985), part 3.

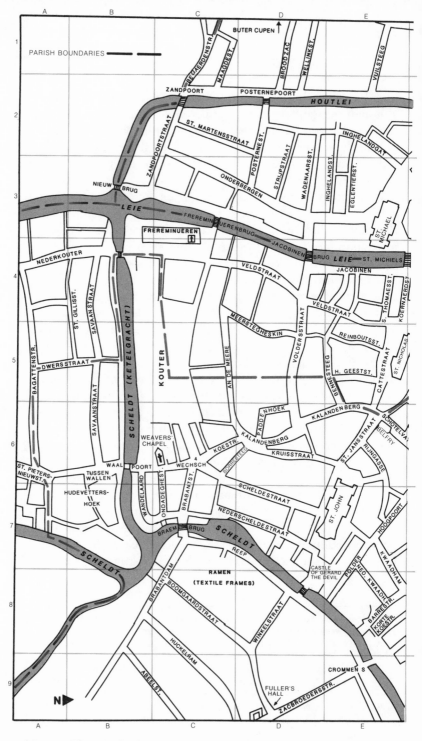

MAP 1. Ghent in the fourteenth century. Adapted from *The Metamorphosis of a Medieval City*, by David Nicholas, by permission of University of Nebraska Press. Copyright © 1987 by the University of Nebraska Press.

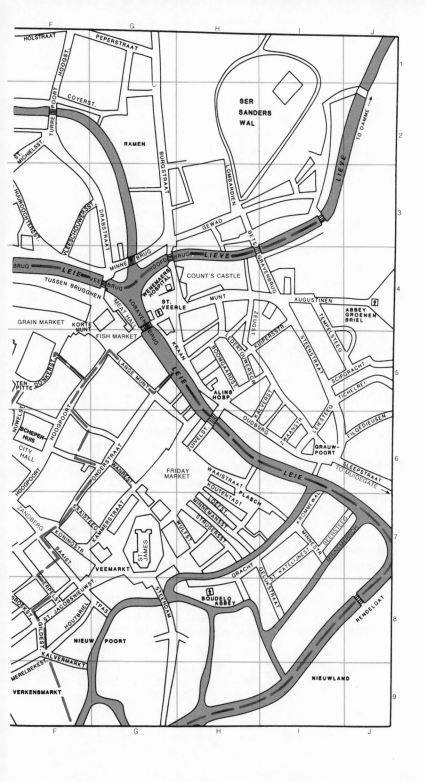

Conflicts between the Flemish cities and the Francophile counts assumed a peculiarly virulent form during the 1320s, when Flanders was torn apart by the revolt of Bruges and the rural communities of maritime Flanders. Count Louis of Nevers was able to crush the rebellion only with the assistance of the French monarch. Ghent sided with the count, evidently to oppose Bruges, and thus was spared the repression after the war ended in 1328. During the confusion of the war, however, Ghent took over much of the count's government in eastern Flanders, including the power to appoint officials and military leaders. Although Ghent was supposed to surrender these functions after 1328, the count complained during the 1330s that in fact the city had continued to fulfill them, particularly in sparsely populated northeastern Flanders. The count in turn offended sentiment in Ghent in the autumn of 1335 when his men insisted on auditing the municipal accounts.[7]

Indeed, Ghent's interests were too tied to England, whose rivalry with France deepened with the extinction of the French Capetian dynasty in the male line in 1328 and the decision by the lawyers at Paris to bypass the claims of King Edward III of England, son of the daughter of King Philip IV of France (1285–1314), to the French throne in favor of the new Valois dynasty. Even apart from the inclinations and ambitions of individual leaders, Ghent simply needed English wool too much for the city to remain long in the good graces of the count or the French monarchy. Wool supplies had been interrupted occasionally even before 1338, and the Flemings' need for English wool gave the English monarch a political lever that he was quick to use. In an attempt to force the Flemish cities to put pressure on Count Louis of Nevers to recognize Edward III of England as king of France, the English placed an embargo on the export of wool in 1336. In late 1337 the Valois king, Philip VI of France, pledged to send the entire French wool export to Flanders, but the

7. Nicholas, *Town and Countryside*, pp. 168–71; Hans Van Werveke, *De Gentsche Stadsfinanciën in de Middeleeuwen* (Brussels, 1934), 65–66.

amount was too small and the quality too mediocre to be of much help.[8]

Unemployment and uncertain food supplies were causing widespread hardship among the working classes of Ghent that had reached critical proportions by late 1337. James van Artevelde addressed a general assembly of the citizenry at the suburban Bijloke abbey on 28 December 1337, and on 3 January 1338 he and four other men were made captains. The very fact that captains were appointed in the middle of the fiscal year shows the gravity of the emergency. An internally inconsistent and overlapping maelstrom of rivalries and antagonisms thus greeted James van Artevelde when he assumed power. How had his background prepared him for this challenge? How did he meet it?

Van Artevelde had served only once in the government of Ghent before 1338, when he collected the fine levied on the rebellious weavers in 1326. He was never an alderman, and his evident lack of public involvement makes his sudden elevation in 1338 all the more puzzling. He was apparently born around 1290, for the daughter of his first marriage, to a lady whose name has not survived, was married in 1341. James's father, William van Artevelde, was a wealthy man who had remained loyal to the Flemish count in his struggle with the French king in 1297. One brother of James van Artevelde was murdered at Mons (Hainaut), while another, Francis, was castellan of Beveren and may be the man of that name who later became captain and alderman at Bruges. A third brother, John, was evidently a draper.[9]

James van Artevelde was probably a younger son, for the father's namesake, William van Artevelde, became watergrave, an official in charge of maintaining the canal network, in northern Flanders in 1341. William's early career was chequered; we shall see that he made a pilgrimage in 1334 for leading an armed

8. Rogghé, *Vlaanderen*, 1:15.
9. Ibid., 1:17.

insurrection of weavers. He may have been an alderman in
1338.[10] He went into exile in England after James's assassination
and was given a pension by King Edward III. He may have
returned to Flanders, however, for a William van Artevelde was
exiled again in 1348, and the 1348 list includes persons who had
gone to England with him in 1346. He probably died in exile,
because his son and namesake married Zwane, the daughter of
Simon van Mirabello, an Italian financier who became regent of
Flanders in 1340. Inasmuch as William van Artevelde was receiver of money repaid in 1360 to persons taken hostage in 1348,
along with the landowner Simon van Vaernewijc and the
weaver Peter Mabenzoon, he was probably affiliated with the
small guilds. He posted bond as a hosteler in 1365. The van
Arteveldes were kinsmen of the van der Pales, their neighbors
on the aristocratic Kalandenberg ([Map 1, D–E 6 and Illust. 1),
but William kept up friendly relations with them after James's
children had quarreled with them in the early 1360s. Despite
this, his relations with James's children were cordial, and Philip
van Artevelde was damaged as his surety in 1375. William lived
in the St. Michielsstraat (*Map 1, E–F 2–3*), an area of Ghent not
frequented by the other van Arteveldes, but he sold his house to
the bakers' guild in 1375 and secured his debt to Philip on the
annuity that the guild had paid him for the property. He seems
to have played no role in Philip's political career and is not
mentioned with the rest of the family after 1375, although he
may have still been living in the St. Michielsstraat in 1385.[11]

The van Arteveldes were landowners, possessing a complex
of lands and houses in the parish of St. John on the Kalanden-

10. CA 122–24; *Rek. Gent 1336–1349*, I:36; 3:147. The sources mention a
wagonmaker named William van Artevelde, but he was the son of a John van
Artevelde and thus was not James's brother. The wagonmaker was alderman in
1347, but whether he or James's brother was the alderman of 1338 is uncertain.

11. CA 130–34, 138–42, 149, 155, 158–61, 583; SAG, K 4, 2, fol. 35r. He
evidently had a son and namesake who took holy orders and had rights on the
St. Michielsstraat property. Although the father definitely sold the property to
the bakers, a "master William" lived there in 1369, and "lord William," a term
that can mean either a priest or the male head of a lineage, held the property in
1385; K 3, 1, fol. 52v; K 10, 1, fol. 34v.

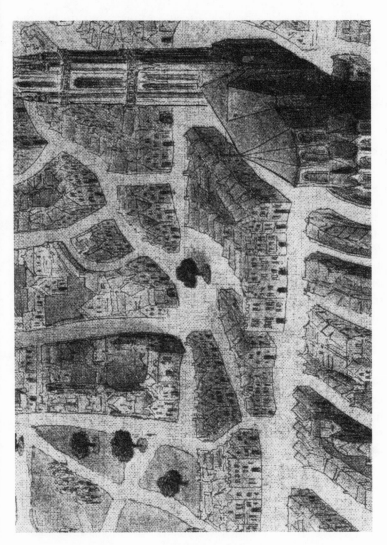

1. The Kalandenberg in Ghent, as shown on the anonymous plan of the city of 1534. Courtesy Stadsarchief te Gent (Municipal Archive of Ghent).

berg (*Map 1, D–E 6*) and adjacent streets, but they may have practiced trades as well as lived on their rents. James van Artevelde was clearly a broker, for at various times during the 1340s he sold animals, fish, wine, and silver implements to the city.[12] He never posted bond as a hosteler, which would have permitted him to do brokerage at the cloth halls. His interests were thus clearly with the victualling trades rather than in textiles, a fact that may explain his land investments and diking and reclamation work at Bornem and Baasrode, in pastoral northeastern Flanders.[13] The chroniclers—notably, van Artevelde's contemporary Giovanni Villani, an anonymous writer who was probably from Ghent and whose work is preserved in a manuscript housed at Bruges, and the nearly contemporary Jean Froissart—all claimed that James van Artevelde was a brewer, and the context shows that this was intended as an insult. It is conceivable that the "mead brewers," the term used for van Artevelde, were a separate group not affiliated with those who brewed beer.[14] The anonymous *Memorieboek* of Ghent states that van Artevelde was a nobleman who did not practice the trade personally but had himself inscribed in the guild "to gain more respect in the community."[15]

Firmer evidence of a tie to the brewers is the fact that a priest named John van Artevelde, apparently James's nephew, owned a house on the Kalandenberg (*Map 1, D–E 6*) adjacent to a property described on 6 June 1352 as "next to the property of Lord John van Artevelde, priest, and his sisters, where mead is brewed, on the corner of the Borresteeg" (*Map 1, C–D 6*). The reference does not make it clear whether the mead brewery was the priest's establishment or was the adjacent property. James van Artevelde had lived on the west side of the Kalandenberg, at

12. Jean Froissart, *Chroniques*. Publiées pour la Société de l'Histoire de France (Paris, 1869–1975), vol. 1, chap. 59, p. 127; van Werveke, *Jacob*, 8; *Rek. Gent 1336–1349*, 1:383–35, when he was paid for two oxen and a bear sent live as a present to the Flemish count in 1339; 2:102.
13. Nicholas, "Weert," 242–45.
14. CA 216–17.
15. Vander Meersch, *Memorieboek*, 1:55.

the Paddenhoek, while the Borresteeg is across the street. This document has caused some speculation that van Artevelde's first wife came from a family of brewers, thus giving rise to the story of her husband's affiliation with that guild. It is true that during the 1350s their children owned properties on the east side of the Kalandenberg in which van Artevelde's children by his second wife had no share. Yet the fact that the priest's family name was also van Artevelde shows clearly that he was not the son of one of the captain's in-laws. James may have possessed the brewery as a rental investment, and certainly if it was the priest's property in 1352 it was being used for rents and not as a profession. The van Arteveldes thus had an extended family complex— which was very unusual in Ghent at this time and in itself shows their wealth—that housed at least two branches of the family, on opposite sides of the Kalandenberg. Parts of it, including a brewery, were rented out by 1352, seven years after James died.[16]

The earliest surviving list of brewers was compiled in early 1362. It apparently contains the names of those then practicing the trade and others who might have a claim to mastership through their fathers. None of James van Artevelde's three surviving sons is on the list, but it does include the name of Baldwin van der Pale, the van Arteveldes' neighbor and kinsman on the Kalandenberg. Baldwin's younger son, Giles, was apprenticed to the weaver Peter Mabenzoon, an ally of van Artevelde in the 1340s who was repatriated with his sons in 1360.[17] The connection is tenuous but may help to explain the legend. The brewers were a growing guild and were persons of considerable standing in the community, with a seat on the town council

16. CA p. 761. For the priest's subsequent career, see SAG, G 1, 2, fol. 59r; K 1, fol. 228r.

17. On Baldwin and Giles van der Pale, see SAG, ser. 160, no. 6, fols. 12r, 13v; G 3, 1, fol. 31r; G 3, 2, fol. 30v. On Peter Mabenzoon, see *Rek. Gent 1336–1349*, 2:46; CA 139. On 29 December 1346 he replaced Giles van Gavere, who had succeeded James van Artevelde as captain from the parish of St. John, a fact that clearly shows he had not been part of the conspiracy to assassinate James.

guaranteed by 1362. The chroniclers to the contrary, enrollment as a brewer would not have prejudiced James van Artevelde's standing in Ghent, whatever the counts and their partisans may have thought of it. Thus the notion that he was a brewer cannot be rejected automatically. It may be more than coincidence that Philip van Artevelde in 1382 assassinated Gilbert de Grutere, one of the most prominent brewers and also a landowner, although we shall see that there were many other points of conflict between the two families.

The weavers' involvement in the murder of James van Artevelde in 1345 and van Artevelde's role as collector of the fine exacted from weavers in 1326 has led historians to assume that the weavers were always suspicious of him, even though he readmitted them to participation in the government in 1338. But an incident involving William van Artevelde in 1334 suggests that his brother James was known as a friend of the weavers before he took power four years later. William van Artevelde had been assaulted at Sleidingen by a man who escaped to Ghent, where the sergeant of the count's bailiff tried to disarm two weavers who were van Artevelde's kinsmen and were attempting to help him in his pursuit. Disturbances erupted, and the knight Fulk uten Rosen intervened to keep William van Artevelde from harm. The aldermen imprisoned Fulk, then freed him under pressure from a mob. Another riot broke out, and the count had to come personally to Ghent to install the new boards of aldermen on 15 August 1334.

A second but undated text says that William van Artevelde served a three-year exile for having led an armed insurrection of weavers. The kinsmen were evidently James van der Pale the younger and Lievin de Crijsschere. Van der Pale senior was alderman in 1326, 1329, 1332, and 1333. Thierry de Maech, whose family was one of the most influential weaver clans, was also exiled for three years, while Fulk uten Rosen was exiled for two years for having plotted to put certain unnamed fullers into the government.[18] Because the weavers, rather than the fullers, were disenfranchised at this time, there must have been a party

18. Documents printed CA 118–24.

split within the fullers' guild. John Breebaert and Giles van Contersvoorde were evidently the fullers whom uten Rosen wanted to promote, but they were acquitted of complicity in the conspiracy. Van Contersvoorde was alderman in 1341 and 1344—the latter year, at least, suggests personal enmity toward van Artevelde—and dean of the fullers in 1348, shortly before being exiled.[19] He was thus clearly of the revolutionary party but a personal enemy of van Artevelde. John Breebaert was chosen dean of the fullers in May 1337 and continued to serve until being replaced for the fiscal year beginning 15 August 1338, the first time James van Artevelde had a chance to dictate the choice of aldermen. Breebaert is not mentioned again in Ghent until 1349 and was thus clearly an opponent both of the revolutionary regime and of James van Artevelde personally.[20]

In 1338 Fulk uten Rosen was a partisan of the count against James van Artevelde. On 2 August 1338, seven months after assuming power, van Artevelde murdered uten Rosen in the count's presence.[21] William van Artevelde had been the weavers' ally by 1334, and his public career suggests that of all his brothers he was personally closest to James. Fulk uten Rosen's offense in the count's eyes was not recommending that fullers be admitted to the government, for they were already in it, but suggesting fullers of whom the count was evidently suspicious. His fatal offense against James van Artevelde lay in furthering the political ambitions of two men who were van Artevelde's pesonal enemies, and the fact that he did this four years before van Artevelde entered public life gives us our first evidence of three personality traits shared by James van Artevelde and his son Philip: they had a strong sense of family, they were extremely violent, and they nursed grudges for many years, waiting for the right time to strike.

James van Artevelde thus became captain in 1338 as the appar-

19. *Rek. Gent 1336–1349*, 2:93; 3:44, 200, 274.
20. Ibid., pp. 24, 39, 275; Rogghé, "Gemeente ende Vrient," 123; SAG, K 1, fols. 91v, 95r; he had died by October 1352, and his widow remarried the hosteler Baldwin van den Walle, who had been alderman in 1339, G 1, 3, fol. 19v.
21. Van Werveke, *Jacob*, 19.

ent leader of a revolutionary party with a history, albeit ill documented, of hostility toward Count Louis of Nevers. His personal affiliation was with the small guilds, for he was a landowner with real estate both inside and outside Ghent. He may have been enrolled as a brewer at some point, and he was active as a broker during his political career, but he was also a partisan of the weavers who was willing to tolerate fullers who opposed the count. In view of the economic interest all groups in the textile industry had in securing the supply of English wool, van Artevelde's policies were guaranteed a broad base of support. Our task now is to examine the character of the man as revealed by the way he ruled Ghent and, through Ghent, Flanders.

CHAPTER 2

The Hero Ascendant:
James van Artevelde
in Power, 1338–1342

James van Artevelde was made chief captain at Ghent on 3 January 1338 (*Illust. 2*). Two days later the city issued a comprehensive set of statutes. Prices of grain were fixed and hoarding was forbidden. Exiles were ordered to leave the sanctuary of the churches of Ghent and the environs, and all citizens outside the city were ordered to return within three days or be fined. Dancing and gambling were prohibited. The concluding clause decreed all feuds at truce "by [order of] the men of the count of Flanders, at the request of the count, and with the consent of the good cities and the common land of Flanders, albeit reserving the liberties of the cities and of each city of Flanders."[1] There was clearly a serious food shortage, and the prohibition of violence is admirable; but the ordinance also reveals a puritanical streak that we shall also see in the statutes of James's son Philip.

Van Artevelde was primarily interested at first in having the city present a united front in the emergency and was accordingly willing to associate persons of various guild affiliations in the magistracy. The twenty-six aldermen who had taken office in

1. Napoléon de Pauw, ed., *De Voorgeboden der stad Gent in de XIVe eeuw (1337–1382)* (Ghent, 1885), 7–8.

2. Salary payment to James van Artevelde and the other four captains, 3 January 1338. Courtesy Stadsarchief te Gent (Municipal Archive of Ghent), ser. 400, 4, fol. 204.

August 1337 continued to serve, and van Artevelde was able to work comfortably with at least eighteen of them. But there are changes of emphasis that suggest an imminent housecleaning. Three aldermen who had not been active on missions outside the city earlier in the fiscal year became so after 3 January 1338, while three who had participated up to then became much less conspicuous, although they remained in the government.[2] The city clerks were cashiered and a new set hired on 27 February, and one was subjected to a formal inquiry. Some were exiled, although others were permitted to remain in Ghent after surrendering their offices.[3] The two city receivers were also removed on 9 January and replaced by the captains Gelnoot van Lens and William van Huusse. The deans were also rotated, and the weavers may have lost their guild rights for a few weeks. Although James van Wackine was paid as "leader" of the weavers for the first fourteen weeks of this fiscal year, or until 21 November 1337, he had an armed escort until 27 February, twenty-eight weeks into the year. His successor, John van der Vloet, served only the final eighteen weeks of this fiscal year; but this leaves a gap between 27 February and 10 April, and an undated reference in the municipal account, the source of our information, mentions payment to two officials to "attend to the weavers' guild." Yet while both van Wackine and van der Vloet later served in the government, van Wackine served in years suggesting loyalty to van Artevelde, 1343 and 1346, while van der Vloet seems to have been implicated in the plot to assassinate James.[4] Apart from the clerks and receivers, men whose loyalties were suspect simply left office in the normal course of events and were not fired en masse.

The weavers were formally admitted to the city council only in August 1338, when the membership of the magistracy was normally rotated.[5] Van Artevelde used this occasion to pack the

2. Lucas, *Low Countries*, 265.
3. Paul Rogghé "De Gentse Klerken in de XIVe en XVe eeuw. Trouw en verraad," *Appeltjes van het Meetjesland* 11 (1960): 62–72.
4. *Rek. Gent 1336–1349*, 1: 158, 161, 164, 225.
5. Rogghé, "Democraat," 56–57.

two boards of aldermen, and departures became noticeably hastier thereafter. Thus, although John Speliaert became first Law Alderman on 14 August 1338, when all aldermen installed were van Artevelde's men, he then apparently left the city. He or his son and namesake became alderman again in 1349, 1353, and 1356, during the fuller-dominated regime installed by the count after he had crushed the revolt of Ghent.[6] The fishmonger Giles de Tolnere was alderman in 1337, the year of van Artevelde's rise, but he then left public life, only to return in 1349. His personal relations with the van Arteveldes were at least correct, for in 1350 he bought a rent for his sister from James van Artevelde's son John and his wife, the lady of Drongen.[7]

The new regime maintained a tenuous neutrality for a time in the developing conflict between France and England, but both monarchs applied pressure on the Flemings to choose between them. Relations with Count Louis of Nevers reached a crisis on 28 March 1338, when Louis, acting on the orders of King Philip VI of France, executed Zeger de Kortrijzaan, the extremely popular military commander of Ghent. Although van Artevelde's policy was generally supported in Flanders, at least in the cities, its potentially revolutionary implications were inescapable. Some of the count's sympathizers from Bruges and the Franc (castellany) of Bruges came to Ghent on 11 April but were forced to withdraw. Biervliet, north of Ghent, became a center of the resistance, and on 24 April 1338 the militia of Ghent marched on it and dispersed the rebels.[8]

In May 1338 van Artevelde personally led a delegation of captains, guild representatives, and count's men to force the governors of the rural jurisdictions and castellanies to swear

6. Rogghé, "Stadsbestuur," 149; *Rek. Gent 1351–1364*, 339. Despite his prominence, he survived the change of government in 1361, dying in early 1379, before the new rebellion broke out; SAG, G 6, 4, fol. 32r.

7. CA 279, 284–87; *Rek. Gent 1336–1349*, 3:327, 397.

8. Lucas, *Low Countries*, 275, after *Rek. Gent 1336–1349*, 1:238–41, assumes that van Artevelde accompanied the militia, but the accounts, while mentioning other commanders, do not note his presence. We shall see that most evidence suggests van Artevelde normally did not leave Ghent except for the direst emergencies.

allegiance to his regime. The rule of the three cities was particularly severe in western Flanders, the center of sentiment favoring the count. Van Artevelde did continue to use "parliaments," discussions with representatives of all subordinate jurisdictions in Flanders, which had been an integral aspect of the count's governance since the thirteenth century. But his agents also ruled with a heavy hand farther east. At Courtrai in 1340 and at Oudenaarde in 1342 there were violent uprisings against the captains whom he had installed.[9] His regime was based on the overt domination of rural Flanders by the three cities of Ghent, Bruges, and Ypres and the domination of the other two by Ghent. The persistent hostility toward Ghent of Dendermonde, Courtrai, and Oudenaarde, the smaller cities of eastern Flanders, would haunt James and particularly Philip van Artevelde. But in the short run, van Artevelde's policies worked. He had eliminated serious open opposition to his regime by the end of 1339.

The other four captains who assumed power with James van Artevelde in 1338 were Gelnoot van Lens, from the parish of St. Michael; Peter van den Hovene, from St. Nicholas; William van Vaernewijc, from St. James; and William van Huusse, from St. Peter. The captains were basically military leaders of the parish musters, but they also had administrative functions within their parishes, such as requisitioning grain in periods of emergency.[10] Ghent had known regimes of captains before, but in 1338 at least three—van Lens, van den Hovene, and van Huusse—and conceivably van Artevelde himself were members of guilds. Although there was a rough occupational balance among the captains, it was an incidental feature that became more noticeable after van Artevelde's death.

9. Rogghé, *Vlaanderen*, 1:23; van Werveke, *Jacob*, 34–35; *Rek. Gent 1336–1349*, 1:185; Lucas, *Low Countries*, 313; Nicholas, *Town and Countryside*, 178–82; Rogghé, "Democraat," 57–58; Napoléon De Pauw, "Enquête sur les abus des capitaines de Courtrai sous Artevelde (1338–1340)," *Bulletin de la Commission Royale d'Histoire* 79 (1910): 219–88; De Pauw, *Conspiration d'Audenarde sous Jacques van Artevelde (1342). Critique historique* (Ghent, 1878).

10. For example, *Rek. Gent 1336–1349*, 3:110–11; see, in general, van Werveke, *Jacob*, 63.

Gelnoot van Lens was a weaver who remained loyal to van
Artevelde to the very end, sharing his deposition from the captaincy but not his ultimate fate. Exiled in 1349, van Lens returned to Ghent when the weavers were restored to power in
the 1360s, but he kept out of public life. Other members of his
family remained in the city during the 1350s. A John van Lens
was a fuller and draper who was alderman in 1339 and 1344. In
December 1349 he served as "overseer" from the maternal side
of the children of the late Peter van Coudenhove, who had
become captain in 1342 as part of a reaction against van Artevelde. Gelnoot van Lens thus may have been the only member
of his family to maintain absolute fidelity to the revolutionary
regime.[11]

Peter van den Hovene is the least known of the five captains
of 1338. He was probably a fuller, for in 1336 he had channeled
money to the fullers through their ward organizations. He surrendered his captaincy to become alderman in 1342, the fiscal
year of John van Steenbeke's conspiracy against van Artevelde,
and he was again an alderman in 1344, the fiscal year during
which van Artevelde was assassinated. He was not taken hostage in 1349 and remained in Ghent during the 1350s, but he was
not in the government again until he was sent with a delegation
from the parishes to negotiate with the count in July 1358. He
was city receiver in 1359, and he disappears from the record
after April 1361.[12] If he had been part of the van Steenbeke
conspiracy of January 1343, he probably would not have returned as alderman in 1344, for van Steenbeke was exiled. Although van den Hovene avoided exile, his early association with

11. SAG, K 1, fol. 4v; K 7, fol. 29r; K 10, 2, fol. 53v; Z 3, 5, fol. 9v; G 2, 5,
fol. 20v; on Peter van Lens, *Rek. Gent 1336–1349*, 1:195; SAG, G 1a, fol. 11r.
12. *Rek. Gent 1336–1349*, 1:26, for his role in 1336; *Rek. Gent 1351–1364*,
339–40, 416. He was related to John van den Hovene, alderman in 1338 and
1352 and thus a man who was involved in van Artevelde's rise, but who later
broke with him; in 1360 Peter van den Hovene was guardian of the children of
Peter van den Zomple, John's son-in-law. John van den Hovene was called "de
Kersmakere" (candlemaker), and such nicknames sometimes signify profession. SAG, K 1, fol. 21v; G 3,1, fol. 18r; RAG, St. Veerle church, charter of
July 1348.

van Artevelde so compromised him in the count's eyes that he could not join the other fullers in the government during the 1350s, and his reappearance in 1358 suggests that he was at least acceptable to the weavers. William van Huusse was a weaver from the parish of St. Peter. Curiously, he paid a fine to the city in 1338 for leaving in violation of van Artevelde's statute, but since he did return when ordered, it was probably a business trip. He and other members of his family sold cloth to the city at various times. Although a weaver himself, he collected the fine from the weavers in St. Peter's abbey village for the city in 1330 and 1336 and may thus have been a weaver who was less than beloved in his own trade. This certainly would explain his elevation to the captaincy in 1338, as a weaver not hostile to the aristocratic previous regime. With Peter van den Hovene, he left the captaincy in 1342 to become alderman, but the fact that he was again alderman in 1345, immediately after van Artevelde's death, shows that he was firmly with the Gerard Denijs faction of the weavers by that time. He was able to stay in Ghent through the 1350s, perhaps as a reward for turning against van Artevelde. As "Old William van Huusse," he is distinguished from his son and namesake, who was exiled in 1349 and killed in 1359. In 1356 he accepted repayment of a loan to support the city militia on behalf of the weavers, who then had no guild organization. He pledged loyalty to the city in 1362, along with persons being repatriated, but this does not necessarily mean that he had been exiled, for he was dean of the weavers in 1361 and 1362. He was dead by February 1369. While the fact that there were two people with this name confuses matters, the ally and later opponent of van Artevelde definitely stayed in the city during the 1350s and resumed public life after the weaver restoration.[13]

William van Vaernewijc was a knight and landowner from

13. *Rek. Gent 1336–1349*, I:5, 261; 3:43; *Rek. Gent 1280–1336*, 588, 732, 827; *Rek. Gent 1351–1364*, 263, 516, 565; SAG, ser. 400, 9, fol. 249r; Z 2, 4, fol. 15v; BB 49, fols. 89v, 90r; EP 2:506; SAG, G 4,4, fol. 46v.

the parish of St. James. A member of one of the most distinguished lineages of the city, he and his relatives were often in the city government. Perhaps because of this, and perhaps also because of his skill in diplomacy and his ability as a knight to deal with aristocrats on an equal footing, he was sent more frequently than his colleagues on embassies outside the city during the 1340s and was the last of the original captains of January 1338 to be replaced, remaining in office until 29 December 1346. He was dead by 6 February 1351, but his kinsmen continued to serve in the city government. Another William van Vaernewijc evidently left Ghent during the tumults between 1379 and 1385, and we shall see that Simon van Vaernewijc was a passionate opponent of Philip van Artevelde.[14]

In 1338 two captains were made receivers of the city's property, but thereafter the deans of the members were receivers until 1341, when the captains again assumed this function. Van Artevelde, van Vaernewijc, and van den Hovene handled the "great receipt," which was by far the more lucrative of the tax farms, while van Lens and van Huusse handled the "lesser receipt," the rents. The deans were receivers again, however, in 1342.[15] Van Artevelde's supremacy as chief captain is shown by the fact that he received an annual wage of 30 lb. gro. (pounds groot), while the other four captains got 12 lb. gro. apiece.[16] But van Artevelde clearly preferred to work behind the scenes. In both 1338 and 1339 he was also repaid "for expenses that he has incurred this year in governing the city." The extra amount was roughly one-third of his salary in 1338 and more than two-thirds of it in 1339. His reimbursements from 1340 are comparable to those of 1339; his expenses were thus stabilizing into a fairly predictable pattern. Van Artevelde received an additional

14. *Rek. Gent 1336–1349*, 1:107; 2:265; 3:43, 147, 274; SAG, G 1, 1, fol. 27r; G 2, 5, fol. 2v; Z 6,2, fol. 21r; K 10, 2, fol. 25v. A charter of August 1384 mentions a house owned by William van Vaernewijc and his wife, but it does not say that they were living in it; RAG, charter Groenen Briel.

15. *Rek. Gent 1336–1349*, 2:94, 155–56.

16. Several moneys of account were employed at Ghent during the fourteenth century. The pounds groot and parisis, abbreviated lb. gro. and lb. par. in this book, contained twenty shillings, abbreviated s., and each shilling contained twelve pence (denarii), abbreviated d.

payment in 1339 for "many letters that [he] had made and written for the profit of the city." The figures are so exact, expressed in pounds payment (one-fortieth of a pound groot), that he was clearly presenting detailed expense vouchers to the city, although the chronicler Froissart claimed that he did not render accounts at all; rather, when he needed money, he simply demanded it, and no one dared contradict him.[17]

Van Artevelde later complained that he had been impoverishing himself on behalf of King Edward III's policy, and the fact that none of his descendants seems even to have approached his wealth gives some substance to his complaint. Yet the accusations against him that led to his death included not only the indisputable claim that he had collected revenues owed to the count, but also the allegation that he had sent them to England, evidently in hope of buying an English alliance. We shall see that his own son was later to revive this claim in an attempt to retrieve the money. James's finances are difficult to reconstruct from the city accounts, for he received payments and repayments from many sources. He received 500 écus from the government of Ypres in 1339–40 for quelling an uprising there, and in 1340 received £1000 sterling from the English.[18] It is also significant that while two or three of the captains normally accompanied the militia and diplomatic missions outside the city, van Artevelde generally stayed in Ghent except when the business was particularly weighty. However, he sometimes did participate in military expeditions; he accompanied the force to Aardenburg in July 1338, to Courtrai on 3 April 1340, and to Cambrai on 14 June 1340, and he was with the Flemish forces when they joined the English at Tournai in the summer of 1340. But he was conspicuously absent from all negotiations with Count Louis of Nevers after 1340.[19]

There was clearly some tendency of the aldermen and cap-

17. Froissart, *Chroniques*, vol. 1, chap. 59, p. 128; *Rek. Gent 1336–1349*, 1:275, 388.

18. CA 232–33. The English source is the Wardrobe Account of 1338–40, but it refers to the fourteenth year of the reign of Edward III, which ended 25 January 1341.

19. *Rek. Gent 1336–1349*, 1:184, 244–45, 404, 455, 474–75, 486, 496; 2:23–24.

tains to have special areas of competence. All city officials, down to the lowest echelon of clerks and menials, received per task repayments for their expenses, and their activities can thus be reconstructed from the city accounts. The alderman John van Steenbeke, who in January 1343 would lead an an abortive revolt against van Artevelde, and the captains William van Huusse and, to a lesser extent, Gelnoot van Lens were used particularly in diplomacy during the fiscal year 1338–39. It is at least possible that van Artevelde's blanket reimbursements at the end of the fiscal year included his travel, while the other four captains were repaid for individual embassies. During the fiscal years 1338–39 and 1340–41 van Artevelde was never reimbursed under the "Discussions and Parleys" rubric of the accounts, although he did go with the other four captains and other magistrates to West Flanders between 1 and 11 October 1338. But while this mission was extended into other regions of Flanders under the leadership of two aldermen and the captain Gelnoot van Lens, as far as we know van Artevelde returned to Ghent on 11 October. The other military forays of this year show John van Steenbeke as the most prominent of the aldermen and van Lens of the captains. Between 17 and 27 February 1339 van Artevelde went with twelve aldermen and three captains (only van Lens was missing) and guild representatives to West Flanders to quell disturbances around Diksmuide; this expedition is referred to as "James van Artevelde and his company." He also went to Bruges to pacify that city during the third week of July. He participated whenever negotiations were conducted with the English. The notion that van Artevelde ordinarily expected to remain at Ghent is confirmed by the fact that one alderman of 1338 was paid for his costs "last year during the war, when he stayed in the city in place of James van Artevelde to govern the good people who remained inside."[20]

Whether under van Artevelde's direct inspiration or not, the practice developed during the early 1340s of having important officials relinquish their duties during one fiscal year, then as-

20. *Rek. Gent 1336–1349*, I:350, 355–57, 346, 422.

sume other important positions when the aldermen were rotated the following August. Although this could signify a fall
from power if the person concerned did not take another office
later—it certainly did when van Artevelde and his partisans left
the government in the spring of 1345—it seems to suggest a
concern for continuity in administration. Virtually all city governments of medieval Europe rotated important magistracies,
and there were inevitably problems of continuity. Perhaps the
most conspicuous institutional innovation of van Artevelde's
ascendancy was the great increase in power of the deans of the
three members of the city, who functioned with their retainers
as diplomats, soldiers, and particularly city guards. During
emergencies the deans and captains circulated with armed
guards, and there thus seems to have been a concern that new
deans should get some practical experience of their new duties
by assuming them at mid-year.

Deans were such crucial figures that when one was absent
from the city temporarily, he was normally replaced for the
duration; John Scettorf, for example, acted as dean of the small
guilds to guard the city while the dean John Yoens was in the
militia at Tournai in 1340. Hence John van der Vloet was replaced as dean of the weavers by John van Steenbeke on 16 April
1340 but continued as city receiver throughout the year. John
van Dessele yielded as dean of the fullers to John Zelle on 1
May. The two new deans and John Yoens, the small guilds'
dean, who was not rotated out, continued to serve for the rest of
this fiscal year and into the next, while van der Vloet and van
Dessele became first aldermen of the two city councils on 15
August 1340. Van Steenbeke, in turn, served as dean of the
weavers only until Easter 1341, and Zelle as dean of the fullers
until 1 May, but both men continued to serve as receivers
throughout the fiscal year. The practice was maintained
throughout the 1340s but was discontinued thereafter.[21] This

21. Van Werveke, *Jacob*, 62; *Rek. Gent 1336–1349*, 1:388; 2:1, 9, 24. It is at
least possible that these events were tied to an anti–van Artevelde reaction.
Although the aldermen were legally the chief officers of the city, they in fact
exercised less power than the captains, and perhaps the deans, during the

suggests some concern about balance between the weavers and fullers and also shows that the identity of the next board of aldermen was almost certainly known several months before their formal installation.

The concern about balance among members becomes more pronounced from 1342, as guild conflicts intensified in Ghent and other cities. The three holders of the great receipt in 1342 were the deans of the weavers and small guilds, together with John van Steenbeke, who may have been representing the landowners at this time, although in other contexts he acted as a weaver. If so, this is one of the earliest instances of separation of the landowners from the small guilds. But the keepers of the lesser receipt were the weaver John van der Vloet and the fuller John de Bake, who at various times were aldermen but were not deans in this year and thus seem to have been representing members. The deans of the weavers and fullers, Gerard Denijs and John de Bake, were joined by dean Peter Zoetaerd of the small guilds in an embassy on 20 May 1343 to Courtrai to settle internecine conflicts among the guilds there. The legal standing of the persons giving occupational balance was not always the same. When problems arose between the weavers and fullers at Diksmuide in the summer of 1343, one captain (the fuller Joseph Aper) and one alderman (the weaver Peter Stocman) went to settle it.[22]

James van Artevelde was a violent man. After his elevation to the captaincy, he lived in considerable state with an armed escort of brawlers maintained at the city's expense. The chronicler Jean Froissart (*Illust. 3*) claims that he ordered his thugs, numbering between sixty and eighty, to kill any suspected opponent

---

emergency. Most members of the city government were at the siege of Tournai when the magistracy was rotated on 15 August 1340. It may be significant that Gerard Denijs, later the dean of the weavers, who brought about van Artevelde's downfall, became alderman at this time following an exile for most of the 1330s, and John Scettorf was apparently an ally of John van Steenbeke. For the discontinuation of the practice, see *Rek. Gent 1336–1349*, 2:152.

22. *Rek. Gent 1336–1349*, 2:216, 155–56, 218. For a suggestive incident of 1341, see 2:46, 105.

Maistre Jehan froissart

3. The chronicler Jean Froissart. Courtesy Bibliothèque Municipale, Arras, MS 266, from the *Receuil d'Arras,* Photographie Giraudon, and Art Resource, NY. G-11925

at a signal from their leader. He had spies, and there were wholesale banishments of persons from all social ranks who opposed his regime. His opponents' property was confiscated, as was standard practice at the time. While this allegation probably contains some rhetorical exaggeration, other sources prove conclusively that the basic delineation of James's character and activities is essentially accurate. In 1342 a Christmas bonus was paid to fifty-one "of his guards," and the language suggests that he had others who were not included. This is an enormous force to have in attendance on one man, and it may be a commentary on his alleged popularity among the masses that he was murdered within two months of losing his bodyguard in 1345. Froissart also noted that he left half the common property of his opponents for their wives and children and attributed this act to generosity, but it actually demonstrates, as do van Artevelde's administrative practices, an overriding concern with preserving legalities, for wives were entitled to half the common property under Flemish law, regardless of their husbands' behavior.[23]

We have seen that the first murder for which James van Artevelde is known to have been personally responsible occurred seven months after his elevation to the captaincy in 1338, apparently as an offshoot of rivalries between his brother and the victim, Fulk uten Rosen. We shall see that the narratives surrounding van Artevelde's assassination in 1345 mention the father of a poor shoe restorer whom van Artevelde allegedly killed. Spies sent to Arras reported in late 1339 that van Artevelde had killed unnamed brokers of Bruges and had taken an oath at Ghent to go to Calais and remove the nest of pirates who were robbing and killing merchants. To lie about such matters in an espionage report would have been gratuitous, and these incidents would certainly help to explain van Artevelde's notorious unpopularity at Bruges.[24]

23. Froissart, *Chroniques*, vol. 1, chap. 59, p. 128; *Rek. Gent 1336–1349* 2:246; Nicholas, *Domestic Life*, 77–79.
24. CA 232–33.

Another murder occurred at the siege of Tournai in the autumn of 1340, where van Artevelde personally led the troops of Ghent. While in King Edward III's tent, van Artevelde killed a Brabantine knight in front of his master for having referred disparagingly to van Artevelde's low birth. This incident may have been confused with a better documented episode at Tournai, the source of which is a letter from the magistrates of Mechelen, in Brabant, to those of Ypres. English troops had arrested some Brabantine pipers who were chatting with French musicians on the walls of Tournai. Van Artevelde tortured one of them until he confessed that the Brabantine merchant and nobleman William van Duivenvoorde had sent him, but the man then escaped to the camp of Duke John of Brabant. The Brabantine forces left the siege soon afterward. The incident is confirmed in the Ghent accounts. On 12 October 1340, a month after the alleged torture, a city sergeant was sent to the duke and city representatives of Brabant "to atone the deed that allegedly was done to a late servant of the lord William van Duivenvoorde."[25] While van Artevelde can be forgiven a case of nerves, such incidents suggest a man of violent temper, and the uten Rosen affair shows that he was capable of harboring grudges for many years.

Even when no violence was involved, van Artevelde often acted arbitrarily. In 1358 two litigants claimed that the aldermen of Boekhoute, north of Ghent, had rendered a judgment, but that James van Artevelde had summoned them before him, ordered a truce, then reversed the judgment. Count Louis of Male restored the original verdict. Van Artevelde owned peat bogs at nearby Zelzate, and he had interests at Weert, across the river

---

25. Van Werveke, *Jacob*, 16–17; Carson, *Artevelde*, 77; *Rek. Gent 1336–1349*, 2:35. Van Duivenvoorde was a merchant of Mechelen and lord of Oosterhout, and eventually chamberlain of the count of Hainaut. He was also acting as an agent of King Edward III in the Low Countries. See Mary Lyon, Bryce Lyon, and Henry S. Lucas, eds., and with the collaboration of Jean de Sturler, *The Wardrobe Book of William de Norwell 12 July 1338 to 27 May 1340* (Brussels, 1983), p. lxvi and literature cited.

from Bornem; the countess of Bar had held the castle of Bornem
in fief of the count, but van Artevelde and the regent van Mirabello seized it during the war.[26]

Van Artevelde was clearly a man of new money but aristocratic social pretensions. His family is first mentioned only at the
end of the thirteenth century. But we have seen that he became
friendly with the English king, loaned him money, and became
his pensioner in turn, and that two of his children married into
the Flemish nobility. The occasion of the marriage of his daughter to the lord of Erpe on 18 October 1341 brought delegations
and gifts from Bruges, Ypres, and Ghent itself. There were
similar festivities when his son John married the lady of Drongen in 1344.[27]

These incidents illustrate van Artevelde's authority in the other Flemish cities. Captains and regents were installed in the
smaller communities of Flanders. Yet while van Artevelde
maintained the pretense that the three cities of Flanders were
acting as a corporate group, most of the captains were in fact
citizens of Ghent, and he even installed a regime of Ghent men
at Ypres, although not at Bruges; that dubious accomplishment
was to be reserved for his son. He collected taxes and import
duties owed to the counts, instituted forced loans, and collected
tribute from the other towns and castellanies. But van Artevelde
maintained to the end the fiction that he was acting on behalf of
the absent count of Flanders.[28]

The position of Count Louis of Nevers thus becomes crucial
in an evaluation of James van Artevelde's career. James stayed
strictly neutral in the early stages of the Hundred Years War, for
Flanders needed both English wool and French grain. But his
personal inclinations clearly favored the English, while Louis of
Nevers was a faithful vassal of King Philip VI of France. The
count's presence was essential to lend legitimacy to van Artevelde's regime. Louis was in Flanders from the beginning of

26. CA 259, 262, 275.
27. CA 269–73.
28. Nicholas, *Town and Countryside*, 175–83.

1338 until mid-February 1339, from early October through December 1339, from September 1340 through June 1341, and from August 1342 through January 1343. Citing his absence for several months, the cities persuaded him to return in October 1339, but they immediately asked Philip VI for the return of the Walloon castellanies surrendered to the French crown in 1305. This demand, which could not have been taken seriously, effectively compromised Louis of Nevers with his overlord, but the return of Walloon Flanders seems to have become a cardinal aspect of van Artevelde's policy.

Meanwhile, van Artevelde had prepared the ground with the English. King Edward III was sending messengers to van Artevelde at Ghent by October 1338. In January and February 1339, van Artevelde received letters under Edward's privy seal, and from June 1339 he was in frequent contact with the English army at Vilvoorde, in Brabant. By September, van Artevelde's brother John was handling "secret business" with Edward.[29] On 3 December 1339 van Artevelde and the cities forced Louis of Nevers to seal an alliance with Brabant. Nonetheless, van Artevelde seems to have been surprised by the count's flight to Paris later that month, for he still thought that Louis could be won over to an English alliance. Indeed, the argument has been raised that since Edward III had made claims on the French throne since 1328 but had not formally claimed the crown, the idea may have come from James van Artevelde, who saw it as a way for Louis of Nevers to preserve his allegiance to the French monarchy. The count's flight deprived van Artevelde of all basis for his claim that the three cities were acting in their accustomed role as the count's advisors, and he thus had to engineer the appointment of a regent. The choice fell on Simon van Mirabello, husband of the count's bastard sister, evidently before 21 February 1340, shortly after the alliance with England was consummated. When Louis of Nevers was back in Flanders briefly in October 1340, the three cities forced him to pledge that he

29. Lyon, *Wardrobe Book*, pp. li, 260, 262, 274–75, 278, 286.

would govern Flanders and appoint officials in the future only with their consent.[30]

Thus Edward III of England entered Ghent on 26 January 1340 and was acknowledged as king of France in a ceremony on the Friday Market. Edward's first personal contact with James van Artevelde came on this visit, which lasted until 20 February. The pregnant queen remained behind at St. Bavo's abbey and gave birth there to the famous John of Gaunt. Edward III pledged a substantial monetary subsidy to the three cities in return for their alliance, together with the transfer of the staple on English wool to Bruges for fifteen years and commercial concessions in England. As "king of France," he pledged to return the three disputed castellanies and also agreed to cede Tournai and Artois to Flanders.

The rupture with France involved a conscious choice of wool over grain, for most of Flanders' food supply came from France. By the end of January 1340 all legal trade between France and Flanders had ended. There was evidently some smuggling, for Edward III conducted a propaganda campaign in the Walloon castellanies.[31] By 22 February 1340, van Artevelde was receiving substantial payments demanded by the king from the city of London, although evidently to repay the expenses that he had incurred on behalf of the English rather than as a pension or bribe. On 2 March the royal Exchequer paid van Artevelde £1500 "for money owed him for doing the king's business."[32]

Van Artevelde's correspondence with England is a fascinating aspect of his career. Even as early as 5 March 1339 he asked for the return of wine that had been seized on a Sevillian ship belonging to two merchants of Poperinge, near Ypres, but which was destined for van Artevelde. The king agreed to return it, but he openly stated as his reason his fear that van Artevelde might yet change sides. Although Flanders was still officially

30. Van Werveke, *Jacob*, 47–51; Rogghe, *Vlaanderen* 2:14; Lucas, *Low Countries*, 348–52; Rogghé, "Democraat," 60.

31. Lucas, *Low Countries*, 358–67, 370; Van Werveke, *Jacob*, 52.

32. Lyon, *Wardrobe Book*, 25, 44; CA 624–26.

neutral, this text refers to van Artevelde's "good services and his assistance given to the King's affairs in parts beyond the sea." In early 1342 van Artevelde had sent his wife to the English queen to explain the situation in Flanders to her. He wrote to the Prince of Wales, asking him to intercede with his father to pay the archers in Flanders, whom van Artevelde had been paying out of his own pocket. Van Artevelde was clearly able to write French, as any Flemish patrician would have been able to do. He intervened when the interests in England of Flemings not from Ghent were involved, notably Giles de Kempe of Oudenaarde. He tried to have cloth belonging to two merchants of Bruges returned to them from a confiscated ship.

On 31 March 1341, Edward III paid a debt to van Artevelde by giving his attorney in London sixty sacks of wool confiscated from the stores of the Peruzzi bank; although other documents mention grants of license to other Flemings to export wool from various English ports, presumably to avoid going through the staple, this shows that van Artevelde was maintaining ties with the London financial community and that he presumably would have had some use for the wool. The wool grants to van Artevelde continued through the summer of 1342, although no other sources suggest that he was a draper.

The extent of van Artevelde's authority in Flanders is shown by the fact that on 15 December 1342 Edward III intervened with him on behalf of an Englishman whose goods had been detained at Bruges after a shipwreck. Edward had been unable to obtain their release from the burgomaster and aldermen of Bruges and thought that van Artevelde could bring sufficient pressure. On 4 January 1343, as Flanders experienced severe food shortages, the king permitted the merchants of Lynn to export substantial quantities of grain and ale to Flanders, but they were first to obtain letters patent from van Artevelde certifying that they were taking their products to Flanders and not elsewhere. On 16 January 1343, van Artevelde and the government of Bruges jointly attested to Edward III that two merchants of Bruges had sent their proxies to Lynn to buy the grain

and take it to Bruges.[33] Van Artevelde was clearly being treated
as the prince of Flanders and relished the dignity.

The English alliance proved a cruel chimera for James van
Artevelde, as it would for his son Philip. It did secure the wool
supply and enough foreign backing to maintain his position in
Flanders for a few years, but the planned English invasion of
France was a fiasco. An Anglo-Flemish army besieged Tournai
in the autumn of 1340 but got no farther. The truce sealed at
Esplechin on 25 September 1340 was later renewed, and the
peace of Malestroit of 8 December 1342 terminated hostilities
until Michaelmas 1346. Only after van Artevelde's death were
foreign troops again in Flanders, and this time they were
French.[34] The reappearance of Edward III himself at Sluis in the
summer of 1345 inadvertently gave the signal for van Artevelde's assassination. Van Artevelde's negotiations with Edward III between 1340 and 1345 were clearly intended to entice
English intervention and to secure the business interests of
Flemings in England, but the result may have been no more
than to earn van Artevelde a reputation for being an English
agent. The English did not pay the promised subsidies, and the
Flemings had to importune them repeatedly as their municipal
treasuries ran low. James van Artevelde's wife even sought out
the English army in Brittany in the summer of 1342 to press her
city's case with Edward III. The lack of foreign dangers caused
many in Flanders to question the necessity for the great captain's
extraordinary powers, and the problem of the grain supply soon
became critical. The problems that led to the death of James van
Artevelde were thus clearly apparent by 1342, and accordingly
we turn our attention to the last three years of his captaincy and
of his life.

33. The extant correspondence is printed in CA 621-62.
34. For the campaigns and diplomacy, see Lucas, *Low Countries*, 408-24,
478-79.

CHAPTER 3

The Hero Redundant: The Fall and Death of James van Artevelde, 1343–1345

THE VAN STEENBEKE CONSPIRACY

Van Artevelde's regime underwent its first serious crisis during the fiscal year of 15 August 1342 to 14 August 1343. Particularly since the names of the incoming aldermen were known several months before the actual rotation, it is likely that the seeds of trouble were present in 1341–42, but the municipal account of that year is a rough fragment that is hard to compare with its predecessors and successors.

The fact that there had been no fighting against foreign troops since 1340 contributed to some relaxation of internal tensions. An accommodation could probably have been reached with the count, but that would have meant sacrificing van Artevelde personally. There had been serious food shortages since the mid-1330s, for Flanders imported most of its grain from France. In 1342 Edward III tried to help by permitting the export of considerable food, but the city accounts of this year show the forces of Ghent scouring the countryside of eastern Flanders, searching for stores of grain. Van Artevelde had staked everything on the English alliance and was now isolated. A substantial body of opinion in Flanders rejected the notion of accepting the Englishman as king of France and sympathized with the count.

Thus, when Louis of Nevers returned to Flanders between August and December 1342, resistance to the three cities' regime was heightened. The count's presence undeniably influenced the choice of the new government in Ghent in August, but in the short run he seems to have strengthened van Artevelde's position in the city. Under obvious pressure from the three cities, Louis confirmed their ancient privileges, prohibiting imitation of their specialty textiles in the smaller towns and villages. Van Artevelde had always received a much higher wage than the other four captains, but now he became distinguished from them further by wearing the same uniform furnished to the aldermen, which suggested that he alone of the captains could bind the city in negotiations. This was Louis of Nevers's last stay in Flanders; he was to die on the battlefield of Crécy in 1346. Simon van Mirabello was again made regent.[1]

We have seen that van Artevelde was circulating with an enormous bodyguard before the revolt, much larger than those furnished to the other captains, which implies that he anticipated trouble. Although the 1341 account mentions a Christmas bonus paid to fifty-one men, the city did not pay them a regular wage. We can only assume that van Artevelde was paying them from his high salary and reimbursements for costs. They were clearly his private bodyguard. This and the distinction in uniform from the other captains lends credence to contemporary accusations that James was behaving as though he were king. But there is another suggestion that he was in serious trouble by August 1342 and may conceivably have lost power briefly. We have noted his tendency to remain in Ghent and to send the other captains and the deans on business outside the city. Neither he nor the three deans received compensation for accom-

---

1. Nicholas, *Town and Countryside*, 152–55, and literature cited, 176; *Rek. Gent 1336–1349*, 2:193–94. Mirabello survived van Artevelde but was murdered by the count's party in 1346; see Paul Rogghé, "Simon de Mirabello in Vlaanderen, "*Appeltjes van het Meetjesland* 9 (1958): 1–52, particularly 43–44.

panying the militia and the other four captains to Bergues in the summer of 1342, a particularly notable omission, since the members of the incoming government for 1342–43 were chosen there, and the admission of several of his opponents to the magistracy was doubtless facilitated by his absence. Yet in 1343 van Artevelde was paid 40s. gro. arrears in connection with the expedition to Bergues the previous year "for a blood price." The government also paid "for arrears of costs that James van Artevelde incurred for the city before Cambrai and Tournai, and then loaned the city, including 40 gro. that he paid for another blood price than the one above." He may have been loaning the city money without being present. "Blood price" suggests homicide, but the amount that he paid is extremely low and suggests that he was probably one of the party of the killers but did not actually commit the deed himself. While it is clear that the city was paying all of van Artevelde's costs, including private vendettas, the fact that he is not mentioned in the formal payment of expenses to the militia, and the delay in repayment until the following year, after the van Steenbeke coup had failed, almost certainly mean that van Artevelde had faced serious opposition in the summer of 1342, that the killing was probably the subject of an inquiry, and that van Artevelde may have been away from the army when the new government was installed in August.[2]

Ghent had subjected Oudenaarde to a brutal repression following an abortive revolt in the summer of 1342, and this may have caused opposition to surface in Ghent.[3] In addition, two of the original five captains of 1338, William van Huusse and Peter van den Hovene, became aldermen in August 1342. They would serve again in this capacity in 1344 and 1345, during and after van Artevelde's fall from power and death, and the change may thus signify an attempt by van Artevelde to purge his

2. *Rek. Gent 1336–1349*, 2:246, 255–57, 335.
3. N. De Pauw, *Conspiration d'Audenarde sous Jacques van Artevelde (1342)*. *Critique historique* (Ghent, 1878); summary in Nicholas, *Town and Countryside*, 186–87.

regime of two unenthusiastic men who later would become open enemies, since the aldermen in fact held less power at this time than the captains.

The new captains were Joseph Aper and Peter van Coudenhove. Aper was a fuller from the parish of St. Nicholas. Despite the defeat of the fullers in 1345, he served as captain until he was replaced by Baldwin van Laerne on 29 December 1346. With his fellow-captain, John de Scouteete, he would go to Sluis in July 1345 under orders from the city to bring James van Artevelde back; we shall see that the van Artevelde clan killed de Scouteete in 1361 because they held him personally responsible for luring their father into an ambush. Aper served the revolutionary regime loyally to the end, probably dying in the final assault on the city in January 1349, for his widow was disputing his estate with his kin on 15 December 1349. His son remained in the city during the 1350s but held no office. He disappears from the record after 1357 and presumably died. Had he been alive, he almost certainly would have shared the fate of John de Scouteete.[4] Since he replaced a fuller from the same parish, there was evidently some concern to give representation to members as well as to parishes in the captaincy by this time. In view of his subsequent conduct, Aper cannot be considered as having been particularly loyal to the interests of his own guild, and certainly not to James van Artevelde.

Peter van Coudenhove was a weaver and draper who had been alderman in 1340 and loaned money to the city in 1342, when his captaincy began. He left the government in 1345, but he was again alderman in 1347 and evidently died during the assault in early 1349. During the fiscal year 1349–50 his widow was awarded money from John van Steenbeke for a horse taken from her husband, which would suggest that he was not an ally of van Steenbeke in 1342–43, since van Steenbeke was exiled and was only able to return after van Artevelde's death. Some members of the van Coudenhove family were exiled in

4. Rogghé, "Gemeente," 208; *Rek. Gent 1336–1349*, 2:195–96, 216, 265; 3:43, 24; CA 245; SAG, G 1a, fol. 11r. SAG, G 1,2, fol. 37r; Z 2, 3, fol. 5v.

1349, but other van Coudenhoves were linked to the van Arteveldes. William van Coudenhove was the bailiff of the countess of Bar at Drongen, a village on the western outskirts of Ghent. She also held the castle at Bornem, where various van Arteveldes held polder lands, and in 1344 the lady of Drongen married John, son of James van Artevelde. The daughter of James van Coudenhove in 1363 inherited various properties from her father, including a fief at Drongen held of James van Artevelde's daughter. Some van Coudenhoves were exiled during the 1350s, but others seem to have remained in the city, and the family continued to be prominent in various branches of the textile trade, with the notable exception of fulling. It is thus likely that Peter van Coudenhove was a van Artevelde partisan.[5]

The first sign of trouble came from Bruges, where van Artevelde was never popular and where his party was called "the Jacobins," a term also used in the Ghent accounts. By September 1342, the three cities had developed a regular machinery for handling complaints from the rural areas and small towns against their regime, but Bruges was always reluctant and had to be prodded to intervene even in western Flanders. The magistrates of Ghent occasionally even settled industrial disputes in Bruges. On 7 September 1342, three aldermen of Ghent went to Bruges "to hear the words of Hank de Pelsenayere, who was executed at Bruges for his maliciousness." The rough draft of this account more specifically says that his execution was "for his vile language about James and the Jacobins." The aldermen were still at Bruges because of the de Pelsenayere affair on 12 September and were joined by the captain Peter van Coudenhove, another confirmation of his pro–van Artevelde party affiliation. In December, Bruges had to be urged to take action against the textile industry of Eeklo, which was in the Franc (castellany) of Bruges but was within thirty kilometers of Ghent, within which distance it was illegal to make certain types

5. *Rek. Gent 1336–1349*, 1:167, 165; 3:147; SAG, G 1a, fols. 11r, 37v–38r; G 1, 5, fol. 40r; K 1, fol. 37v; CA 275, 307. See also SAG, G 2, 1, fol. 6v; BB 49, fol. 89r; G 3, 1, fol. 46v; Z 6, 4, fols. 3r, 15r; G 7, 3, fol. 22r. Giles van Coudenhove was dean of the lamb pelt workers in 1392, SAG, ser. 172, no. 12.

of cloth. In October the magistrates of Ghent appealed to the count, who was then in Bruges and obviously would serve as a rallying point for opposition, to obtain the release of "some Jacobins who had been captured at Bapaume."[6] There was clearly considerable discontent at Bruges, but contingents from Bruges and Ypres would rescue van Artevelde from van Steenbeke's adherents the following January.

The only complete surviving account of the van Steenbeke affair is contained in the sixteenth-century chronicle of Jacobus de Meyere, but he is generally accurate, and some aspects of his story of the rebellion can be confirmed from the Ghent accounts. De Meyere reports that just before the count left in December, van Artevelde repressed a rebellion at Aardenburg and personally killed Peter Lammins, a noble accused of plotting it.[7] Van Steenbeke was joined in January by the alderman John Borluut, Solomon Borluut, and Peter Damman. When van Artevelde besieged van Steenbeke in the latter's house, his partisans assembled on the Friday Market (*Map 1, G–H 6–7*) and then marched on the town hall, where they proclaimed sole allegiance to their natural prince, which could only mean Louis of Nevers. Pending an investigation, van Steenbeke was confined in the count's castle (*Map 1, H 4*) and van Artevelde in the castle of Gerard the Devil (*Map 1, D–E 7–8*), the two most imposing stone fortifications of the city. But on 8 January troops from Bruges appeared at the city gates and were joined on 11 January by a contingent from Ypres. Van Artevelde's partisans then gained the upper hand in Ghent, exiled van Steenbeke and his allies, and confiscated their property.[8]

The careers and family alliances of van Artevelde's opponents in 1343 show a network of ties pregnant with implications for the future. The Borluuts were an ancient, aristocratic lineage

6. Nicholas, *Town and Countryside*, 182–87, 196–98, and on the textile monopolies of the three cities, 98–116; *Rek. Gent 1336–1349*, 2:206–10.

7. The accounts mention this foray in November but do not say that van Artevelde participated personally. *Rek. Gent 1336–1349*, 2:259.

8. Cited by Carson, *Artevelde*, 78–79.

that generally opposed the van Arteveldes. They are difficult to trace, for there were numerous persons of this name not connected to the wealthy family. The appearance of John Borluut on the council in August 1342 suggests that van Artevelde's opponents may have hoped to ease him out peacefully. John van Steenbeke's career before the episode of 1343 suggests a man of property and principle. Although van Artevelde's murder in 1345 was the result of personal hostility without an ideological base, van Steenbeke was a wealthy member of the governing aristocracy of the city who genuinely felt that Ghent had to repair its relations with the count to avoid disaster. Van Steenbeke was a landowner and alderman in 1338, becoming dean of the weavers at Easter 1340. His ties to the weavers were not purely a politically inspired formality, for he sold cloth to the city for uniforms in 1340. He was city receiver between 7 October 1340 and 14 August 1341, was out of office the next year, then was receiver again in the year of his rebellion. He was married to the daughter of Peter Damman, his ally in 1343. In addition to his functions at Ghent, he was a member of the count's council, accompanying Louis of Nevers in that capacity on 11 November 1339 to negotiations with the Duke of Brabant.

Although Ghent undertook considerable diplomatic activity during the 1339–40 fiscal year, van Steenbeke served the city at Rupelmonde, on the border with Brabant and the site of a strategically vital castle of the count. He was made castellan for thirty-one days but was evidently imprisoned there and had to be rescued by a force from Ghent. He was exiled after his revolt failed but was allowed to return in the spring of 1346. The men leasing his rural property paid the city for the terms of 15 March and 22 June 1346; but then, in return for a final payment of 18 lb. gr., "John van Steenbeke and his friends may have full use of his property henceforth without claims being raised on the city's account." Peter Damman and Solomon Borluut, his allies, were also repatriated under this formula. This background and the fact that only 17s. 8d. gr. worth of his property, probably the chattels, was confiscated immediately after his rebellion suggests a man whose assets lay largely outside the city.[9] He was not exiled in 1349 and continued to live in Ghent in the Onderstraat (*Map 1, F–G 5–7*) until at least 8 February 1375. He was evidently the father of James van Steenbeke, who was alderman during the second and less revolutionary magistracy of late 1379. James may already have been terminally ill, for on 17 October 1380, shortly after leaving the government, he made a bequest to his two bastards and had died by 8 August 1381.[10] The son's early death make it impossible to determine his attitude toward Philip van Artevelde's assumption of power in late 1381.

The Damman connections are important for showing the interlocking ties of family and governance during this time. This family was one of the oldest of Ghent. Peter Damman, whose daughter Beatrice married John van Steenbeke after the rebellion of 1343, had disliked van Artevelde's regime from the beginning. Peter was arrested on 9 March 1338 on van Artevelde's orders but escaped on 8 April. He evidently had a fortified establishment at Evergem, northwest of Ghent, which was besieged by the city guards between 28 March and 16 May 1338. His position until 1343 is unclear, but he was repatriated with van Steenbeke in 1346 and was dead by 31 August 1350.[11]

The situation of other Dammans is more ambiguous. A Lievin Damman stood surety in 1368 for William van Artevelde and Henry Yoens against several butchers. Although a Lievin Damman was a broker in dyestuffs, a draper, and dean of the small guilds in 1356, the man who stood surety for William van Artevelde in 1368 was almost certainly the Lievin Damman who was dean of the brewers in 1363 and 1364, further confirmation

9. *Rek. Gent 1336–1349*, 1:179, 228, 404, 410, 476, 479; 2:25; 3:15–16; CA 101.

10. SAG, K 1, fol. 105r; G 1, 4, fol. 1r; Z 1, 4, fol. 10v; K 5, 1, fol. 20r; G 5, 4, fol. 6r; K 7, fol. 47v; K 8, 2, fol. 3v; G 7, 1, fol. 36r.

11. *Rek. Gent 1336–1349*, 1:226; 2:353, 163; 3:15–16; SAG, G 1a, fol. 5v; K 1, fol. 81r; G 1, 1, fol. 1v.

of a van Artevelde link with the brewing trade.[12] The branch of the family associated with Gelnoot Damman had even closer ties with the van Arteveldes. Gelnoot Damman was married to Marie van Artevelde. He was alderman in 1337, but he evidently died during his term of office. His widow loaned money to the city several times during the van Artevelde ascendancy and owned a loge on the Kalandenberg (*Map 1, D–E 6*) that James van Artevelde himself had built. She still owned the land in 1373, when van Artevelde's daughter and son-in-law, John de Scoteleere, mortgaged the house.[13]

The careers of Gelnoot Damman's children show the problem of facile identification of persons with programs in the tangled politics of Ghent at this time. While service in the government during 1345 does suggest personal opposition to James van Artevelde, it does not necessarily mean opposition to his policies. Simon Damman was the only member of his family who leased tax farms from the city during the van Artevelde ascendancy. Families were divided. John, son of Ser Gelnoot Damman, evidently left Ghent during the van Artevelde regime but returned in 1349 and was alderman several times during the 1350s. But another John Damman, this one the son of John, was also in the counterrevolutionary regime that assumed power in January 1349. One of these gentlemen stood surety for William van Artevelde in 1349. John son of Gelnoot was surety for John van Artevelde, James's son, when he murdered John de Scouteete in 1361. In 1357, John son of Gelnoot Damman and Henry Alin and his wife sold a house that had belonged to the van Arteveldes to the fuller John de Maech. He was among the kinsmen agreeing to the transaction when the property of the younger James van Artevelde was detached from that of his siblings in 1362. The position of the Damman family thus seems to have been personal kinship and friendship to the van Arteveldes but

12. SAG, K 3, 1, BB fol. 1r; WD fol. 24r; G 1, 2, fol. 55v; K 1, fol. 218r; G 5, 1, fol. 5r; *Rek. Gent 1351–1364*, 239; *Rek. Gent 1336–1349* 1:41, 169.
13. *Rek. Gent 1336–1349*, 1:378; CA 192–93, 325.

some hostility toward their revolutionary stance in government.[14]

Gelnoot Damman's son Simon was evidently a business partner of the moneychanger Lievin Rijnvisch, who was active in Ghent throughout the 1350s. Lievin Rijnvisch and his son loaned money to the city in 1380, however, and their evident opposition to the van Arteveldes did not include distaste for the rebel regime per se.[15] But while Lievin Rijnvisch's opposition to the van Arteveldes must be deduced indirectly, other members of his family were clearly their opponents. The hosteler Giles Rijnvisch was alderman in 1339 and 1341 and was banished with van Steenbeke in 1343. In 1349 he was an elector of the magistracy on behalf of the count. James Rijnvisch became alderman in January 1349. He lived in the Drabstraat (*Map 1, F–G 2–4*); and although evidently not a butcher himself, his house was in a neighborhood dominated by that trade, which was extremely hostile to the van Arteveldes. In 1353, James Rijnvisch in the Drabstraat joined no less a figure than John van Steenbeke as guardian of the daughter of John Houdhoers and Juete van Drongen; the families of both parents were butchers. A month later Rijnvisch became guardian of the children of Simon Parijs, the dyer and dean of the small guilds who had been an embittered opponent of van Artevelde in 1345. The family was related to Gilbert and William de Grutere, members of a brewer lineage who opposed the van Arteveldes. In 1355 Rijnvisch stood surety for Catherine Parijs, the widow of Walter van Merlaer; in chapter 4, we shall see the fateful role that the van Merlaers and Catherine Parijs played in the tangled history of the van Arteveldes. The Rijnvisch family owned property at Berlare, near van Artevelde holdings. In view of all of this, it is somewhat surprising that several documents show that James Rijnvisch did not leave the city during the 1380s.[16]

14. CA 302, 304; SAG, BB 49, fol. 91r; Z 2, 4, fol. 1r; K 1, fol. 166v.

15. On Lievin Rijnvisch, see *Rek. Gent 1351–1364*, 145, 430, 485; *Rek. Gent 1376–1389*, 1; SAG, K 1, fol. 197r; K 6, fol. 16r.

16. *Rek. Gent 1336–1349*, 1:262; 3: 397, 327; *Rek. Gent 1351–1364*, 257; Rogghé, "Gemeente," 123; SAG, K 1, fol. 79v; G 3, 5, fol. 12r; K 1, fol. 79v; G

Three conclusions emerge from our study of the major opponents of James van Artevelde in 1343, but none of them holds true for the events of 1345. First, his opponents were convinced that his foreign policy was suicidal; although in 1345 the pretext was used that van Artevelde was conspiring to make the Prince of Wales the count of Flanders, van Artevelde had effectively lost power on the basis of domestic issues some months before his assassination. Second, they came from the old and wealthy families of Ghent, while the van Arteveldes were parvenus. Finally, there is a neighborhood basis for pro- and anti–van Artevelde sentiments that becomes even stronger in the feuds of the next generation. The Borluuts had an enormous castle that still stands on the Grain Market at the corner of the Donkersteeg (*Map 1, F 5*), together with smaller properties nearby, and most of their allies were elsewhere on the Grain Market, the Fish Market (*Map 1, G 4–5*) (the financial center of the city), and the end of the Hoogpoort (*Map 1, F–G 5–6*) toward the Fish Market. The Hoogpoort was a long street linking the two primitive nuclei of the city, along the Scheldt and Leie rivers.[17] Many of van Artevelde's allies lived on the eastern end of the Hoogpoort and the Zandberg (*Map 1, F 7*). The Kalandenberg (*Map 1, D 6*), where the van Arteveldes themselves lived, was near the Waalpoort (*Map 1, B 6*), site of the Weavers' Hall and the area where most of the prominent weavers of the city, including Gerard Denijs, resided. The allegiance of this area seems to have been pro–van Artevelde in the beginning, but James's arrogance alienated his neighbors. In 1361 John van Artevelde, representing his siblings as the eldest son, sued Nicholas van der Pale and his wife, claiming that James the elder had bought a house from Nicholas's mother between his own residence and the house "ter Pale" and had made a kitchen of the property. Nicholas denied that she had sold the house to him; John then began

---

1, 1, fol. 8v; Z 1, 4, fol. 2v; K 2, 1, fol. 19r; G 1, 4, fols. 1r, 5v; G 2, 1, fol. 1v; K 1, fol. 169r; G 2, 5, fol. 2r; Z 2, 2, fol. 12r; K 4, 2, fol. 36v.

17. For the social geography of fourteenth-century Ghent, see Nicholas, *Metamorphosis*, chap. 4.

shifting his ground when ordered to prove his case, claiming that he should at least be compensated for his father's improvements on the building. The aldermen admitted this argument; but it is clear that James the elder had had a falling out with the van der Pales, who were his kinsmen and had been his family's allies in the 1330s, and had simply seized the property between his establishment and theirs. Since the house had passed to his heirs, the van der Pales could do nothing about it until the van Artevelde sons were repatriated.[18]

James van Artevelde's position seemed superficially strengthened in the aftermath of van Steenbeke's failure. His preeminence became even more stridently overt. The domination of Ghent over Bruges and Ypres is demonstrated by an increasing amount of intervention in the internal affairs of those cities from 1343. It was evidently in November 1343 that the troops of Ghent put down a disturbance at Bruges and, according to a Ghent chronicle, came with deployed banners into the Steenstraat at Bruges.[19] On 21 June 1343 the largest cities formally divided Flanders into spheres of influence, in which one of the three was to rule (*Map 2*). The regime of captains in each city was confirmed, although van Artevelde was given no special authority over the others. The rural areas were thus represented in dealings with foreign powers by the cities and subjected to them.[20] In fact, however, the cities had dominated quarters since the beginnings of van Artevelde's ascendancy, if not earlier. In 1482, representatives of Ghent read privileges, allegedly given to the city about one hundred and fifty years earlier, stating that no assemblies could be held or taxes collected in its quarter without its consent. The exact chronology would place this in the early 1330s, but the use of "quarter" suggests that it

18. CA 299.
19. Lucas, *Low Countries*, 490; vander Meersch, *Memorieboek*, 1:48, a work notorious for its erroneous chronology, places this expedition in 1339 but includes the detail concerning the division of Flanders into quarters, which, with the references from the Ghent accounts cited by Lucas, shows that the street fighting at Bruges occurred in 1343.
20. Nicholas, *Town and Countryside*, 178.

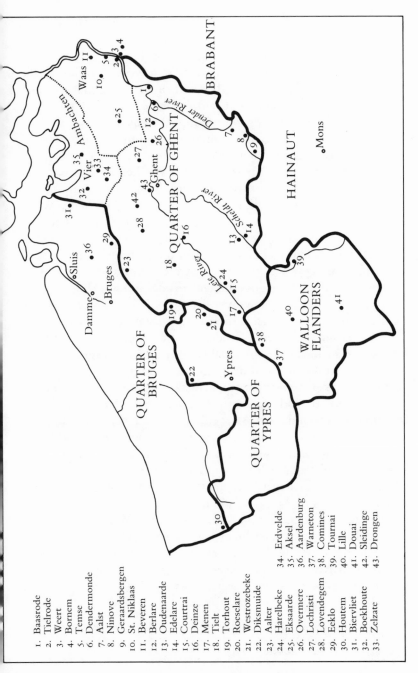

1. Baasrode
2. Tielrode
3. Weert
4. Bornem
5. Temse
6. Dendermonde
7. Aalst
8. Ninove
9. Geraardsbergen
10. St. Niklaas
11. Beveren
12. Berlare
13. Oudenaarde
14. Edelare
15. Courtrai
16. Deinze
17. Menen
18. Tielt
19. Torhout
20. Roeselare
21. Westrozebeke
22. Diksmuide
23. Aalter
24. Harelbeke
25. Eksaarde
26. Overmere
27. Lochristi
28. Lovendegem
29. Eeklo
30. Houtem
31. Biervliet
32. Boekhoute
33. Zelzate
34. Aksel
35. Erdvelde
36. Aardenburg
37. Warneton
38. Comines
39. Tournai
40. Lille
41. Douai
42. Sleidinge
43. Drongen

MAP 2. Flanders in the fourteenth century

dates from van Artevelde's period, probably from 1340, when the count was in Flanders and agreed to govern according to the wishes of the three cities.[21] The text of 1482 does not mention van Artevelde by name, but to do so in dealings with the count would have been the height of studied insolence.

The years 1343–44 also witnessed an important change of internal organization at Ghent, for none of the five receivers now was a captain. This arrangement was kept in 1344–45, but by then at least two of the receivers, Simon Parijs and Lievin van Veurne, were definitely enemies of van Artevelde. While van Artevelde had received a higher wage than the other captains through 1343, all captains received a 10 lb. gro. payment in 1344, with additional compensation for costs. Another notable change this year was the appearance of more open enemies of van Artevelde in the government. In addition to Denijs and the dyer Simon Parijs, the weaver Peter de Clerc reappeared for the first time since 1338, this time as first Estate Alderman.[22]

Other changes were considerably more ominous. Economic problems added to van Artevelde's difficulties. Despite the truce of Malestroit of 1342, little grain was coming down the Scheldt to Flanders. Grain prices at Ghent skyrocketed, and the magistrates had to send expeditions into eastern Flanders to bring supplies overland. Van Artevelde's always pronounced tendency to stay in Ghent became exaggerated after the troubles of 1342–43. When a rebellion at Oudenaarde was quashed in the summer of 1342, delegations from the weavers, fullers, and small guilds participated, as did the other four captains and their guards, but van Artevelde did not. There were more problems at Oudenaarde in October 1343. The three deans, the captain Joseph Aper, and sixty men from each member were sent to pacify the town until a new revolt was crushed on 22 November. Van Artevelde was repaid 7 lb. gro. for money given "to those who were there," clearly proving that he was not. The

---

21. F. Blockmans, *De Volksvertegenwoordiging in Vlaanderen in de overgang van Middeleeuwen naar Nieuwe Tijden (1384–1506)* (Brussels, 1978), 124.
22. *Rek. Gent 1336–1349*, 2:291; SAG, G 2, 1, fol. 8r.

payments in the accounts show that Gerard Denijs, the dean of the weavers, assumed a leading role in this expedition, and van Artevelde's increasing isolation in Ghent could not have gone unnoticed by the rank and file.[23]

Gerard Denijs had succeeded Peter Mabenzoon, van Artevelde's ally, as dean of the weavers by 20 May 1343 at the latest. Mabenzoon was to be aldermen the following year and the other two deans were not rotated, so the change is technically only another example of the mid-year alternation that was common during this period. But the accession to power of van Artevelde's most embittered opponent shortly after the failure of an armed insurrection against him is unlikely to have been coincidental.

Little can be said with certainty about Gerard Denijs, who has generally been considered the person most directly responsible for van Artevelde's fall and death. He had been exiled in Holland during the 1320s, when the weavers were excluded from power. His family name was unusual, and he may have been related to a shearer named Eustace Denijs. He tried to reenter the city with some other exiles in 1330 but failed, and he was only allowed back in Ghent in 1338 by van Artevelde's regime. By 1340 he was alderman. It may be more than coincidence that he represented the weavers on a military expedition to Tournai in April 1340, a foray on which van Artevelde participated personally; the weavers' dean at that time was none other than John van Steenbeke, who was busy in East Flanders. As was true of most prominent drapers, Denijs sold cloth for uniforms to the city, but in 1340 his cloth was rejected as too short. This may have given him cause for a grudge, and he did not sell cloth to the city again during van Artevelde's lifetime. He served as dean until 13 February 1347, when he was replaced by John van den Velde, but he remained in favor with the regime. He died when the count's forces stormed Ghent on 13 January 1349. He lived in the Waalpoort (*Map 1, B 6*), which was the property of the

23. Lucas, *Low Countries*, 480–83; for grain prices at Ghent, see Nicholas, *Metamorphosis*, chap. 3; *Rek. Gent 1336–1349* 2:145, 249, 335–37.

weavers' guild and was near van Artevelde's complex on the Kalandenberg (*Map 1, D–E 6*). On 5 July 1345, less than two weeks before van Artevelde's assassination, he bought an estate at Landegem that would eventually be acquired by the Weavers' Hall. His daughter and evidently only child married Guillaume Pilard of Ath (Hainaut), and his heirs played no political role in Ghent.[24]

James van Artevelde was thus clearly losing power after the abortive van Steenbeke revolt of 1343, and the accounts suggest a man who had delusions of grandeur and was becoming paranoid. His position in Flanders depended on the count's continued absence, but his regime in Ghent had been based on the more or less harmonious relationship among the members—the weavers, fullers, and small guilds and landowners—with each serving in the government. Van Artevelde had probably come to power in 1338 as an ally of the weavers, but he was unwilling to dismiss the fullers as a group; yet most persons who left the city after 1338 were either fullers or landowners loyal to the count. Whatever practical considerations may have moved van Artevelde to attempt a government of civic unity, it was a noble experiment. But it was coming apart by 1342. The other towns and cities resented the domination of Ghent, and throughout Flanders the fullers, who were much poorer than the weavers and depended on them for their incomes, were demanding wage increases. Matters were moving toward a crisis by mid-1343. On 18 July 1344 an alderman who was a draper accompanied two fullers to Bruges, "where the fullers wanted a wage increase." On the same day the three deans went to Oudenaarde, and on 22 July the captain Gelnoot van Lens and one alderman went to Bruges and Damme "because of the fullers."[25] Inevita-

---

24. *Rek. Gent 1336–1349*, 1:26, 486; 2:25, 246–47; 3:44; SAG, K 2, 1, fol. 10r. For the estate at Landegem, see SAG, Wollewevers godshuis, charters. In August 1370, John and Nicholas Denijs atoned for two homicides, but they were the sons of the cloth tenterer John Denijs, who had died in 1355, and were not related to Gerard Denijs as far as can be determined; SAG, Z 4, 5, fol. 19r; G 2, 1, fols. 13r, 40r.
25. *Rek. Gent 1336–1349*, 2:305–8.

bly, the hostility between the weavers and fullers reached Ghent, and it was one of the developments that precipitated van Artevelde's downfall.

THE ASSASSINATION OF JAMES VAN ARTEVELDE

James van Artevelde was deposed from his captaincy in the spring of 1345 and was assassinated in July, evidently as he returned from a mission to Sluis undertaken on behalf of the new rulers of Ghent. The hostilities produced by his murder would have little immediate impact on public policy but would be carried into the next generation by his sons.

There were signs of trouble as early as the change of magistracy on 15 August 1344. The weaver Peter Stocman, who had been alderman in the year of van Steenbeke's revolt, returned as receiver. He was married to Elizabeth van der Pale, evidently the sister of James van der Pale, van Artevelde's by now estranged kinsman and neighbor on the Kalandenberg (*Map 1, D-E 6*).[26] The weaver Lievin van Vuerne had been replaced as alderman at midyear 1342, almost certainly because he was a van Steenbeke ally; but he was city receiver in 1344 and first Estate Alderman from 15 August 1345.[27] Relations between the weavers and fullers were still formally correct as late as 28 February 1345, when both groups were included in a delegation to Dendermonde to stop the guilds there from imitating Ghent textiles. But their wage dispute reached a climax on 2 May 1345 in a pitched battle on the Friday Market (*Map 1, G–H 6–7*), the largest public square of Ghent. The fullers suffered a complete

26. Rogghé, "Stadsbestuur," 150; *Rek. Gent 1336–1349*, 1:25; 2:155; 3:147. He was alderman again in 1347 and succeeded James van den Zomple as captain from St. James parish at mid-year. Although the establishment of wardship for his children John and Elizabeth in 1351 calls them the children of John Stocman, this is almost certainly a scribe's error, for a John, son of Lord Peter Stocman, is mentioned in 1359; SAG, G 1, 1, fol. 22v; G 2, 5, fol. 18r.

27. Rogghé, "Stadsbestuur," 149; *Rek. Gent 1336–1349*, 1:152; 3:44, 200. He was alderman in the first magistracy of 1348 but was then exiled.

defeat on "Bad Monday," as it was called in contemporary Flemish historiography, which was strongly biased in favor of the count. But they were not deprived of political rights, and one captain remained a fuller. Van Artevelde had come to power as a champion of the weavers, but he seems to have tilted toward the fullers after the van Steenbeke rebellion of early 1343. Nonetheless, he sided with the weavers in the wage dispute, perhaps fearing the count's influence among the fullers. By 13 June, an embassy to Bruges included representatives of the weavers and small guilds, but no fullers.[28]

Van Artevelde was definitely deprived of his captaincy at some point during the fiscal year 1344–45, along with Peter van Coudenhove and Gelnoot van Lens, his most loyal partisan of the original captains of 1338, and modern historians have generally assumed that they surrendered power on or shortly after 2 May. The new captains continued to serve during the fiscal year beginning on 15 August 1345, but they received back pay for four months, which would mean that they assumed power around 15 April 1344 rather than 2 May.[29]

A closer reading of the municipal accounts, however, suggests that van Artevelde was deposed even before 15 April. Van Artevelde's salary priority over the other captains, which had been discontinued during the fiscal year 1343–44, was restored in August 1344. The city apparently paid its obligations as they were incurred, since most of its income was derived from tax farms payable at the beginning of the year, for van Artevelde, rather than his heirs, is stated to have received 26 lb. 6s. 8d. gro. in wages and costs; but the "costs" supplement means that we cannot use this figure as an indication of when he stepped down. The amount was "in partial payment," but there is no indication in the later accounts that the unpaid remainder was ever paid to his heirs. The deans were now receiving 12 lb. gro. per year, giving them salary parity with the lesser captains for the first

28. *Rek. Gent 1336–1349*, 2:361, 474–75, 386, 390–91; Rogghé, "Gemeente," 109.
29. Van Werveke, *Jacob*, 81–85.

time. Curiously, both Gerard Denijs of the weavers and John de Bake of the fullers received the full amount, although de Bake died on 2 May and was replaced by Giles van Gavere, a weaver who was evidently made dean to keep the fullers in line. With the new fiscal year in August 1345, all captains received a salary of 10 lb. gr., a clear reaction against the higher position of van Artevelde. Giles van Gavere, in addition to his duties with the fullers, received 4 lb. "arrears of his wage from last year, when he was chosen captain in place of James van Artevelde" in the parish of St. John, and the same rate was applied to John de Scouteete, who replaced Gelnoot van Lens. The case of Peter van Coudenhove is more ambiguous, for his arrears included not only his wages but also costs on embassies. It thus cannot be stated absolutely that he was deposed with van Artevelde and van Lens, although it is probable. This rate would suggest that the change of power occurred 146 days into the previous fiscal year, or 23 March 1345.

This timing is confirmed by the fact that in March the three cities decided in principle to try to get Count Louis of Nevers to return to Flanders. Realizing that he would be sacrificed in any arrangement calling for the return of Louis of Nevers, van Artevelde had opposed the return of the count since 1342. Van Artevelde and Gelnoot van Lens may have had to surrender their captaincies in connection with this development.[30] Yet he was still a man of great influence, and as late as 28 April the city paid the costs of a messenger sent "from outside to James."[31] Peter Zoetaerd, who was probably a furrier, was deposed at the same time as dean of the small guilds and replaced by the dyer Simon Parijs, whom the chroniclers portray along with Denijs as van Artevelde's most determined personal opponent. Zoetaerd, in contrast, had been a firm ally of van Artevelde. Indeed, their families had probably been neighbors at Ertvelde, north of Ghent, the van Arteveldes' ancestral home, although

---

30. *Rek. Gent 1336–1349*, 2:406. On Giles Van Gavere, compare *Rek. Gent 1336–1349*, 2:385 and 372.
31. Rogghé, *Vlaanderen*, 2:30–31.

there is no evidence that any van Arteveldes as late as James held land there.[32] The weaver-fuller agitation thus undoubtedly contributed to van Artevelde's death, but it is not tied directly to his fall from power, which occurred some months earlier.

No contemporary document gives the precise date of James van Artevelde's death, but most have assumed that he was killed on the evening of 17 July 1345. He had been at Sluis negotiating with the English king on behalf of Ghent. Although he had no formal tie with the city government by that time, the city frequently used the services of specialists not in the magistracy, particularly moneychangers and hostelers, in conducting official business, and van Artevelde's personal friendship with Edward III was useful. Most chroniclers claim that Edward III wanted the Flemish cities to recognize the Prince of Wales as count of Flanders if Louis of Nevers persisted in his alliance with the Valois of France, and that all Flemish political leaders except van Artevelde objected to this scheme. The usually accurate Giovanni Villani, who died only three years after van Artevelde, gives this version and suggests that van Artevelde's assassination at Ghent was more the result of his own haughty behavior than of any fundamental disagreement over policy. Credence is given to Villani's account by the fact that he mentions the death with James of his brother and nephew, and no other source mentions Francis van Artevelde after this date.[33] Of modern historians, only Léon Vanderkindere has accepted this version, although

32. Most of the Zoetaerds were butchers, but on 16 September 1351 the furrier Peter Zoetaerd atoned the killing of John de Duutsche or von Tryren of Ypres. In early 1342, as dean of the small guilds, Zoetaerd represented them in a mission to Ypres to "help" choose deans and guild councillors and thus almost certainly became involved in the affairs of the furriers' guild; *Rek. Gent 1336–1349*, 2:46, 105; SAG, Z 1, 2, fol. 2r; Z 3, 1, fol. 3r. The butcher is first mentioned independently in a text of 1364, RAG, SN 118, fol. 151r. The ties with Ertvelde appear in 1359, when a Giles Zoetaerd, who was living at Ertvelde, leased all land in that parish belonging to the church of Our Lady of St. Peter's of Ghent, and his surety was his son, the baker Giles Zoetaerd, whose bakery was in the Scelstraat on the corner of the Koutersteeg in Ghent, very near the Van Artevelde complex on the Kalandenberg; SAG, K 1, fol. 241r; K 5, 2, fol. 39r.

33. Quoted CA 250–51.

van Werveke seems to have leaned toward the view that van Artevelde may have thought in such radical terms.[34]

As soon as van Artevelde's assassination became known outside Ghent, Froissart relates that delegates of the other Flemish cities sought an audience with Edward III to assure him that Ghent alone was responsible for the killing and that they had considered him a wise leader. Yet the fact that van Artevelde was no longer in the government of Ghent when he died and that the English had no choice except to maintain the Flemish alliance makes one suspicious of the personal side of this story. It is true that shortly after van Artevelde's assassination Edward III allied directly with Bruges and Ypres, while Ghent only joined the union a few days later. But this probably reflects English uncertainty about whether the government at Ghent intended to maintain the old alliance, not a greater willingness of Bruges and Ypres to admit the claims of the Prince of Wales.[35]

The chroniclers were basing their work on nearly contemporary original records. It seems clear that whether van Artevelde actually intended revolution or not, his fellow citizens at Ghent believed it of him, and his personal and political opponents were more than willing to use the resulting disenchantment as an excuse to get rid of him. It cannot be denied that restoring Louis of Nevers would have cost van Artevelde his life and that he may have thought that he could recover his lost position at Ghent with English aid. The parallel of Walter of Brienne, who transformed the extraordinary office of "war captain" into a short-lived tyranny in Florence in 1343, the very year of the van Steenbeke conspiracy, cannot be overlooked, for van Artevelde was no more oblivious to developments in Italy than Villani was

---

34. Van Werveke, *Jacob*, 85–87; Léon Vanderkindere, *Le Siècle des Artevelde. Etudes sur la civilisation morale et politique de la Flandre et du Brabant* (Brussels, 1879), 37–38.

35. N. de Pauw, "L'Assassinat d'Artevelde et l'instruction de ce crime," *Cour d'Appel de Gand* 4 (1905): 30; Froissart, *Chroniques*, vol. 3, chap. 237, pp. 103–5. Froissart, however, adds that Bruges and Ypres did mention that they disagreed with van Artevelde about recognition of the prince of Wales as count, for the Prince would eventually have such a magnificent inheritance that he had no need of Flanders. The king evidently accepted that argument.

to those in Flanders. The estrangement from the weavers after 1342 also suggests that van Artevelde may have been thinking of himself as lord of his native city, for the Flemish counts had traditionally supported the poorer and less numerous fullers as a counterpoise to the weavers. But the weavers were firmly in control in Ghent in 1344–45 and demonstrated this by crushing fuller demands for higher wages in the other Flemish cities as well as in Ghent. Van Artevelde's attitude had thus alienated both the weavers and the fullers by the spring of 1345. But it also cannot be denied that whatever Gerard Denijs and his allies may have thought of having the Prince of Wales declared count of Flanders, they continued the English alliance forged by James van Artevelde. Short of submission to the French, they had no choice, and no one in his right mind wanted to offend Edward III and cut off the wool supply.

Human attitudes are rarely consistent. Ghent depended upon English wool, but van Artevelde was widely distrusted as an English agent. The weavers naturally favored an English alliance in principle, as the shippers would favor France. We shall see that conflict between these groups, so dependent on imports from the two rival kingdoms, would have fateful consequences in 1379. Van Artevelde had certainly spent considerable sums from his own pocket in furthering English political interests. On 16 January 1345, Edward III granted him a yearly pension of 100 lb. as his reward "for the trouble and enormous costs that he has incurred in the land overseas in order to preserve our rights, exposing his life to many dangers." Nothing was said about the Flemish countship as a quid pro quo, but this was a great deal of money. Despite his fall from power, van Artevelde may have underestimated the extent to which public opinion at Ghent had turned against him; but other indications, notably the fact that he sent his wife and children away from Ghent shortly before his death, suggest that he knew that his time was short and that he was really hoping for an exile in England rather than a restoration at Ghent. The pension would have provided him a comfortable income. That Edward III thought of the pension as compensation for the loss of van Artevelde's assets in Flanders is suggested by his confirmation on 13 November 1345 of the pension to the captain's widow until the Flemings returned her property or he regulated matters differently. She ordinarily would have had no rights on money granted to her husband alone, but the king knew her personally, since she had conducted diplomacy for Ghent in England. In 1346 nine of van Artevelde's servants, his brother William, and some partisans were given asylum in England and small sums of money. But the property of Catherine de Coster, the widow, was not confiscated. She returned to Ghent after a short time in England and by 24 June 1349 had remarried, to the knight Zeger Bornaige. Her stepsons, John and James, her nine-year-old son, Philip, and her brother John de Coster went into exile in England.[36]

The accounts of Ghent mention both the duties performed by municipal officials outside the city and the amount of their reimbursement. This information permits us to reconstruct the diplomatic activity of James van Artevelde's last days. On 1 July 1345 the captains van Vaernewijc and van Coudenhove went to Bruges for four days to negotiate with William of Weston concerning a subsidy that Edward III had promised. They were thus back in Ghent by 5 July. The same men were again in Bruges between 7 and 9 July. On 7 July 1345, presumably starting at the same time that the captains went to Bruges, van Artevelde was sent to Sluis, the outport of Bruges to the king himself to thank him for coming. But the costs of this expedition included men sent after him to bring him back toward Ghent, and a separate payment was made to Lievin van Veurne, the first Estate Alderman and a prominent weaver, who was also sent to him.[37]

All under the rubric of Thursday 7 July, James van Loevelde, the aldermen's clerk, was sent toward Sluis to fetch van Artevelde but met him coming back toward Ghent. We are not told when these various persons returned, but van Artevelde must have made it back to the city, since his costs were repaid.

36. CA 660–61, 664–65, 669.
37. *Rek. Gent 1336–1349*, 2:391.

But on Monday, 11 July, three aldermen, including the former captain Peter van den Hovene, two clerks, and the captains William van Vaernewijc and the fuller Joseph Aper (the former having returned from Bruges on 9 July) went to Sluis, where van Artevelde was stated to be. Aper had been at Aalst, thirty kilometers east of Ghent, between 7 and 11 July, so he must have been sent to Sluis the moment he got home. They were out two days, "and when they got back home, there was sent back on Wednesday and Thursday [13 and 14 July]" a delegation consisting of four of the same people, aldermen, and seventeen men from the guilds, evidently summoned because they had power to act on behalf of the city, as van Artevelde and the captains did not, "for the job of sealing that our lord the king wished done." Gerard Denijs, Giles van Gavere, and John de Scouteete were conspicuously absent from this embassy; de Scouteete and one alderman were sent on the same day to the fair at Houtem, southwest of Bruges. The Ghent accounts are obviously composites from rough drafts and receipts, for after the entry about Houtem, we are told that van Vaernewijc and the clerk van Loevelde were sent "toward Sluis to the good people of Bruges and Ypres for the same purpose." Some members of the Sluis delegation were away from Ghent for two days, others three. This embassy must have left on 12 July, for on 11 July the magistrates leased a horse "that Loevelde rode around the city." Although we are not told the purpose of the ride, the implication is that he was summoning the citizens to an assembly. All men sent to Sluis would have been back in Ghent before Sunday, 17 July.

But the account then shifts back to John de Scouteete, "who was sent to James van Artevelde with a delegation of twelve horses [horsemen] when he first went to Sluis to our lord the king." It was obviously a quick trip, for de Scouteete was away from Ghent for only one day, and Sluis and Ghent are forty kilometers apart. But the "first" reference shows that van Artevelde in fact went to Sluis at least twice. He went on 7 July and was summoned back, but the references to those sent for him say that they met him coming "toward Ghent," which does not mean that he actually got back. He was at all events back in Sluis doing something to make the magistrates suspicious, and at an early enough date to give them time to send a delegation on Monday, 11 July. Thus it is likely that van Artevelde did not in fact get all the way back to Ghent on 7 July, but rather returned to Sluis after meeting van Loevelde on his way back to the city. He may at most have gone to Ghent long enough to present his expense vouchers, since he was reimbursed for this trip then left again. The delegation of 11 July was sent "to hear the king's wish," which may have been relayed by van Artevelde to van Loevelde.

On 13 July, the day when the larger delegation went to the king, the captains de Scouteete and Aper were sent "urgently" to van Artevelde at Sluis. There is no overlap in personnel between these embassies. The captains were gone for two days; they evidently went to van Artevelde while the larger group went to the king, suggesting that the city was trying to disassociate itself from van Artevelde in Edward III's eyes. On 16 July 1345 another expedition, some of whose personnel were also on the mission of 13 July, returned "there to speak about the letters of my lord of Flanders [Edward III, who was recognized as king and thus as the lord of Count Louis of Nevers] for the unity of the common land." An undated reference follows this in which van Artevelde's wife was paid for an embassy to England, and William van Vaernewijc thereafter went to England for the same purpose.[38] Indeed, on 11 June 1345, after van Artevelde's fall from power but a month before his assassination, Edward III had agreed to repay the costs incurred for the war by van Artevelde and William van Vaernewijc through payment of the enormous sum of 1000 lb. gro. by book transfer through merchants of Lucca.[39] While this shows the extent to which van Artevelde had used his own resources on behalf of

38. All references and quotations are in *Rek. Gent 1336–1349*, 2:412, 392–94.
39. CA 661–62.

the English alliance, it also shows that sympathy for England was not per se his undoing, for van Vaernewijc remained in power until late 1346. The last dated entry of the "Meetings and Parleys" rubric of the municipal accounts for this fiscal year is for 16 July 1345, nearly a month before the fiscal year ended. This is rather peculiar under any circumstances and suggests that the magistrates wanted to conceal from future investigation just what role particular individuals had played in the events leading to van Artevelde's murder. We shall see that they were not thorough enough.

The figure of John de Scouteete thus assumes central importance in the drama of James van Artevelde's assassination. Gerard Denijs was dead by the time the van Artevelde sons were repatriated, leaving only a female as his heir, and women were generally exempted from blood feuds in fourteenth-century Ghent. But John van Artevelde, James's oldest son, killed John de Scouteete in the autumn of 1361, shortly after returning to Ghent from exile. He obviously felt that his father had been betrayed. He undoubtedly heard rumors that have escaped the written record of what passed between the two men at Sluis, and the fact that John de Scouteete was not exiled in 1349, despite his intimate association with the revolutionary regime, would have fueled the van Arteveldes' suspicions. John de Scouteete was apparently a carpenter, for he, his brother Zeger, and a Henry de Scouteete are in a list of carpenters dating from 1352 through 1367. He replaced the draper Gelnoot van Lens as captain from the parish of St. Michael. His service was brief, for he was succeeded on 29 December 1346 by John de Bastaert.

Although John de Scouteete had living relatives who would ordinarily have arranged the atonement of the death, the blood price was set in 1361 by Henry Goethals int Hout, a wood merchant and carpenter who was dean of the small guilds that year, a fact that suggests that the homicide had been a consequence of John de Scouteete's performance of his official duties. The various de Scouteetes who pledged to keep the peace after the atonement in 1361 were not required to furnish sureties, which was highly unusual and suggests that the captain's survivors may have agreed that he had compromised himself. Goethals first appears in the government in July 1358, when he was sent to a conference with the count, who was investigating the misdeeds of the fuller regime that was about to end. He and other members of his family were in the magistracy frequently thereafter. The Goethals and de Scouteetes thus seem to have been carpenter families who disliked the counterrevolutionary regime, but John de Scouteete had been too compromised by his association with the rebels of the 1340s to be able to assume public functions again.[40]

The exact date and circumstances of James van Artevelde's death are disputed. Nothing in the Ghent accounts places him at Sluis later than 13 or 14 July. Messengers who came to him from outside the city on 20 July were sent back, suggesting that he was dead by that time. Villani places his death on 19 July.[41] To reestablish the circumstances of his death, it is thus necessary to turn to the chronicle evidence and check it against the indirect suggestions of the official sources.

The anonymous Flemish chronicler who was probably from Ghent but whose work is known only in a Bruges copy of the fifteenth century claims that van Artevelde wanted the Prince of Wales to be recognized as count of Flanders and sent messages to the other cities urging this. At an assembly at Ghent, perhaps the meeting called by van Loevelde on 11 July but conceivably another meeting on 16 or 17 July, since van Artevelde cannot be proven still to have been at Sluis at that time, Gerard Denijs spoke against this and also made a personal point against van Artevelde: "This James wants to deceive us, and it is clear that he is a liar. For he once said that if he ever married [his] children to golden spurs [nobles], or had imposing houses built, or kept big steeds to ride, or acquired great wealth, nobody should ever

40. CA 302–03; SAG, Z 3, 5, fol. 2v; G 3, 5, fol. 38v; ser. 190–1, no. 1, fols. 2r–4r; *Rek. Gent 1336–1349*, 3:43; *Rek. Gent 1351–1364*, 340.
41. *Rek. Gent 1336–1349*, 2:413; CA 251.

trust him again and or respect him in the community." Van
Artevelde's daughter had in fact married a nobleman, and the
municipal accounts lend credence to the other allegations.

Defeated in the assembly, van Artevelde withdrew to his
house on the Kalandenberg (Map 1, D–E 6) and had a meal with
his personnel. Denijs seized his advantage and came to the house
with "his weavers" with banners deployed, calling "Kill the
false sealer, who wants to deseal [sic] our legitimate prince from
his land." This language is so strongly reminiscent of the passage in the city account that we have discussed that it suggests
that Denijs's accusation was probably accurate. Van Artevelde
tried to escape through the barn into the Paddenhoek (Map 1, D
6) behind his house; but the Flemish chronicler then adds that a
restorer of old shoes whose father van Artevelde had killed lived
in the Paddenhoek and dispatched him with an axe blow to the
head, thus avenging his father's death. The chronicler reports
this as done on the eve of Saint Mary Magdalene, or 21 July.[42]
Van Artevelde's obituary at the church of St. John (Map 1, D–E
6-7) was celebrated on 17 July; but if a copier of this chronicle
made xvij into xxi, and the Flemish scripts of this period often
have a tag on "x" that could easily be confused with "vj," this
account would correspond very nicely to other accounts of
James's death. Even the reference to the shoe restorer rings true,
for a rent book of the Weavers' Hall from the 1390s mentions
"shacks at the Waalpoort (Map 1, B 6) where the shoemakers
sit."[43] The Waalpoort is near the van Artevelde complex on the
Kalandenberg and Paddenhoek, the site of Gerard Denijs's residence, and the shoe restorers were a poor group who may well
have disliked van Artevelde's aristocratic pretensions. It is indeed likely that the legendary haughtiness of van Artevelde and
his documented propensity to violence simply caused him to
lash out at a "trashy" neighbor who interfered with him. We
shall see that Philip van Artevelde apparently thought that a
shoemaker had been involved in his father's death.

42. Documents quoted CA 246–48.
43. SAG, Wollewevers godshuis 268.

The chronicle of the Burgess of Valenciennes, who died around 1370, also has some information that can explain the superficial discrepancies in the city accounts.[44] This version has van Artevelde summoned to Sluis by Edward III rather than being sent by the government of Ghent. This is clearly inaccurate, since the city was reimbursing van Artevelde's travel expenses. He went with his entire entourage of about one hundred persons, but the king advised him to send them back to Ghent except for his small private guard, for he had great things to discuss with him. When this became known at Ghent, it was discovered that he had taken all his property and his family with him when he left. The aldermen then sent two officials to ask him to return because they needed his advice. He said that he would be back within five days, by the Sunday before Mary Magdalene, or 17 July. This would mean that he was speaking on 12 July; we have seen that the city sent an embassy to him at Sluis on 11 July, and it took a day to get there, so this version is probably correct. The officials carried this message back to Ghent, where the masters of the city decided that it was too suspicious, and that van Artevelde would have to be executed when he returned.

As this embassy returned on 16 July, an assembly on 17 July to "set up" van Artevelde is thus very probable. Edward III then

44. Printed CA 248–50. The chronicler of Saint-Dénis claims that van Artevelde asked Edward III for a guard of five hundred to kill Gerard Denijs for him, but the decision was taken to send van Artevelde into the city with only twenty-six men and have the five hundred storm the gates. Denijs heard of it, killed van Artevelde, then shut the gates against the English (CA 253). A version of this story has been accepted in a recent biography of Edward III; see Michael Packe, *King Edward III* (London, 1983), 142–43. In view of the obvious risk to van Artevelde of such an undertaking, this version is highly improbable. A variant of the story is given by an anonymous Walloon Flemish chronicler whose history ends with the death of Count Louis of Male in 1384. He, too, mentions the assembly at which van Artevelde and Denijs debated; but although "a great part of the commune sided with James, the landowners and even the dean of the weavers, named Gerard Denijs, disagreed and said that it would be dangerous to abandon one's true lord for another." In this, most of the commune sided with the landowners. Van Artevelde then went to transmit the assembly's wishes to Edward III and at this point asked for the five hundred men to kill Denijs; CA 254.

offered him an armed escort, but van Artevelde declined it because he thought that no one would do him harm, and here is a crucial feature of the problem. Van Artevelde definitely returned to Ghent without a substantial guard; most of his private retainers had already been sent back. He may have been overconfident, but in that case he would hardly have removed his family and belongings. In all probability, one of the emissaries who was sent to recall him—and the evidence of the municipal accounts suggests that this was John de Scouteete—misled him into thinking that there was no risk. Van Artevelde's heirs obviously thought that this had happened. Again following the Burgess of Valenciennes, when van Artevelde entered the city with his twelve remaining guards, he noticed that persons who normally doffed their hats to him now were hanging their heads. He went directly to his house, where Denijs led the mob. This version says nothing about the shoemaker but claims that van Artevelde was trying to reach sanctuary in the Franciscan convent (*Frereminueren, Map 1, B-C 3–4*), which was some distance away, but the logical route for a man trying to escape detection would have been through back alleys such as the Paddenhoek (*Map 1, D 6*). The final version of Froissart's Chronicle gives this basic version of events as well, but adds the detail that the mob outside van Artevelde's house demanded an accounting from him for the money that he had allegedly sent to England. Froissart also quotes a speech by the captain from an upstairs window in which he allegedly claimed, "You have made me what I am, and you swore once to defend me against all men, and now you want to kill me for it."[45]

The fall of James van Artevelde may thus be tied to foreign-policy considerations but certainly not directly to the weaver-fuller rivalry. It was personal, the result of his excesses and private rivalries inside the city. His death brought no fundamental changes in policy. This fact makes it difficult to determine in all cases who his friends and enemies were. It is safe to say that those who entered the government in August 1345 were his

45. Froissart, *Chroniques*, vol. 3, chap. 237, pp. 100, 102.

enemies, but this was no longer true by 1346. In avenging his father's death, Philip van Artevelde was more concerned with tracking down people who had been in the government in the fiscal year 1344–45; but since James van Artevelde started that year as captain, he still had friends in the administration at that time. There does not seem to have been a general proscription of van Artevelde's allies after his death. The benches of aldermen that took office on 15 August 1345 were stacked with his opponents, and this year saw a return to the earlier practice of having the captains function as receivers. Van Artevelde's opponents had clearly wanted his hand out of the treasury in 1342 and 1345, but the captains were not receivers in 1346.[46] There was a further reaction in December 1346, and some van Artevelde partisans returned. Most notable among them was Peter Mabenzoon, who succeeded Giles van Gavere, van Artevelde's successor as captain from the parish of St. John. Mabenzoon, like van Gavere, was a weaver. He was alderman in 1339 and receiver in 1342. But he was also alderman in 1343, showing clearly that he was in the pro–van Artevelde party of the weavers' guild, not the Denijs faction. He was exiled in 1348, and, with William van Artevelde, he was in charge of money for the hostages in 1360. Yet the fact that young Giles van der Pale became his apprentice in 1362 suggests that by then he had distanced himself somewhat from the van Arteveldes, as the van der Pales had done.[47]

The change of 1346 also suggests that there was now more desire to keep professions balanced among the captains, for the replacement of van Artevelde by van Gavere had involved a weaver succeeding a small guildsman. But this did not mean that the same profession had to be represented in the same parish. Gelnoot van Lens, a weaver, had been succeeded by a carpenter, who in turn was succeeded by another carpenter, replaced on 29 December 1346 by Jan de Bastaerd, whose profession is uncertain. Curiously, the fuller Joseph Aper repre-

---

46. *Rek. Gent 1336–1349*, 2:444; 3:2.
47. Ibid., 2: 46; 3:43; CA 139; SAG, G 3, 2, fol. 30v.

sented the parish of St. Nicholas, the richest parish of the city and a place where few fullers lived, and he was succeeded in the December revolution by another fuller, Baldwin van Laerne. The linen merchant James van den Zomple replaced the landowner William van Vaernewijc in St. James parish. The fiscal year 1346–47 witnessed rapid changes of personnel, notably three deans of the weavers: Gerard Denijs until 13 February 1347, John van den Velde until 7 April, and Lievin van Vuerne until 14 August. Yet in each of these cases, including that of van Vaernewijc, the displaced officials remained loyal to the regime and continued to perform services for it. Simon Parijs, however, who was first Estate Alderman this year, was deposed and banished at this time for reasons that are uncertain. The count himself was in Ghent briefly in March 1347, and the change of 7 April was probably the result of a meeting at Bruges that same day, made necessary because the the count had left Flanders again. A more extreme group became deans, for now the deans, rather than the captains, were the real source of power. Gerard Denijs was never captain, and his domination of the city was neither as long-lived nor as blatant as van Artevelde's. While he had a larger force of bodyguards than did the captains and the other deans, the largest number ever mentioned for him is five, in contrast to over fifty for van Artevelde.[48]

The weaver-dominated regime that came to power shortly before James van Artevelde's death in 1345 thus continued to control Ghent until the final capitulation to the Flemish count on "Good Tuesday," 13 January 1349. But there can be no question of a dictatorship of the weavers. The fullers were back in the city government by August 1345, although in considerably reduced numbers.[49] The sources agree that the factions in the city favoring capitulation to the count were led by fullers, butchers, fishmongers, and shippers. All of these trades were to

48. *Rek. Gent 1336–1349*, 3:1, 24–25, 43–44, 60, 66 ff., 70–71, 117–18; Julius Vuylsteke, "De goede Disendach, 13 Januari 1349," *HMGOG* 1 (1895): 17.

49. Rogghé, "Gemeente ende Vrient," 108–09.

suffer the vengeance of Philip van Artevelde, and all except the fullers were groups growing in numbers and economic power as a consequence of the economic reorientation that Ghent was experiencing during the fourteenth century.[50] The butchers, indeed, seem to have been the count's most trustworthy allies in Ghent. His great-grandfather had probably given them a privilege in 1302 by making mastership in the guild hereditary. When Count Louis of Male confirmed this grant in 1356, the butchers complained that the weavers had withdrawn it while they were in power, and this can only mean about the time of van Artevelde's assassination or shortly thereafter.[51] The weavers resisted the count to the bitter end, and we shall see that Philip van Artevelde came to power as their ally in a purge of the small guilds, and particularly the butchers. The van Arteveldes were firmly allied with the English and the textile guilds dependent on English wool. Opposition to them, and particularly to Philip, came from the food guilds, which needed the French trade, even though James van Artevelde evidently began his career as a broker in comestibles.

Although Jean Froissart claimed that Philip van Artevelde instituted a purge of his father's opponents, he concluded his account of James's assassination by saying that he thought it peculiar that the blood of James van Artevelde was never avenged.[52] But Froissart was wrong. Just how tragically mistaken he was is the principal theme of the rest of this book.

50. Vuylsteke, "Goede Disendach," 15, 25–28. It is also true, however, that each of these guilds had minorities that favored the weavers' extreme position; see Rogghé, "Gemeente ende Vrient," 117–18.

51. The confirmation of 1356 is printed by Frans de Potter, *Gent van den oudsten tijd tot heden*, 8 vols. (Ghent, 1883–1901), 2:397–401.

52. Froissart, *Chroniques*, vol. 3, chap. 237, p. 320.

CHAPTER 4

The Brood of Vipers:
The Children of James
van Artevelde, 1345–1370

Accounts of the van Artevelde family have understandably focused on the spectacular career of James the elder.* But his widow was obviously a very interesting and able woman, and the careers of James's six children provide important information about their father's legacy.

Figure 2 traces the descendants of James van Artevelde the elder. He was married twice. The name of his first wife is not known. Her sister or more probably her daughter, whose name is also unknown, married Godfrey de Roede, for John van Artevelde, her son, later became guardian from the maternal side of Wivine, Godfrey de Roede's daughter. When the parent of a minor child died, his or her personal estate and all common property were divided immediately between the surviving

---

*Parts of this chapter will remind musically inclined readers of Ralph Vaughan Williams's description of the finale of his Sixth Symphony: "whiffs of theme drifting about." Although I have made every effort to simplify, the family relationships of persons involved with the van Arteveldes and their blood enemies are extremely complex and difficult to reconstruct coherently from the sources. But they are a necessary prologue to themes that will be developed in chapters 5 and 6. Readers are therefore urged to make liberal use of the Dramatis Personae provided at the beginning of the book and the genealogical tables accompanying this chapter.

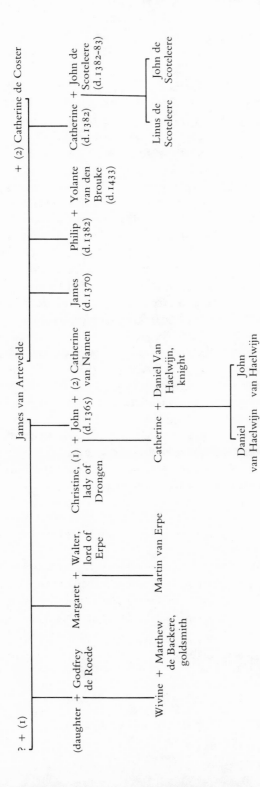

FIGURE 2. Genealogy of the van Artevelde family

spouse and the child. The Estate Aldermen appointed a guardian from the deceased parent's family to manage the orphan's property, and an overseer, who could come from either side of the family, to assist and check on the guardian. The identity of guardians and overseers thus gives us important information about family affiliations.

Godfrey de Roede had leased the stalls in the wool hall from the city in 1347 and was exiled the next year. He was a neighbor of the van Arteveldes on the Kalandenberg (*Map 1, D–E 6*), probably living in his wife's property, in what seems to have been an enormous family complex given over to the food trades, for by July 1355 the house there that had belonged to him was a bakery belonging to John van den Hoernicke, who was not related to the van Arteveldes. Godfrey de Roede was almost certainly related to the baker John de Roede and perhaps to the brewer William de Roede.[1] When we remember that James van Artevelde had owned a brewery in the Kalandenberg complex, although perhaps as a rental property, it becomes clear that he was engaged in an enormous operation of food provisioning that may be tied to his interests in rural Flanders, which we shall discuss in this chapter.

Margaret, another daughter by James's first marriage, was married in 1341 to Walter, lord of Erpe. From the date of her marriage, we can assume that Margaret was probably born around 1320. Her son, Martin van Erpe, lived until some time after 1382, but the line died out with him. John, the captain's oldest son, is usually thought to have been the child of his second wife, Catherine de Coster, but there are reasons for attributing him to the first marriage.

James van Artevelde the younger was also probably the child of his father's first marriage, but conceivably of the second. He was substantially older than Philip and Catherine, who were definitely Catherine de Coster's children, but younger than

---

1. SAG, G 3, 2, fol. 12r; G 3, 1, fol. 39v; G 3, 3, fol. 2v; G 4, 3, fol. 40r; G 1, 5, fol. 41r; G 5, 3, fol. 24r and K 4, 1, fol. 29r; ser. 160, no. 6, fol. 10v.

John. James the younger was called by the diminutive name Coppin in 1350, when his older brother John and their cousin, the son of John van Artevelde, paid expenses that he had incurred in prison at Geraardsbergen. Diminutives were occasionally used for persons as old as twenty, the minimum age for young James in 1350 if he was a child of his father's first marriage. Later in 1350 he is stated to have acted personally in selling peat bogs at Assenede. His share of the bogs was still not separated from those of "the children of James van Artevelde," who are not named. The language suggests that they may have been his half-siblings, particularly since the mother of Philip and Catherine van Artevelde, both of whom were still quite young, would normally have been entitled to a share of this property if she and her husband had held it jointly; but she is not mentioned.[2] The most conclusive evidence that James the younger was a child of his father's first marriage is the fact that when Wivine de Roede, whose maternal guardian had been John van Artevelde, died in 1369, James the younger became the guardian on the maternal side of her daughter by the goldsmith Matthew de Backere, and this would have been unlikely if John and James van Artevelde had had different mothers.[3]

James van Artevelde the younger never married and was murdered in 1370. Philip van Artevelde, who would follow his father's career in public life, was born on 18 July 1340 to James van Artevelde and his second wife, Catherine de Coster. He was married to Yolante van den Brouke, evidently after he took power, and died childless at the battle of Westrozebeke on 27 November 1382. Catherine, the second child of James the elder and Catherine de Coster, was born in 1341 and married the

2. CA 288–89; Nicholas, *Domestic Life*, 110.
3. See CA 298, 315. On Matthew de Backere's profession, see SAG, G 3, 2, fol. 29v. He furnished wine and cloth for the uniforms used in the Tournai procession in 1379, and he was reimbursed by the city for past debts in 1382 and 1386, although we have no direct evidence of association with Philip van Artevelde during these years. For his involvements during the 1380s, see *Rek. Gent 1376–1389*, 163, 320, 368. The gold and silversmiths were in the same guild, and there were close ties between workers of iron and of precious metals.

prominent but impecunious John de Scoteleere. They had two sons, Linus and John, and Catherine died in 1382.[4]

John de Scoteleere seems to have been a ne'er-do-well. He had been married previously, and he and his first wife were victims of an assault in 1356. The arbitrators for his side included the tanner John Heinmans, who later would be the overseer of the property of de Scoteleere's sons by Catherine van Artevelde, and Giles Soyssone, whose family were ancestral enemies of the van Arteveldes. James Heinmans's widow had married Lievin Soyssone by April 1388. John de Scoteleere and his wife inherited a share of her parents' polderlands, but by 1371 John was heavily in debt, owing Jordan Ser Sanders 450 lb. gro. He and Catherine sold Ser Sanders a substantial amount of land from her parental estate in Baardonc and Baasrode to cover part of this, but they still owed him 240 lb., due over twenty years. They secured this on all their property in Ghent, mentioning particularly the houses "de Vos," on the Kalandenberg (*Map 1, D–E 6*), "den Hert," adjacent toward the Belfry (*Map 1, E 6*), two houses behind them in the Bennesteeg (*Map 1, E 5*), and the houses left by James van Artevelde on the Kalandenberg and in the Paddenhoek.[5]

John de Scoteleere evidently survived his wife, but he had died by 29 January 1383, and his children were placed under wardship. Their overseer was the tanner James Heinmans, whose widow would marry Lievin Soyssone five years later. John, the older boy, was apprenticed to another tanner that May. In 1389 John de Scoteleere the younger and his brother Linus agreed to liquidate the rest of their father's debt to Jordan Ser Sanders's heirs by mortgaging again their houses on the Kalandenberg and the Paddenhoek and surrendering all claims to the estate at Baardonc to the Ser Sanders. On 20 August 1390 John de Scoteleere finally sold the van Artevelde houses on the

4. See van Werveke, *Jacob*, genealogical table on p. 5. Although whether John was the son of van Artevelde's first or second marriage must remain uncertain, the roughly fifteen-year age gap between John and Philip suggests the former.

5. SAG, Z 2, 2, fol. 15r; Z 2, 3, fol. 18r; CA 320–26.

Kalandenberg and Paddenhoek to the Ser Sanders family.[6] Thus the ties of the can Arteveldes to the ancestral home on the Kalandenberg were broken through the son-in-law's incompetence.

Apart from the tie to the Soyssones in 1356 and the eventual marriage of Lievin Soyssone to the widow of James Heinmans, whose family was in constant financial dealings with John de Scoteleere, nothing ties de Scoteleere directly to the enemies of Philip van Artevelde, and indeed it is likely that he died at Westrozebeke. Relations between van Artevelde and his feckless brother-in-law remained correct; but there is no suggestion that Catherine van Artevelde was personally responsible for the debts that led to the disposal of the Kalandenberg properties, and it is hard to believe that de Scoteleere's problems would not have caused hard feelings. For a grandson of James van Artevelde to become a tanner was a social comedown, even granted the allegation by contemporaries that the great man himself had been a brewer.

Catherine de Coster, James the elder's widow, returned to Ghent after a brief exile and married the knight Zeger Bornaige. She had performed important diplomatic missions for her husband during the 1340s and was apparently not in Ghent when he was assassinated. The new regime of 1349 fined 250 persons, and she had to pay the highest amount, followed by the widow of Gelnoot van Lens, the captain who had been deposed with James van Artevelde. Catherine de Coster also had to return 60 lb. gr. that James had taken from the city treasury, and her sons had to refund the blood price that the government had paid for Fulk uten Rosen, whom James had killed.[7]

The sons of James van Artevelde and their uncle William were taken hostage and went into exile in England in 1349. The widow was allowed to keep her share of their common property. There are problems in trying to account for the whereabouts of

---

6. CA 380; SAG, G 7, 3, fols. 32v, 61v; G 7, 4, fol. 21r; G 8, 4, fol. 44r; K 11, 2, fol. 74r; K 13, 1, fol. 55r; G 8, 3, fol. 76 bis r.

7. Van Werveke, *Jacob*, 91–93.

James's sons during the 1350s. It has been assumed that their exiles continued until they were recalled in 1359 and 1360, but in fact the count released the hostages to the government of Ghent on 23 August 1349 on condition that the aldermen would judge their misdeeds.[8] Edward III of England took the van Artevelde sons under his protection on 12 September 1350, so they apparently did not return immediately.[9] But the van Arteveldes continued to manage their property before the aldermen of Ghent without using proxies. It is likely, indeed, that the brothers were in Ghent for at least part of the 1350s, for on 21 October 1360 the count, at the request of the English king and with the consent of the aldermen of Ghent, remitted a fifty-year banishment issued by the alderman against John and James van Artevelde and Walter Grijp; Grijp was a tailor who was in the city until at least 14 August 1357.[10] The city had been racked by disturbances from mid-1358, and numerous prominent people were exiled, only to be recalled in the early 1360s.[11] The exile from which the van Arteveldes were recalled in late 1360 thus seems to have been imposed later, conceivably as late as the beginning of 1360, while the banishment of 1349 had been either repealed in an act that has not survived or was tacitly ignored.

This chronology is confirmed by John van Artevelde's marital history. His first wife, the noble lady of Drongen, Christine van Steenland, is first mentioned as deceased on 23 May 1359, but in fact John had been married by 9 August 1358 to Catherine van Namen, whose brother John was an armament maker. The context of this document, in which she and her brother act on behalf of themselves and of her absent husband John van Artevelde, suggests a recent marriage and shows that John van Artevelde had indeed returned to Ghent after his banishment, had been widowed, remarried, and then re-exiled. The second

---

8. T. de Limburg-Stirum, ed., *Cartulaire de Louis de Male, comte de Flandre, 1348 à 1358*, 2 vols. (Bruges, 1898–1901), 1:79.

9. van Werveke, *Jacob*, 91–92.

10. SAG, Z 2,2, fol. 14v.

11. On the banishments of the late 1350s, see Nicholas, *Metamorphosis*, chap. 1. The other documents referred to in this paragraph are in CA 288–89, 295.

marriage produced at least one child, who died young. The mother probably died during its birth, for on 13 January 1361 John de Jaghere, a nickname of John van Namen, and Philip van Artevelde acquitted John van Artevelde of his child's estate. As John van Artevelde's banishment was only remitted in October 1360, his wife either shared his exile or the sentence could not have been issued before January 1360.

Catherine, John's daughter by his first marriage, who suc-ceeded her mother in the lordship of Drongen, had been mar-ried by 21 October 1361 to the knight Daniel van Haelwijn.[12] This marriage produced two sons, Daniel and John. In view of John van Artevelde's comparative youth in 1361, he probably first married a woman older than himself and had a single child, a daughter, who must have been born no more than a year or two after her parents' marriage to have married when she did; and then to a woman of uncertain age but probably considerably younger than he, who died in childbirth. The relative equality of men and women in Ghent at this time, which has been noted in a recent study,[13] is demonstrated by the fact that John van Artevelde and Christine van Steenland were a fertile couple who, unless she suffered an injury during childbirth, must have deliberately decided not to have more children after the birth of one girl. The youth of Catherine van Artevelde when she mar-ried—she could have been no more than sixteen and was proba-bly younger—is atypical of the population at large, but quite usual for persons of noble standing or pretensions to nobility, who were anxious to preserve and advance their lineages by early betrothals.[14] Catherine, James van Artevelde's youngest child, was also married before she was twenty.

John van Artevelde was definitely the eldest son and, as such, bore the principal responsibility of avenging the family's griev-

---

12. CA 193, 305; SAG, G 2, 3, fol. 38v; G 3, 1, fol. 31v. It is possible but unlikely that van Artevelde's brother-in-law was the schoolmaster John van Namen, nicknamed Naemkin; Z 6, 3, fol. 21r.

13. Nicholas, *Domestic Life.*

14. Compare Peter Laslett, *The World We Have Lost. England before the Indus-trial Age,* 3d ed. (New York, 1984), 90 ff.

ances. He wasted no time after returning to Ghent. On 10 August 1361 he atoned the murder of John de Scouteete, whom he suspected of having betrayed his father. The killing must have occurred some months previously. His only surety was John, son of Lord Gelnoot Damman, who in turn was the son of Marie van Artevelde, who owned properties with the other van Arteveldes on the Kalandenberg.[15] But apart from the killing of John de Scouteete and his first marriage to a noblewoman, John van Artevelde seems to have been an essentially private man. The few references to him in the sources after 1361 have no political overtones. He is last mentioned on 11 January 1363. He was almost certainly dead by the spring of 1365, when Philip and Catherine van Artevelde acknowledged receipt of their property from an unnamed guardian. As their oldest sibling, John van Artevelde had been their guardian in 1362.[16]

The younger van Arteveldes divided the estate of their recently deceased mother with their stepfather on 20 June 1361.[17] This division mentions for the first time the extensive van Artevelde properties at Weert and Bornem and nearby Baardonc, in the polders of northeastern Flanders. They settled the estate as a group, without dividing their individual shares. The children received the polder of Baardonc in the estate at Bornem, held of the countess of Bar, but Bornaige received one-quarter in jointure. The van Artevelde children also received four houses and their land in the Paddenhoek (*Map 1, D 6*), but Bornaige got the rest of his and Catherine's common property in return for a money payment to his stepchildren. The document refers to Catherine de Coster as the "mother" of James, John, and of Philip and Catherine, but the diminutive form is used for the latter pair, who were twenty-one and twenty, respectively, at this time. Flemish kinship terminology was imprecise, and it is not unusual to find persons being called parents when they were clearly stepparents.[18]

15. Nicholas, *Domestic Life*, 200; document CA 302–3.
16. SAG, G 3, 1, fol. 39v; Z 3, 2, fol. 9v; CA 306, 311.
17. CA 301–2.
18. On the terminological problem, which reflects the absolutely bilateral nature of Flemish kinship, see Nicholas, *Domestic Life*, 175.

Curiously, young James's property was only separated on 18 September 1362 from that of Philip and Catherine, who were emancipated jointly only two and one-half years later, on 28 March 1365.[19] James kept an estate of 12 *bunderen* (about 35 acres) at Bornem, while Philip and Catherine received three-quarters of the polder of Baardonc, 44 *bunderen* (128 acres) in size, and the last quarter at the death of Bornaige, together with lands at Deinze and Lederne, the peat bogs at Zelzate noted above, and their father's residence on the Kalandenberg (*Map 1, D–E 6*), the outbuildings in the Paddenhoek, and the four houses in the Paddenhoek that had figured in the estate division with their mother; the elder van Artevelde thus had evidently owned the Kalandenberg residence before his second marriage but acquired the buildings in the Paddenhoek during it. Philip van Artevelde also paid ground rent to the count for two parcels of land with a total area of nine *bunderen* (26 acres) at Bornem.[20] That James's share was worth considerably less than those of Philip and Catherine is further evidence that he was the son of his father's first marriage and that the polderlands were acquired during James the elder's marriage to Catherine de Coster.

James van Artevelde had ties to the gold- and silversmiths of Ghent, and it was through them that the fateful connection to the de Mey family first appears. We have seen that the cousin of John and James the younger married the goldsmith Matthew de Backere. On 10 April 1367 the silversmith John de Mey stood surety for money that the younger James van Artevelde was holding for young John van Revele, the ward of his uncle William van Artevelde. De Mey eventually had to pay this money as damaged surety to van Revele on 30 August 1376, at

19. CA 304–5, 311.
20. ARA, RR 2041, fol. 7. This register is undated, and the inventory of the roll accounts dates it around 1350; H. Nélis, *Chambre des Comptes de Flandre et de Brabant. Inventaire des Comptes en Rouleaux* (Brussels, 1914), 130. Comparison of the rent payers with the Weert accounts, however, suggests a date of the early 1360s, and a clearly later section at the end refers to the plague of 1368. The fact that van Artevelde is called "Filips," rather than the diminutive "Lippin," also suggests that the document was not compiled in the 1350s, when van Artevelde was still a teenager and under wardship.

least six years after James's death.[21] James's relations with the powerful and wealthy silversmiths suggest financial difficulties; it is at least conceivable that his property had been separated from that of Philip and Catherine, whose estates were kept together until her marriage, because they wanted to escape liability for his debts. In June 1367 James, the silversmith Peter Heinric, and the knight John Brecht stood surety in a homicide case for James Loys. On 6 October 1368 James was guardian and the smith Arnold van den Borne overseer of Simon and Catherine Wieric. The children's father is not named, but a silversmith named John Wieric lived in Ghent in the late 1380s. On 12 January 1370 he acquitted the younger John de Groete of money belonging to these children, and a John de Groete was a smith. James's brother Philip stood surety for him in 1369, but another hint of young James's financial problems comes on 4 August 1369, when he acknowledged an enormous debt of 100 lb. gro. to Philip, payable on demand.[22]

James van Artevelde atoned the death of Eustace van den Ackere in February 1368; I have been able to find no political or family involvements of the van den Ackeres that suggest anything other than a private quarrel. James, in turn, was evidently killed in the early autumn of 1370. He was still alive on 11 March 1370, but on 5 October Matthew de Backere became his own daughter's guardian, suggesting that James was probably dead by that time. On 10 February 1371 Daniel van Haelwijn, acting for his wife, the decedent's sister, acquitted Philip van Artevelde of James's estate, and the language suggests that it was complicated.[23]

James van Artevelde the younger thus seems to have been the family "problem child." His assassination is linked to the van Artevelde holdings in northeastern Flanders, which by the 1360s were considerably more important to the sons than the houses

---

21. CA 314; SAG, G 6, 2, fol. 1v.
22. CA 315, 317; SAG, Z 4, 2, fol. 9v; G 4, 5, fol. 21r. On the profession of Matthew de Backere, G 3, 2, fol. 29v; for Arnold van den Borne, see G 1a, fol. 2v; for John Wieric, G 8, 1, fol. 49r; for John de Groete, G 5, 2, fol. 19v.
23. CA 318–19, 745.

in Ghent, which were controlled by their brother-in-law. Weert was an estate acquired by the abbey of St. Bavo, located in a village suburb just east of Ghent, in 1240. It was an island surrounded by the "Old Scheldt" and the present bed of the river, the result of a diversion in the thirteenth century. James van Artevelde the elder and his heirs had interests at Bornem, across the Old Scheldt from Weert, and the heirs were still buying land there in the 1370s. He also diked a substantial amount of land at Weert, called "Middle Sand" and "New Sand," described variously in the charters as five to six *bunderen,* 288 *roeden* (15.52–18.72 acres). He did this over the abbey's protests, however; and in litigation during the 1370s, St. Bavo's received the land thus reclaimed but had to compensate James's heirs for his costs. Van Artevelde also maintained a permanent farmstead at Weert, and his heirs were leasing tithes there from the abbey by 1360. James van Artevelde had evidently been dissatisfied with the way that St. Bavo's drainage system was serving his estate. St. Bavo's account for Weert in 1354 mentions the dike of Zeger Bornaige, the husband of van Artevelde's widow, who held the six *bunderen* of meadow reclaimed beyond the dike. In 1360 the abbey gave Bornaige the tithe of five *bunderen* of meadow, and this had passed to Philip van Artevelde by 1366.

The van Arteveldes were distinctly unpopular in the area, but the hostility seems to have been directed mainly at James the younger rather than at Philip. John van Merlaer and John Panneberch, who had connections with Weert, paid one-quarter of James's blood price. The major perpetrators of the deed were the de Mey clan, who may also have had interests in this area. The de Meys and van Merlaers were related, and their ties of kinship, both to one another and to two ancestral enemies of the van Arteveldes—the Parijs and de Grutere families—are shown on figure 3. A Giles van Merlaer, almost certainly a kinsman of John, had lived at Weert in the 1350s, while John Panneberch was actually living there through 1371. Then his property passed to William Panneberch, while John moved to Temse, across the Scheldt. Both John Panneberch and Philip van Artevelde were paying rent on recently acquired property at

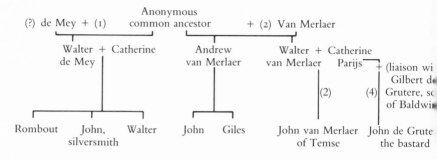

FIGURE 3. Genealogy of the de Mey and van Merlaer families

Bornem in 1367. The Panneberch property was along the dike, as were most homesteads at Weert, while Giles van Merlaer's land was along the beach. We do not know whether van Artevelde's dike caused the lands of these people to flood, but the involvement of so many people from Weert in the killing of James the younger seems too much to be coincidental.

In 1372–73 Philip van Artevelde was involved in a legal action before the count's court in Ghent against the residents of Lupegembrouke, near Bornem, and in the same account Giles van Merlaer, who had just been released from jail, complained that the bailiff had confiscated his property illegally. As late as 1380 the bailiff of the lady of Cassel at Bornem went to Ghent to warn Philip van Artevelde and Daniel Ser Sanders and his brothers that the dike at Baardonc, on the Old Scheldt, was about to break.[24] Daniel Ser Sanders was a cloth wholesaler and hosteller who took German lodgers. He served as alderman in 1371, 1374, and 1378. He lived on the Kalandenberg, in a property described in 1378 as two doors from that of the late James van Artevelde, which may explain Jordan Ser Sanders's interest in

24. Nicholas, "Weert," especially 242–47. This article is based on the manuscript charters and accounts of St. Bavo's and the accounts of the bailiff of Bornem.

acquiring the van Artevelde properties from John de Scoteleere and his wife. Ser Sanders evidently had property near van Artevelde's at Bornem, but they were not joint owners. Indeed, Daniel Ser Sanders was probably not a political ally of the van Arteveldes, for he left Ghent during the fiscal year 1380–81 and is next attested there in August 1385, shortly before the final peace was sealed.[25]

It may be significant that Simon Damman handled the liquidation of the estate of Godescalc Breedevelt between 1366 and 1374 on behalf of Breedevelt's creditors. Breedevelt was a German who had married Lisbette van der Pale, a member of the Kalandenberg family. She had been married first to Alvin van Revele, and William van Artevelde had been guardian of her three children by him. John van Artevelde, in turn, had been Breedevelt's surety for the marriage arrangements. There clearly were conflicts between the van Arteveldes and their neighbors on the Kalandenberg, including the family who eventually bought them out.[26]

But the families of each of the three assassins of James the younger also had important ties at Ghent. In July 1360 Giles and John Panneberch stood surety for the party of Nicholas Wederic, who had been killed by John van Meeren. Andrew van Merlaer was one of the receivers of the blood price and in 1360 became guardian of Wederic's children. In August 1382, Panneberch became the guardian of Simon, Martin Wederic's son.[27] Nicholas Wederic was a baker on the Kalandenberg and the Paddenhoek, the van Arteveldes' neighborhood, and owned one-half *bunder* of land at Tielrode, directly across the Scheldt from Weert and south of Temse.[28] Martin Wederic was married twice. His first wife evidently died in 1362, and the guardian of their daughter, who would have come from the mother's side,

25. SAG, K 2, 2, fol. 37r; K 5, 1, fol. 38r; K 7, fol. 15r; Z 7, 5, fol. 19r; RAG, charter of St. Michael of March 1378; *Rek. Gent 1376–1389*, 176.
26. SAG, K 1, fol. 152r; G 3, 1, fol. 52r; G 3, 2, fol. 22r; K 2, 2, fols. 37r, 40v; G 4, 1, fol. 35r; K 5, 1, fol. 14r; CA 300.
27. SAG, Z 2, 5, fol. 17r; G 7, 2, fol. 38v.
28. SAG, G 3, 1, fol. 40v; RAG, charters of St. Michaels, January 1362.

was Francis van Hansbeke, who had been dean of the fullers during the 1350s.[29] The genealogy of the van Meeren family is difficult to decipher, but in August 1353 the barrister Jan van Meeren, who probably lived in the Burgstraat (*Map 1, G 1–4*), near the count's castle (*Map 1, H 4*), was overseer of the property of the orphan of Zeger van Meeren, and William van Artevelde, brother of James the elder and supposedly an exile, stood surety for the van Meeren clan. There were numerous persons named John van Meeren, but the most likely culprit is a cheese merchant who is last mentioned in the records as the victim of an assault in 1354.[30] John Panneberch was holding a tenement in the Onderstraat (*Map 1, F-G 5–7*) in 1370, the year of young James's murder. Somewhat surprisingly for an outspoken enemy of the van Arteveldes, he does not seem to have left Ghent during the war of the early 1380s, for he and his wife were still in the city in 1384.[31]

We have seen that Andrew van Merlaer, of the second family implicated in James the younger's death, had been a kinsman of Nicholas Wederic, who had been killed by the van Artevelde ally John van Meeren. Van Merlaer was the only person not named Wederic who received the blood price, which clearly identifies him as a maternal-side kinsman. He is stated to have held a tenement on the Friday Market (*Map 1, G-H 6–7*) in 1370, while John Panneberch was in the nearby Onderstraat (*Map 1, F–G 5–7*).[32] But Andrew van Merlaer was killed in 1364 by John Ebbin, a linen weaver of Ghent, and Walter de Mey pledged the peace as guardian of Andrew's children. The killer's sureties were from Waasland, the area of Weert and Tielrode. When the property of John and Giles, Andrew's two sons, was probated, it included land at Tielrode and shares of three houses north of the Friday Market in Ghent, one in the Wulfsteeg (*Map 1, H 7*) and the others not identified more pre-

29. SAG, G 3, 3, fols. 11r, 42r.
30. SAG, Z 1, 3, fol. 14r; G 1a, fols. 16v, 23r; G 1, 3, fol. 16v; Z 1, 4, fol. 12v.
31. AJC, no. 647, fol. 2v; SAG, Z 7, 4, fol. 12r.
32. SAG, Z 2, 5, fol. 17r; AJC, no. 647, fol. 5r.

cisely; but one of them must have been the house owing ground rent in 1370. All the Ghent properties were rented to tenants. The van Merlaers were thus obviously living outside the city at this time, presumably at Tielrode. These boys were still under wardship in 1369. John was emancipated on 26 April 1372, but this is so long after the van Artevelde killing that it identifies the assassin as the son, not of Andrew, but of Walter van Merlaer, who had property around the castle of Gerard the Devil (*Map 1, D–E 7–8*) and the Zandberg (*Map 1, F 7*) but seems to have lived in the Lange Munt (*Map 1, G 5*) at the corner of the Breidelsteeg, while the Andrew van Merlaer branch was around the Friday Market (*Map 1, G–H 6–7*).[33] Andrew's son Giles is mentioned in several documents during the next few years, once when John de Mey, presumably the man of Weert, acted as his surety against the knight Philip van Steenland, a kinsman of the lady of Drongen. Giles van Merlaer appears last in the Ghent records on 18 July 1379 as having bought a house across the Friday Market from the other van Merlaer and Panneberch properties.[34]

Walter van Merlaer, Andrew's brother and the father of young James van Artevelde's assassin, was allied with the Parijs family. The dyer Simon Parijs had been dean of the small guilds in 1345 and an embittered opponent of James van Artevelde the elder. James Rijnvisch in the Drabstraat (*Map 1, F–G 2–4*), whose family also had been John van Steenbeke's allies and thus opponents of van Artevelde, had become guardian of Parijs's children in 1353. On 23 August 1355 he stood surety for Catherine Parijs, the widow of Walter van Merlaer, when Walter's estate was probated. The Parijs family was thus connected through the father's mother's side to the Rijnvisch, one of the oldest lineages of Ghent. The connection of factional strife at Ghent with northeastern Flanders is strengthened by a reference, in June 1374, to another James Rijnvisch, probably the son

33. SAG, Z 3, 4, fol. 6r; G 3, 5, fols. 40r, 28r; G 3, 4, fol. 28r; G 4, 4, fol. 45r; G 5, 2, fol. 52v.
34. SAG, K 5, 2, fol. 43v; K 6, 2, fols. 9v, 14v; K 7, fol. 55r.

of James in the Drabstraat, and his two sisters buying out the collateral heirs of half an estate in the parish of Berlare, just north of the Scheldt, eleven kilometers west of Dendermonde. The other half belonged to William de Grutere, whose family, as we shall see, also opposed the van Arteveldes and was related to the Parijs and by marriage to the van Merlaers.[35] The van Merlaer, Parijs, Rijnvisch, and de Grutere families, all of them personal enemies of the younger van Arteveldes, thus were related to one another and had property in northeastern Flanders, near the van Arteveldes.

Walter van Merlaer had died in 1355, and on 26 May 1362 his son John, the later killer of James van Artevelde the younger, acquitted his guardian, Walter de Mey, who was also involved in the assassination. De Mey was a kinsman from the father's side and thus almost certainly a maternal half brother of Walter van Merlaer. John's mother had remarried by 1362, to Lievin de Beere. Most of the de Beeres seem to have been van Artevelde allies, and Lievin himself loaned money to the city in 1380 and represented the landowners on a mission to the count's council in August 1381, which clearly establishes his credentials with the revolutionary regime. Lievin began settling Catherine Parijs's estate in 1370 with John van Merlaer, who is stated there to have a maternal half brother, John de Grutere, who surrendered his rights on her estate to the van Merlaers in May 1370. The final accounting of her estate was only made in June 1372. We shall return to the de Grutere connection in chapter 6, for it has fateful implications for the career of Philip van Artevelde.[36]

The estate that John van Merlaer inherited from his father included an establishment of 15 *bunderen* (46.34 acres) at Tielrode, an exceptionally large concentration of property for this part of Flanders, together with half a house in front of the castle of Gerard the Devil (*Map 1, D-E 7-8*) at Ghent, between the gates and the steps leading to the river, which places it on the

---

35. SAG, G 1, 4, fol. 5v; G 2, 1, fol. 1v; K 1, fol. 169r; K 4, 2, fol. 36v.
36. SAG, G 4, 5, fols. 50r, 56r; G 5, 2, fol. 57v; *Rek. Gent 1376–1389*, 177, 271.

southern side, toward the Kalandenberg (*Map 1, D–E 6*). The house is described in March 1372 as in the Nederscheldestraat (*Map 1, C–D 7*), opposite that sold by the children of Robert van Eeke, one of the most prominent weavers of Ghent, to Nicholas Vijt, the count's castellan of Beveren in Waas. In November 1373 van Merlaer was described as living by the castle beside the house sold by his kinsman Zeger Parijs to John van Ravenscoet. He had died by May 1391 at the latest, and the house is again described as "behind," or south of, the castle.[37]

This John van Merlaer was known at Ghent as "John van Merlaer of Temse," and on 25 February 1366 he bought a house on the Zandberg (*Map 1, F 7*) from Godfrey de Roede, the van Arteveldes' in-law. John van Merlaer and his former guardian Walter de Mey already owned real estate jointly on the Zandberg, for they sold a different property there on 21 April 1369.[38] John van Merlaer thus held property on both sides of the castle of Gerard the Devil. He was obviously wealthy and relatively young, and he shared the propensity for violence of this age and income group. He was sent on a pilgrimage in 1364 for assaulting Henry van Kerleghem, who retaliated by mutilating him in what seems to have been a general brawl involving, among others, a de Beere kinsman of van Merlaer's stepfather. In May 1365, however, Andrew van Merlaer joined van Kerleghem as surety in a homicide case, for relations between the two branches of the van Merlaers were not totally amicable. John van Merlaer and the brothers John and Walter de Mey were declared in truce by the aldermen in August 1367 against the son of John Heinric, because the boy could not prove his allegation that they had maimed him. The boy's father was "John Heinric at the Count's Castle." He was evidently related to the van Merlaers, for a text of September 1369 lists him and John van Merlaer as kinsmen of the same minor. It may be more than coincidental that a John Heinrixzoon was sued for arrears on a lease of peat bogs on 31 July 1350 by none other than John

37. SAG, G 2, 1, fol. 1v; K 3, 2, fols. 22v, 37r; K 4, 2, fol. 11v; K 7, fol. 32r.
38. SAG, G 3, 2, fol. 35v; G 2, 1, fol. 1v; K 2, 2, fol. 21r; K 3, 1, fol. 36v.

van Steenbeke, James van Artevelde's old enemy. [39] The time gaps between these texts are too substantial to permit firm conclusions, but the van Merlaers and de Meys definitely had a large concentration of property in Ghent on both sides of a fortification near the van Arteveldes' ancestral complex, as well as property near theirs at Weert, and kinship with several families of Ghent that had opposed James van Artevelde during the 1340s.

In late 1372 the count's bailiff fined a "Johnny" [Hannin] van Merlaer and John Beys 15 lb. par. and 24 lb. par. respectively for knifing Nicholas de Roemere. John Beys and Nicholas de Roemere were both pursemakers; de Roemere lived in the Munt (*Map 1, H 4*), near the count's castle, and this may explain the bailiff's taking jurisdiction in the affair. In 1381 Nicholas de Roemere was a major heir of the estate of the fisherman Godfrey Scakelin, who lived at Ser Sanders Wal (*Map 1, H–I 1–3*), near the canal behind the castle, and in February 1384 he bought out the rights of Ywein Panneberch's wife on Scakelin's estate. A William Panneberch still had land at Weert in 1395, and it would be logical to assume ties between a polder village specializing in animal husbandry and presumably fishing and the fishing interests of Ghent, although the link cannot be proven absolutely in this case. [40] The supposition is strengthened by the fact that although this John Beys was a pursemaker, who would probably have imported his leather from northeastern Flanders, another John Beys was one of the most prominent fishmongers of Ghent and served as their dean. In 1353 he stood surety for one Matthew van Tielroden, obviously a man of Waasland. The John Beys who joined van Merlaer in the assault in 1372 was himself named "Johnny van Biervliet, called Beys" in an assault case of 1368. Biervliet, a small town directly north of Ghent, had been a sanctuary for the anti-van Artevelde party during the 1340s. In 1373 Beys was identified as the son of Hugh Beys, and

39. SAG, Z 3, 4, fol. 8v; Z 4, 1, fol. 22v; Z 4, 2, fol. 11v; G 4, 5, fol. 9r; G 8, 3, fol. 74v; K 1, fol. 42 bis.

40. ARA, Rolrekening 1367, fol. 1; SAG, ser. 400, 10, fol. 41v; SAG, Z 3, 5, fol. 5v; G 7, 2, fol. 10r; G 7, 4, fol. 45v; RAG, K 2533, fol. 9r.

in 1357 Hugh Beys was holding property in the Wulfsteeg (*Map 1, H 7*), the same street north of the Friday Market in which the descendants of Andrew van Merlaer were holding rental property after 1364.[41]

John van Merlaer apparently curbed his propensity to violence after 1372. A John van Merlaer was receiver of the city's property at some point between 1377 and 1380 and represented the landowners in an embassy in the summer of 1380. He was captain of the city between 5 December 1380 and 28 February 1381. He succeeded James de Rijke as dean of the landowners midway through the fiscal year 1382, which would probably mean after Philip van Artevelde's death on 27 November. In the lists of persons from whom property was confiscated after the battle of Westrozebeke in 1382, he is definitely identified as a landowner and as the son of Walter, the man who killed young James van Artevelde, rather than the son of Andrew van Merlaer.[42] The fact that Walter's son held land in the city in addition to houses, while the Andrew van Merlaer branch owned only the houses, confirms the identification of this John van Merlaer as dean of the landowners.[43] Although Philip van Artevelde pursued the descendants of his father's assassins with cold-blooded relentlessness, he apparently felt that John van Merlaer had paid his debt for killing his older brother by agreeing to the blood price and did not molest him.

The de Mey family also had important connections at both Weert and Ghent. But while the names Panneberch and van Merlaer were quite distinctive and unusual at Ghent, and thus their appearance suggests family relationships, de Mey was a very common name and is confused with de Meyere in some sources. We have seen that the silversmith John de Mey stood

41. SAG, G 1, 3, fol. 48v; WD fol. 12v; RAG, charters of St. Michael's church, July 1359; *Rek. Gent 1351–1364*, 460; G 5, 3, fol. 40r; Z 4, 2, fol. 12v; AJC 928/37.

42. Angeline van Oost, "Sociale stratifikatie van de Gentse Opstandelingen van 1379–1385. Een kritische benadering van konfiskatiedokumenten," *HMGOG*, n.s. 29 (1975): 89.

43. *Rek. Gent 1376–1389*, 339; CA 355.

surety for James van Artevelde the younger in 1367 and eventually had to pay damages. It may be pure coincidence, but the cloth wholesaler John van der Pale, the van Arteveldes' relative, neighbor on the Kalandenberg, and later rival, was married to an Amelberghe de Mey in 1376. John de Mey and James van der Pale were sureties for one John Deillade in 1349.[44] The blood price of James van Artevelde the younger was fixed on 20 January 1372 but was only recorded with the aldermen on 5 November 1373, presumably when its terms had been fulfilled (*Illust. 4*). It assumes the character of a neighborhood settlement, for it was handled before Baldwin van Zwijnaarde and Peter Hughszoon, two landed men who were close neighbors and evidently kinsmen of the antagonists.[45] Van Zwijnaarde was a sometime alderman who often stood surety for moneychangers. He lived in the Lange Munt on the end toward the Fish Market (*Map 1, G 4–5*), as did the de Meys, and had other property in the Munt (*Map 1, H 4*). His father had been owed a debt in 1363 by Margaret, daughter of Giles de Clerc and widow of Thomas de Mey, and had confiscated her house for it from her heirs in 1369. He was acquitted in July 1372 as guardian of James van Kerleghem, whose family had been enemies of the van Merlaers. In 1373 James sold to van Zwijnaarde his share of a house in the Hoogstraat Buten Turre (*Map 1, F 1–2*), beyond the count's castle. In October 1373 he was included in a list of kindred of the children of John van Steenbeke, whose name crops up with dismal regularity in the kinship network of the de Meys and van Merlaers. Hughszoon was an armorer sometimes called Peter de Zwertvaghere [swordsmith] who had a rental property in the Lange Munt (*Map 1, G 5*) and property in the Munt (*Map 1, H 4*) and, by 1387, in the Onderstraat (*Map 1, F-G 5–7*). He was released from wardship in 1363, which probably made him about the same age in 1372 as Baldwin van Zwijnaarde and John de Mey. His son killed Vincent Bailliu, a

44. SAG, K 6, 1, fol. 16v; BB 49, fol. 91v.
45. Document printed CA 321.

4. Record of atonement for the murder of James van Artevelde the younger, 1373. Courtesy Stadsarchief te Gent (Municipal Archive of Ghent), ser. 301, 4, 1, fol. 8v.

kinsman of the Bornaige family, whose members included the van Arteveldes' stepfather.[46]

The blood price arrangement of 1372 bound John van Merlaer and John Panneberch to pay one-quarter of the blood price at no cost to Walter de Mey and his children, "on condition that Walter and his children come to an entire atonement." For himself and his children, Walter pledged that all of his maternal kinsmen except his brother would help van Merlaer and Panneberch pay this quarter share. Normally the two sides of an assassin's kindred assumed equal liability, but in this case the paternal side was apparently responsible for three-quarters. The Panneberchs may thus simply have been acting as agents who would be compensated for their liability by all members of the maternal clan except for a maternal half-brother, who had no liability. John Pauwels and Paul and Simon de Westerlinc, the latter also acting on behalf of his father, also agreed to help pay the blood price "according to their degree of kinship." The ancestry of Walter de Mey and his sons is thus crucial to our understanding of the van Artevelde involvements.

The John Pauwels mentioned here is difficult to identify positively. A John Pauwels on the Steendam (*Map 1, G 8–9*), a long street behind the church of St. James that led to St. Bavo's abbey village, is mentioned in 1364. He is probably the same man as the John Pauwels the cooper at St. Bavo's who is mentioned in 1375. In the spring of 1364 he and Walter de Mey were receivers of the blood price of Andrew van Merlaer. A John Pauwels without reference to the Steendam and William Parijs, whose family had a maternal-side bond to the van Merlaers, as we have seen, were sureties for John van Merlaer against Simon Parijs's son in a civil matter in 1376. In 1386 the bailiff of Ghent held John Pauwels responsible for the blood price of John de

46. For Baldwin van Zwijnaarde, see SAG, K 1, fol. 118v; BB 68, fol. 1r; K 3, 1, fol. 50v; G 5, 2, fol. 60r; K 4, 1, fol. 24v; G 5, 4, fol. 6r; G 6, 2, fol. 5v; K 6, 2, fol. 49v; *Rek. Gent 1351–1364*, 434. For Peter Hughssone or Zwertvaghere, see G 1a, fol. 22v; G 1, 2, fol. 8v; G 2, 2, fol. 35r; G 3, 1, fol. 67v; G 3,4, fol. 9r; K 3, 1, fol. 21r; Z 5, 1, fol. 14v; K 3, 2, fol. 29v; K 5, 2, fol. 49r; K 10, 2, fol. 53v.

Mey, a doublet maker of Antwerp, but the nature of his kinship with the de Meys cannot be ascertained absolutely.[47]

John Pauwels and Simon de Westerlinc were obviously distant and collateral relatives. A John de Westerlinc of Waas, the area of Weert and Bornem, paid the "issue" fee to the city in 1356, suggesting that he was leaving but probably maintaining interests in Ghent. He committed a housebreak at St. Niklaas in Waas in 1377. On 21 November 1368 Baldwin, son of John de Westerlinc, acquitted Walter de Mey and his *zwagher*, John van Lovendeghem, of the estate of his father, John.[48] *Zwagher* can mean brother-, son-, or father-in-law in Middle Netherlandish, but we clearly have a van Lovendeghem tie to the de Meys.

As if our genealogies were not complex enough already, John van Lovendeghem also opens a number of intriguing possibilities. On 15 December 1371 John and Andrew van Lovendeghem renounced their rights as heirs of James and another Andrew van Lovendeghem on a house on the Zandberg (*Map 1, F 7*), where Walter van Merlaer also had property. This holding is identified in February 1374 as the residence of the lord of Lovendegem, a village northwest of Ghent; but he was not the owner, for it was part of a property sold by another man. We have seen that the widow of Thomas de Mey, from whom Baldwin van Zwijnaarde confiscated a house in 1369, had been Margaret, daughter of Giles de Clerc. On 16 December 1373 the estate that another Margaret, daughter of Henry de Clerc, called van Lovendeghem, had inherited from her mother, Margaret, was probated; it contained properties north of the Friday Market (*Map 1, G–H 6–7*), including the father's residence. In late 1355 John van Lovendeghem paid compensation to Lievin de Mey for an assault. Walter de Mey was a landowner in Ghent. After his death, his heir, Peter de Smet, recorded with the alderman a document of 1373 found in Walter's possessions in which John, son of the late Bertram van Lovendeghem, acknowledged

47. SAG, G 5, 5, fol. 21r; G 5, 2, fol. 56r; G 3, 4, fol. 24f; Z 3, 4, fol. 6v; K 4, 2, fol. 13v; K 5, 2, fol. 43v; G 6, 1, fol. 47v; G 8, 1, fol. 75r; G 8, 2, fol. 66v.
48. SAG, G 4, 4, fol. 24v; *Rek. Gent 1351–1364*, 256; CA 742.

a debt to his mother and sister. The Westerlinc tie appears in September 1351, when John van Lovendeghem and John Zeghers of Lochristi acquitted John de Westerlinc, who was evidently his brother-in-law, of his wife's estate. It is likely but thus unprovable that the de Meys were connected to the family of the lords of Lovendegem, perhaps as retainers, for in March 1360 John de Mey the younger was among the persons pledging truce for the party of Soy van den Velde, who had been killed by retainers of the van Lovendeghems.[49]

The de Meys also had property on the Kalandenberg through their ties with the de Schachtmakere family. John, son of Walter de Mey, the van Artevelde assassin, had owed money to John, the son of the baker Philip de Schachtmaker. He was married to Philip's daughter Catherine, but they separated in 1377. Their property division mentioned nothing in northeastern Flanders, for this would have come from the de Mey side, but it did include property on the Kalandenberg and the Paddenhoek left by Philip de Schachtmakere.[50] We have seen that the van Artevelde holdings on the Kalandenberg included a bakery used as a rental property by 1355, and it is thus extremely probable that this is the same building.

Walter de Mey was clearly the principal culprit in the killing of James van Artevelde the younger. The settlement bound him to secure an annuity to provide a lamp to burn in the Bijloke hospital for James's anniversary. On 16 May 1375 he secured it on a property in the Breidelsteeg, near his residence in the Lange Munt (*Map 1, G 5*). He was a cheese merchant who in 1355 became the guardian of John, son of another Walter van Merlaer. He was joint owner of a property described in 1357 as being in the Breidelsteeg but in 1361 as in the Lange Munt on the corner of the Breidelsteeg at the gate of Ser Lievin Rijnvisch, whose family, as we have seen, was antagonistic toward the van Arteveldes and was involved with the Parijs clan. He still owned

49. SAG, G 5, 2, fols. 25r, 19r; K 4, 2, fol. 26v; G 5, 4, fol. 26r; G 5, 5, fol. 13r; Z 2, 1, fol. 4v; G 1, 2, fol. 5v; G 2, 5, fol. 22v; G 4, 4, fol. 41r.

50. SAG, G 4, 4, fol. 51 bis; G 5, 2, fol. 35v; K 6, fol. 44v; RAG, SN 118, fol. 114 r–v.

this property in 1387. The dairy market of the city was nearby, in the Korte Munt (*Map 1, F 4–5*). He seems to have specialized in importing cheese of Tienen, in central Brabant, to Ghent; and in 1368 he and the shipper John Jacquemins were owed jointly a debt by a man of Oudenaarde. Walter's son John was owed a debt in 1378 for Hamburg beer, although, as was true of the van Arteveldes, he was never in the brewers' guild and may have simply imported the German product.[51]

The interests of a dealer in Brabantine cheeses in the animals raised at Weert and Bornem, on the border of Flanders and Brabant, would be obvious. It seems clear, therefore, that Walter de Mey, the father of van Artevelde's assassins, had important business interests in the northeast, as did van Artevelde; that he lived in a region of Ghent near the food markets and close to the van Merlaers, to whom he was related, and the Panneberchs, who also participated in the van Artevelde assassination. The branch of the van Merlaers with property near the van Arteveldes' ancestral complex on the Kalandenberg was involved in the killing only as kinsmen, not as principal perpetrators of the deed. Members of each of these families held land at Weert and were enemies of the van Arteveldes. There are indications also that the assassins may have been tied to John van Steenbeke, who had led a revolt against James van Artevelde's captaincy in 1343, and noble factions inimical to James van Artevelde the younger.

One other source demonstrates clearly that the van Merlaers as well as the de Meys were active in the food trades at Ghent. The accounts of the Holy Ghost of the Church of St. Nicholas for 1362, 1369, and 1374 show a Peter van Merlaer selling pigs to the foundation. Although Peter is not mentioned in other Ghent, Weert, or Bornem material, most purveyors of pigs to the Holy Ghost were, curiously, bakers of Ghent rather than butchers. The de Meys, although evidently not the van Merlaers, were in-laws of a baker, Philip de Schachtmakere. The

---

51. SAG, K 1, fols. 233r, 240v; G 2, 1, fol. 1r; G 2, 2, fol. 28v; G 3, 2, fol. 35v; K 3, 1, fols. 1v, 20v; K 5, 1, fol. 35r; K 7, fol. 32b v; K 10, 2, fol. 131v.

account of 1362 shows a direct Ghent tie with Weert, for John
de Scoteleere, son-in-law of the elder James van Artevelde, who
had interests at both Weert and Bornem, sold linen to the foundation, and clothmaking seems to have been well established in
that vicinity.[52]

Our connections are infuriatingly fragmentary, difficult to
follow, and often do not permit more than superficial analysis.
We generally know only that kinship existed but cannot specify
its degree. But the coincidences have become too overwhelming
to be dismissed as accidents. A strong network of personal and
proprietary ties linked the foodmongering trades of Ghent with
northeastern Flanders, where the van Arteveldes had large estates, and the assassins of James the younger were close neighbors not only at Weert but also at Ghent. Much of the hostility
toward the second generation of the van Arteveldes stems from
their involvements in the polders since at least the time of James
the elder, who as we have seen dealt in animals and agricultural
products. But the most prominent van Artevelde of the second
generation was also involved in these dealings, and we must
now turn to the antecedents of his public career.

52. RAG, SN rolls 122, 128, 131. On the identification of sellers of pigs to
St. Nicholas as bakers, see Nicholas, *Metamorphosis*, chap. 9. On animal husbandry and clothmaking in the villages of the northeast, see Nicholas, "Weert,"
263, and note. In 1372 the bailiff of Bornem fined one Giles de Visschere "for
making cloth of different type wools," ARA, B 2407, fol. 2.

CHAPTER 5

"Filthy Phil": The Background and Rise of Philip van Artevelde, 1340–1381

THE CHARACTER OF THE MAN

The most celebrated of James van Artevelde's sons, and the only one who had a public career, was the youngest, Philip. Born in 1340, he was named for Philippa of Hainaut, queen of Edward III of England, who raised him from the baptismal font.

Philip van Artevelde acquitted his guardian in 1365, just before he turned twenty-five, a long but not unheard of period of tutelage. He and James the younger attested a document as "landed men" on 20 January 1366, although they seem soon afterward to have transferred their interests in the Kalandenberg properties (*Map 1, D–E 6*) to their sister Catherine and her husband.[1] Historians have been unanimous in seeing Philip as a historical accident who was thrust into a political role for which he was totally unprepared and unsuited only because his father's memory was still cherished. We shall see that this view, though perfectly understandable, is utterly erroneous. The political and social situations that produced Philip van Artevelde were vastly different from those of the 1330s.

1. CA 312.

We have seen that Philip van Artevelde was involved in the divisions of his parents' properties among their children. This meant that he had substantial estates in northeastern Flanders, notably at Weert, Bornem, and Baasrode, particularly after James the younger died. But he had little property in Ghent. Aside from this, however, most of what we know of his career before 1381 must be deduced from material surviving from the period of his political career and the litigation over his estate.

One of his actions while captain seems to have been to contract a marriage with Yolante van den Brouke, nicknamed Lente, and the nature and circumstances of that marriage carry important implications for our evaluation of Philip's character and circumstances. Although earlier authors have assumed that Philip had married Yolante in 1375 or 1376, I find no basis for that assumption in any document.[2] They are never mentioned together by name during his lifetime, and the terms of the settlement of his estate suggest a recent marriage. Although the natural assumption is that he married the daughter or sister of someone whose alliance he needed in early 1382—he was certainly going out of his way to pay off old scores with his enemies—the evidence suggests that he married later, shortly before leaving for Edelare on the militia expedition that would take him to his fate at Westrozebeke.

A striking feature of the van Arteveldes' careers is the extent to which they appear to have been outsiders among the ruling elite of Ghent. Other clans display marriage alliance patterns. Groups of families stayed together and intermarried as they feuded with other parties. But for no other prominent Ghent family of the fourteenth century is the surviving documentation concerning property and marriage ties so scanty as it is for the van Arteveldes. Contrary to accepted practice among those who had considerable property to entail and preserve, the van Arteveldes were "not the marrying kind." James the elder was married twice, but his second wife's family name, de Coster, was so common that it is impossible to reconstruct her family

2. Van Werveke, *Jacob*, genealogical table p. 5, following CA 268.

background. Yolante van den Brouke's ancestry is also unclear, although we shall see in chapter 7 that she probably came from a family of shipwrights. James the younger died a bachelor, and after 1370 the only male descendants of James the elder were Philip and his nephews Linus and John de Scoteleere and Daniel and John van Haelwijn, the sons of his younger sister and grandsons of his older brother, respectively. When Philip van Artevelde's estate was settled in 1385, the heirs' share was divided into thirds, one each going to the de Scoteleere boys, the sons of his sister Catherine; to Martin van Erpe, the son of his half sister, Margaret; and to the van Haelwijn descendants of John van Artevelde, whose share was seized by the city, as the van Haelwijns had left and served the count and France.[3]

Yolante van den Brouke was remarried around 28 June 1384, within two years of Philip's death, to Peter Diederic, who was evidently a shipwright and often served as alderman, including for the term beginning 15 August 1384. Numerous other members of his family practiced this trade. The son of Matthew Diederic, Peter was part of a gang that assaulted John de Ram in 1375 and escaped trial in Ghent on the technicality that the deed had occurred outside the city. The language identifies him by his father's name, which would suggest a young man, probably a teenager about the same age as his future wife. He bought a house beyond the Grauwpoort (*Map 1, I 6*) in August 1384, shortly after his marriage, located between the houses of two shippers, one of whom was his kinsman Ferrant Wandaert. Diederic's blood heirs in 1431 were members of the Boele family, one of the most prominent of the shippers. He and Yolante later moved to a large house at the Groenen Briel by the Augustinian convent (*Map 1, J 4*), at the opposite end of the Steenstraat (*Map 1, I 4–6*). Although many remarried widows identified themselves legally by their first husbands' names, Yolante evidently preferred to bury the memory of her marriage to Philip van

---

3. CA 384. The van Haelwijns were restored to civil rights after the peace, but they renounced Philip van Artevelde's estate on 3 June 1389; SAG, G 8, 4, fol. 63v.

Artevelde, for by 1404 she was being called simply "Peter Diederic's wife."[4]

The law of Ghent required widows and widowers, as holders of their deceased spouses' property, to offer a division of assets with the blood heirs within a year and a day of the death, and most did so within a month or two. Yolante van den Brouke did not propose a division until 19 November 1383, nine days before her time would have elapsed.[5] This text is our first evidence that Philip van Artevelde had even been married, and the fact that she waited so long suggests that there may have been some question about the validity of the marriage. Since Yolante survived until 1434, dying three years after her second husband, it is most unlikely that she was born before 1360, and probably later. We know that Philip van Artevelde was born in 1340, and it is thus clear that he married a woman considerably younger than himself. Given Yolante's probable date of birth and the fact that teenage marriages seem to have been unusual although occasionally countenanced, it is unlikely, although conceivable, that the marriage could have occurred much before 1382. The fact that Philip's marriage to her was childless does not in itself prove that it was of short duration, for she was probably infertile; she also had no children by Diederic. The division of Philip van Artevelde's estate between the widow and his heirs notes that she had sent a horse to her brothers to compensate them for their expenses of 3 lb. gr., which included but were not limited to supporting Philip and her.[6] It was not unusual for the families of newly married couples to support them for a while, but such arrangements rarely lasted longer than a year or two. Three lb. gro. was no more than a year's support for a childless couple—considering the van Arteveldes' social position it was probably less—and the money was given both for costs and support.[7]

4. CA 418–22; SAG, K 5, 1, fol. 30v; K 10, 1, fol. 1v; K 11, 2, fol. 43v. For the reference of 1404, see SAG, ser. 152, no. 5, fol. 47v.

5. In separate enactments of that day, Yolante was mentioned alone, in an agreement to divide Philip's estate with his blood heirs and as Diederic's wife. CA 383–88, 416–22.

6. CA 400.

7. Nicholas, *Domestic Life*, 27, 134.

Since both Philip and Lente had some other property, all of this points to a brief marriage. But there is no suggestion in any of the documents that Lente van den Brouke was a wealthy woman; had she been, we almost certainly would have more information about her ancestry. She remarried rather rapidly after Philip's death a man who was evidently about her own age. By 1384 he could not have married van Artevelde's widow from political ambition, and her property was no issue. Thus it is likely that a love match between Yolante van den Brouke and Peter Diederic was being set but was broken off when, for political and family reasons, she was married rather hastily to Philip van Artevelde, perhaps scarcely knowing him.[8]

Confirmation of our conclusions about the length of Philip van Artevelde's marriage is found in an unlikely source, Froissart's Chronicle. Froissart introduces Philip by saying that when he was called to power, "he and his mother were living quite comfortably on their rents." Since van Artevelde's mother is known to have died in 1361 and Froissart's informants could hardly have mistaken the youthful Lente for a woman who would have been at least in her sixties, Philip was evidently sharing his house with a female servant in January 1382. Froissart also tells us that Philip van Artevelde remained for several days in Bruges after seizing the city on 3 May 1382, acting as a prince all the while; but he mentions no wife. It is true that Yolante was unlikely to have accompanied Philip on a military expedition whose major component was surprise. But during the summer, before beginning the siege of Oudenaarde, Philip allegedly lived extremely well and entertained the ladies of Ghent lavishly. Froissart then reports that a "girlfriend from Ghent" was sharing Philip's tent on the eve of the battle of Westrozebeke in late November.[9] Froissart does not say this in a

8. That her marriage to Diederic was affectionate is shown conclusively by the fact that when he died in 1431 his blood heirs granted Yolante life use of their comfortable house and furnishings rather than insisting on an immediate division; CA 419. On the practice at Ghent of immediately dividing the assets of a deceased kinsman with his or her spouse, see Nicholas, *Domestic Life*, 192–94.

9. Froissart, *Chroniques* vol. 10, chaps. 207, 279, 283, pp. 82, 235, 279; vol. 11, chap. 334, p. 41.

tone of moral recrimination, for there was nothing out of the ordinary about keeping a mistress. Yolante must have been the damsel in question, but Froissart did not know that she was Philip's wife, a logical mistake if the marriage had been recent. The notion that Philip van Artevelde and Yolante van den Brouke were married by 1375 apparently is based on the fact that, as his widow, she was awarded half interest in his two houses in the Minnemersch area (*Map 1, I–J 7–8*) when his estate was settled in 1385. But if Philip had been married to Lente when he acquired these properties, she would have been entitled under the inheritance law of Ghent not only to half the property in outright ownership—which she received—but also to dower rights on one-half of the remaining half.[10] Thus Lente's share would not suggest common property under the law of Ghent.

The question hinges on the date when Philip van Artevelde acquired the houses in the Minnemersch. We do not have a sale contract transferring this property to him, but he apparently bought it just before 1375. He owned only the houses, not their land, but he seems to have used them as his residence when he was in Ghent. The Minnemersch is extremely close to the van Merlaer houses in the side streets just north of the Friday Market (*Map 1, H 7*). Although the de Scoteleeres still owned the heavily encumbered Kalandenberg properties (*Map 1, D–E 6*), Philip van Artevelde is last known to have acted as a "landed man" on 6 January 1366.[11] Except for the reference to the Minnemersch property and his legal action of 1372 with the bailiff of Bornem before the count's court, no other surviving source even places him in Ghent between that date and 1380. The city rent books were kept for several years at a time. Marginal insertions and crossings out were used to show changes in ownership before a new book was compiled. The first book of relevance to the van Artevelde property was written in late 1360 or early 1361. It is in an extremely corrupt state, but most of the changes in it seem to

10. Nicholas, *Domestic Life*, 28.
11. CA 311.

have been entered during the plague years of 1368–69. The next book is dated 1375, and a third has no date but was probably compiled around 1400.[12]

The book begun in 1375 lists Philip van Artevelde as the owner of two tenements next to the fortification in the area between the Beersteeg on the Leie (*Map 1, I–J 7*) and Boudelo abbey (*Map 1, H 8*). The book begun in 1361 has him succeeding two previous owners, and a note in the margin beside the second owner's name is dated 1371. Thus he acquired the property between 1371 and 1375. By the time the last register was compiled, the houses were in the hands of an Arnold de Backere and his wife; the de Backeres were probably relatives of Catherine, daughter of the goldsmith Matthew de Backere, the van Artevelde in-law who in 1361 had inherited property on the canal behind the Friday Market (*Map 1, H–I 7*), near enough to the Minnemersch to make the location attractive. Since Yolante van den Brouke had remarried by the time the estate was probated and van Artevelde's blood heirs did not live in Ghent, they probably sold their interests in the properties. Furthermore, the account of the receiver of Flanders for January through 3 May 1382 mentions a payment to a man for setting fire to Philip van Artevelde's home, so the property was probably uninhabitable when Yolante and the heirs settled his estate.[13] That Yolante van den Brouke was awarded half interest on the houses without dower on the rest thus suggests that they were Philip's marriage gift to her, not that they had been married when he bought them.

The virtual certainty that Philip van Artevelde married at the age of forty-two confirms other suggestions that he may at one time have been destined for holy orders. This is an extremely advanced age for a first marriage. He was a youngest son, and it was still common for the youngest to be destined, albeit infor-

12. On the dating of these registers, particularly the first, see Nicholas, *Metamorphosis*, chap. 2.

13. SAG, ser. 152, no. 3, fol. 6r; no. 4, fol. 6r; G 3, 1, fol. 39v; CA 358. The extent to which the count's men had infiltrated Ghent is one of the most striking features of the events of early 1382.

mally, for the priesthood. He did not play a prominent role in the property transactions of his family until after James the younger was murdered in 1370. Most of James the elder's property evidently went to his daughters in dowry. Had it not been for the peculiar circumstances of the division of the family holdings at Weert and Bornem, we might have no information about Philip's property at all. The estate settlement with Yolante mentions lands and other property, but these were couched in the general terms of standard formulas used in such documents. The only real estate in Ghent identified specifically was the pair of houses in the Minnemersch (*Map 1, I–J 7–8*). The lands at Bornem and Baasrode went to the heirs alone, although Yolante got half the income for life as dower. The widow had been plagued by Philip's creditors and had had to pawn some personal possessions, including silver.

Thus, despite his political prominence, Philip van Artevelde was not a wealthy man.[14] It would seem that the political career of the elder James van Artevelde, perhaps in combination with the chequered careers of his sons, had seriously compromised the family fortunes. No text uses the "der" title customary with priests for Philip van Artevelde; indeed, he could not have married if he had ever taken his vows. But it is likely, in view of other evidence, that he was in minor orders, or at least was considered the family intellectual, until the unexpected death of his older brother thrust a secular role upon him.

One old canard, however, must be laid to rest. In December 1382 the count's bailiff at Bruges referred to the by then late Philip van Artevelde as "Filthy Philip" (*Philips sLodders*) and in a different context as "Lippin" (Phil), a diminutive form grossly insulting to the memory of a man as old as Philip van Artevelde had been.[15] The adjective does not mean Lollard, which is *Lollaert* in Flemish and means a cell brother. *Loddere* is extremely unflattering, but it means a voluptuary or a vagabond, not a heretic. Belgian scholars have rightly dismissed the use of the word as a personal slur on a political opponent.

14. CA 399–400.
15. CA 378.

But other terms of the estate settlement do make it seem likely that Philip van Artevelde was destined at some time for the priesthood. At the time of his death he had in his possession two chalices, four ampules, and a piece of gold cloth. He entrusted these to Yolante to give to the church of St. Maria of Baasrode, although the settlement does not say that he had removed these articles by force. Baasrode is in a bend of the Scheldt east of Dendermonde and due south of Bornem. Baardonc, where Philip van Artevelde and his siblings held property, was in the parish of St. Maria of Baasrode.

The division also mentioned a reliquary with a silver base that Lente was "to give to the church to which she knows it belongs, the church at Elsegem, and the documents that go with it, and this to acquit Philip's soul."[16] The document thus strongly suggests that Philip had taken this jewel without the permission of the church authorities. The village of Elsegem is 3.5 kilometers southwest of Oudenaarde, while Edelare, where van Artevelde spent most of October and November with the army, is on the eastern outskirts of Oudenaarde. He thus proceeded from Edelare to Elsegem as he moved west toward Courtrai en route to his final battle at Westrozebeke, picking up the reliquary for good luck. Since he obtained documents for it, it was evidently on loan, and Lente, who had accompanied him, knew where he had gotten it. But although he had intended to return it, it was tied up in his estate. The settlement suggests not only that the donations to St. Maria of Baasrode were charity rather than repayment, but also that Philip considered this his home parish church. The city accounts also mention twelve silver dishes and two salt vessels found at Philip's house. Two men stood guard over the valuables, which were kept in the accounting chamber at the city hall.[17] Since Philip was not an enemy of the city whose property would be confiscated, he must have taken them from someone else.

Philip van Artevelde was obviously receptive to educated men. We shall see in chapter 6 that some contemporaries

16. CA 325, 498–99.
17. *Rek. Gent 1376–1389*, 325, 345.

thought that he relied heavily on an obscure clerk. Still another suggestion of priestly or at least intellectual inclinations is found in Froissart's account of the eve of the battle of 3 May 1382 at the Beverhoutsveld, outside Bruges. Most of Froissart's descriptions of pre-battle prayers are quite perfunctory, but he goes into great detail about the religious preparations undertaken in the Ghent militia at van Artevelde's express orders. They included prayers, masses held at seven places in the army followed by a sermon lasting an hour and a half, and confession by all. Philip himself gave several speeches on the occasion.[18] Although all of this evidence is circumstantial, taken together it suggests a very religious man with a level of artistic consciousness unusual in a public man of Ghent at this time, and this in turn may suggest a priestly vocation that had been abandoned before Philip had taken his final vows.

THE HISTORICAL SITUATION

Count Louis of Nevers, James van Artevelde's unequal nemesis, had died at the battle of Crécy in 1346 in the service of his Valois lord, King Philip VI of France. His son and successor, Louis of Male, was a much shrewder and more calculating politician than his father. Not yet sixteen when he became count, he managed in his early years to honor his obligations to the French without totally alienating the English. Although the Flemish burghers hoped that he would marry an English princess, instead he married the daughter of Duke John III of Brabant, and the complications of that marriage led him into a war with Brabant between 1356 and 1358 that severely taxed the financial resources of the Flemish cities. The marriage of his daughter and only heir, Margaret, became an issue in the 1360s. Though the cities again wanted an English alliance, Louis married her to Philip of Burgundy, younger brother of King Charles V of France, in a great ceremony at Ghent in 1369. This

18. Froissart, *Chroniques*, vol. 10, chap. 272, pp. 221–22.

marriage was to lead to the absorption of Flanders into the Burgundian state after Louis's death in early 1384.[19]

In 1349 Louis of Male installed a regime at Ghent based on the fullers and small guilds. The weavers were excluded from the boards of aldermen and were forbidden to assemble publicly in groups. Many weavers emigrated, but most seem to have stayed in Flanders. Their absence meant that the city's export textile trade suffered. As early as 6 December 1349 the magistrates were ordering weavers to return, clearly believing that the weavers were close enough to the city to find succor and be able to get word of their pronouncements. Armed guards several times the size of those used in peacetime patrolled the streets during the 1350s. There was a serious uprising in 1353 in which the weavers were joined by the millers in a plot that implicated the dean of the small guilds. Many exiles went to northern Flanders, and at least one attempt was made to storm the city from the north at the Muide gate (*Map 1, J 6*). While the count had ample reason to be irritated at the weavers, the exclusion of the largest occupational group of the city, constituting about one-quarter of the work force in 1357, could only be disastrous. The textile industry of Ghent began a sharp decline in the 1350s that became a catastrophe during the 1360s and 1370s. The wealth of the city came to be centered more in shipping and the grain trade, although the textile trades taken together still constituted the largest single occupational group. Thus the economic and social structure of Ghent underwent a fundamental reorientation between the periods of James and Philip van Artevelde, becoming based much less on textiles and more on the primordial function that Ghent had always served as a center for local and regional marketing and merchandising.

The policies of Louis of Male thus appear in retrospect to have been extremely unfortunate for Ghent. Louis evidently hoped to

---

19. On Louis of Male, see M. Vandermaesen, "Vlaanderen en Henegouwen onder het Huis van Dampierre, 1244–1384," *Algemene Geschiedenis der Nederlanden* 2 (Haarlem, 1982): 399–440; M. Vandermaesen and D. Nicholas, "Lodewijk van Male, graaf van Vlaanderen, Nevers en Rethel," *Nationaal Biografisch Woordenboek* 6 (1974): cols. 575–85, and literature cited.

strengthen the smaller Flemish communities at the expense of Ghent, Bruges, and Ypres, but he managed only to annoy the cities. His devaluations of the Flemish coinage contributed to severe inflation. Unrest in all the major cities and the disruption caused by Louis's war with Brabant led the merchants of the German Hanse to leave Flanders. By this time western Flanders was as severely dependent on the Germans for grain as Ghent was on France, and Louis had to agree to their terms in 1360. Troubles began at Ghent in the summer of 1358. In 1359 some old partisans of James van Artevelde returned to the government, including the captains William van Huusse, Peter van den Hovene, and John Ser Pieters, John van Vaernewijc, the son of the late captain, and several former aldermen and city clerks.[20] By February 1361 the weavers were firmly in control of the city and excluded the fullers from power. But while the count-backed fuller ascendancy in 1349 had meant exile or death for many weavers, the latter seem to have used their power with discretion. There was continuity at the lower levels of administration, in contrast to the proscription of the weavers and their allies during the 1350s. The fullers struck for higher wages in 1373, and many left the city and went to the villages south of Ghent, whereas the weavers had gone north in the 1350s. Louis of Male gave them a substantial raise. Although the weavers and fullers clashed briefly in the summer of 1379, most fullers evidently acquiesced in the revolutionary regime that took power that August, although there were some conspicuous exceptions.

At some point after 1361, and conceivably as early as 1359, the twenty-six members of the two boards of aldermen came to be chosen on the basis of guild affiliation, with the weavers and the small guilds receiving five seats per council and the landowners three. The city reinstituted a three-person receivership in 1361, with a weaver, a landowner, and a brewer representing the small guilds, but the practice was then discontinued until 1369. The position of the landowners as a separate member remains unclear, for many of them were not simply men who

20. Rogghé, "Gemeente ende Vrient," 128–29.

lived on their rents but also practiced trades included among the small guilds. A separate dean of the landowners is mentioned in 1349 and 1352 but not thereafter, although the landowners did occasionally serve in a corporate capacity at other times, notably in the discussions with the count that led to the reestablishment of the weavers in power. A text of 1368 mentions the deans of the weavers and of the small guilds as "overdeans of the two members of the city at this time," showing that the landowners were not then a separate group. They finally became a separate member only in the early 1380s, evidently at the expense of the small guilds, and their rise seems to have been one of the issues involved in the struggles surrounding Philip van Artevelde's ascent to power.[21]

Ghent had exercised a staple privilege since the 1320s on all grain coming down the Scheldt and Leie rivers from France (*Illust. 5*). The grain had to be recharged to boats of Ghent, taken through the halls, and all the needs of Ghent provided for before the shippers of Ghent could reexport the unsold remainder. The regulations for the staple were formalized in 1358, and thereafter Ghent acquired considerable capital by forcing the peasants of the environs to buy on the city market and by reexporting immense quantities of grain down the Scheldt. Although Bruges bought most of its grain from the Hansards, it also purchased some at Ghent. Thus the commerce of Ghent would be seriously compromised by any attempt of the other Flemish cities to channel into the Leie or the Scheldt south of Ghent and thus divert grain to other destinations before it could pass through the halls. Ghent was still insisting on its right to prohibit all canals into the Leie in the fifteenth century and even claimed to be able to hinder canal trade from Damme to the interior of West Flanders. Thus when Count Louis of Male authorized Bruges to dig such a canal in 1361, the authorities at Ghent grew uneasy. But they could do nothing until August 1379, when the canal reached Aalter and thus crossed into the

21. These interpretations are based on sources discussed in Nicholas, *Metamorphosis*.

5. The grain staple at Ghent. Courtesy Stadsarchief te Ghent (Municipal Archive of Ghent).

quarter of Ghent. The paramilitary "White Hoods" of Ghent then attacked the workmen and precipitated a new civil war.[22]

The canal was an issue that united the shippers and indeed the entire city, but the outbreak of civil war was also tied to personal rivalries within the shippers' guild. From this point on, much of our story is based on the famous chronicler Jean Froissart. Although the early part of his work is drawn from previous chroniclers, notably Jean le Bel, and contains many demonstrable inaccuracies, his second book was written while he was a curate at Les Estinnes, in neighboring Hainaut. He obviously knew Flanders very well and had numerous sources of information. He is our only source for many events in the war in Flanders between 1379 and 1385. Froissart undeniably exaggerated the size of armies, confused chronology, and had a bias in favor of the landed aristocracy; but on topics where his version can be tested against the municipal accounts of Ghent and the records of the aldermen and the count's bailiffs, his account stands up extremely well.[23]

The grant of the grain staple had made the shippers the count's most reliable allies, after the butchers, among the guilds of Ghent. Even in 1436, after all the disorders of the previous years, the count was able to speak with a straight face of their established tradition of loyalty. Of the shippers, the Yoens family had been among the count's staunchest allies during the period of James van Artevelde the elder. John Yoens, apparently the father of the rebel leader of 1379, was alderman in the counterrevolutionary year 1349. According to Froissart, John at some point killed a citizen of Ghent whom the count wanted dead. Although the city government banished Yoens for four years, the count was able to get the sentence of exile commuted

22. Ibid., chap. 9, and particularly D. Nicholas, "The Scheldt Trade and the 'Ghent War' of 1379–1385," *Bulletin de la Commission Royale d'Histoire* 144 (1978): 189–359. For cases from the 1420s, see Blockmans, *Volksvertegenwoordiging*, 474–76.

23. I shall have occasion in the coming pages to demonstrate Froissart's remarkable knowledge of points of detail. See, in general, J. J. N. Palmer, ed., *Froissart: Historian* (Totowa, N.J., 1981), particularly the contribution of Jan Van Herwaarden, "The War in the Low Countries," pp. 101–17.

early and to engineer Yoens's election as dean of the shippers. The Ghent records show that John Yoens, whether father or son is not clear, killed one Peter Donker in October 1352 and paid a blood price. Yoens is not mentioned again in the records until July 1364, but he was dean of the shippers in 1366, and no other source gap has him absent from the city for as much as a year before 1379. He was in severe debt during the 1370s and even had to pawn his boat for a time.[24]

But Gilbert Mayhuus, another shipper of Ghent and a member of the count's council in 1376, was able to undercut Yoens with the count, who engineered Mayhuus's election as dean. Mayhuus was in office when the rebellion broke out in early August 1379. But as the workmen of Bruges drew close to the border of Ghent's quarter, the members of the shippers' guild turned to Yoens, since Mayhuus was perceived as the count's tool, and Yoens evidently inspired the White Hoods to attack. When the count retaliated by sending his bailiff, Roger van Hauterive, into Ghent to capture Yoens, the White Hoods killed van Hauterive. Although the White Hoods had functioned as early as James van Artevelde's time as a posse-type militia, they assume particular importance in the early stages of the rebellion of 1379. Yoens became dean of the shippers on 15 August 1379. The real basis of his power, however, came from his appointment as one of five captains. The captaincy was kept until the end of the war in 1385; thus, whereas James van Artevelde had inaugurated a new regime of captains, Philip simply succeeded another man.[25]

24. De Potter, *Gent* 3:8–9; Froissart, *Chroniques*, vol. 9, chap. 102, pp. 159–63; SAG, WD fol. 29v; Z 1, 3, fol. 3r; G 3, 4, fol. 48v. For a discussion of his fortunes in the 1370s, see Nicholas, *Metamorphosis*, chap. 9. Although there is no evidence that the Yoens family had property at Douai, where John is supposed to have spent his exile, some Ghent shipping families did maintain residences in the cities of northern France, through which they shipped grain into Flanders.

25. Froissart, *Chroniques* vol. 9, chaps. 103–8, pp. 163–77. Gilbert Mayhuus was alderman in 1367, 1370, 1374, 1377, and again in 1390. See also SAG, K 6, 1, fol. 1v; Z 6, 4, fol. 5v; *Rek. Gent 1376–1389*, 126–27; R. de Muynck, "De Gentse Oorlog (1379–1385). Oorzaken en karakter," *HMGOG*, n.s. 5 (1951): 314.

After Yoens's unexpected death in October, evidently from natural causes, power in Ghent passed to the weavers, whose traditional posture against the counts now was exacerbated by the declining fortunes of the textile trade of Ghent and widespread unemployment. The count initially seemed willing to compromise on the issue of the Bruges canal, but personal rivalries in Ghent prevented a settlement. The White Hoods roamed the streets, and after Yoens's death they chose four leaders: the nobleman Raes van Herzele, the shipper John Boele, and two men of such obscure backgrounds that it is not even possible to ascertain definitely their professions before the war but who were to be of considerable importance in the public career of Philip van Artevelde: John Parneele and Peter van den Bossche. A peace was arranged, however, on 1 December 1379. Amnesty was declared and all old privileges confirmed. A general inquest was to be held by judges approved by the three cities of Ghent, Bruges, and Ypres. New magistrates would be appointed in all communities, and in accordance with this, two new boards of aldermen took office in Ghent on 21 December.[26] Several of the leading families of Ghent were split over the issue of the rebellion. Gilbert the son of Gilbert de Grutere was on the first board of aldermen and Gilbert the son of Baldwin on the second, while the butcher Henry Yoens, whose degree of kinship to John is never made explicit, served in the second magistracy.[27]

The problems that had led to the rebellion under James van Artevelde, the threat to the wool supply and a clear distaste for the extent to which Louis of Nevers was subordinating his foreign policy to the interests of the French crown, had affected all

26. Henri Pirenne, ed., *Chronique Rimeé des troubles de Flandre en 1379–1380* (Ghent, 1902), 25; Froissart, vol. 3, chaps. 110, 116, pp. 180–82, 191–94; *Rek. Gent 1376–1389*, 115, 313. The text of the agreement of 1 December is given in *Rek. Gent 1376–1389*, 442–45.

27. SAG, G 8, 3, fol. 8r; K 6, 2, fol. 6r; K 3, 1, BB fol. 1r; G 3, 3, fol. 8r; Z 5, 1, fol. 1r; Z 5, 4, fol. 1v; G 6, 3, fol. 3v; K 8, 1, fol. 23r. A Henry Yoens is mentioned in 1357 as owning a boat, but he had a son named Henry who was evidently the man in public life. No text ties the son to the shippers. He was dead by 22 December 1380; BB 57, fol. 207r; K 8, 2, fol. 7v.

Flemish cities. Thus, although the rulers of Bruges and Ypres had disliked van Artevelde personally and distrusted his overweening ambitions, they essentially supported the rebellion until it had become abundantly clear that it had no chance of success. The war of 1379, however, developed over an issue of concern only to Ghent, for Bruges and Ypres stood to benefit if the Ghent shipping staple could be curtailed. Factions favoring the revolt came to power in the other cities, but they could only maintain their positions with armed assistance from Ghent. By the summer of 1380, power at Bruges and Ypres had returned to the upper bourgeoisie, which favored the count, and Ghent stood isolated. The smaller towns of eastern Flanders, Oudenaarde and Dendermonde, had always disliked Ghent's domination over them and thus stood firmly for Louis of Male.

The count began a siege of Ghent in September 1380, but the operation was broken off quickly because he was unable to control the Scheldt and Leie rivers and thus to starve Ghent out. On 11 November he granted another truce and amnesty, this time on condition that those who had led the rebellion be punished by judges from their places of residence, which meant that rebels of Ghent would be tried locally.[28] The count was more successful in 1381, and Ghent had to send numerous expeditions into eastern Flanders to obtain food from merchants of Brabant. But Brabant grain was only used at Ghent during emergencies, for it had to come by the difficult overland route. By 1381 most of the grain was coming through Aalst, because the count controlled the fortress at Dendermonde, on the Scheldt. Negotiations continued, however, in a conference at Oedelem in July.[29]

Control of Ghent swayed between fluctuating factions. The landowners and weavers had three deans apiece during the fiscal year ending 14 August 1381, but both finished the year with firm allies of the van Arteveldes, James de Rijke and Lawrence

<hr />

28. Printed *Rek. Gent 1376–1389*, 449–50.
29. On 25 July the count gave safe-conduct to one hundred negotiators from Ghent; *Rek. Gent 1376–1389*, 450–51.

de Maech. Peter van den Bossche was dean of the small guilds throughout the year. But by the end of 1381 the situation in Ghent was becoming desperate, and this led in January 1382 to the establishment of a new captaincy dominated by Philip van Artevelde.[30]

In other publications I have explored the extent of violence in Ghent during the fourteenth century.[31] Party warfare pitted factions against each other and often divided kinsman from kinsman. Much of the problem was simple personal hostility and family feuding, but matters were complicated by the presence of gangs of nobles and the practice on the part of prominent men of the city of maintaining bands of retainers wearing their uniforms and thus identifiable by all. Apart from those supported by prominent men on a more or less regular basis were bands of mercenaries. Premeditated homicide was a contract legally enforceable in the courts. Neighborhood bullies added to the conflicts through petty harassment. Street gangs also presented problems; in 1372 a man was assaulted for stating publicly that he was a member of the de Paeu party.[32]

The patriarch of the family was responsible for enforcing its rights and avenging its grievances. The eldest brother of a murdered man was responsible for forcing the killers to pay the blood price, and the major share went to him unless the decedent had a son. This man, the *montzoener*, should have been Philip van Artevelde when James van Artevelde the younger was assassinated, for James outlived his other brothers and died childless. Curiously, although the complete records of the aldermen of Ghent have survived from the years in question, we do not have a record of the blood price paid and the pilgrimages and other penalties undergone for young James's death; nor is

30. Nicholas, *Town and Countryside*, 139–41; de Muynck, "Gentse Oorlog," 305–18; Pirenne, *Histoire de Belgique*, 3d ed., 2:206–18; and Fritz Quicke, *Les Pays-Bas à la veille de la période bourguignonne, 1356–1384* (Brussels, 1947), 303–20; *Rek. Gent 1376–1389*, 238–40.

31. See particularly D. Nicholas, "Crime and Punishment in Fourteenth-Century Ghent," *Revue Belge de Philologie et d'Histoire* 48 (1970): 289–334, 1141–76; and idem, *Domestic Life*, 17–23, 198–206.

32. SAG, Z 6, 4, fol. 6v; Z 6, 2, fol. 4r; Z 6, 1, fol. 8r; Z 5, 2, fol. 8r.

Philip ever expressly called his *montzoener*. We have only the agreement among the killers concerning the extent of responsibility of each family. Since the deed evidently occurred at Weert or Baasrode, the formalities were probably handled there, for the transcripts no longer exist.

The fact that Philip van Artevelde was on such good terms with the van Merlaers, James the younger's assassins, and with the branch of the de Gruteres descended from Baldwin de Grutere, who, as we shall see, had ties with the van Merlaers through Catherine Parijs, is disturbing enough to raise the possibility that Philip may have been in league with his brother's killers. The silence of the documents about the division of the blood price is particularly suspicious. Philip van Artevelde was not the sort of man to be squeamish about murder. But he arranged the division of James's estate with the other heirs, and this would have been impossible if he had been suspected of complicity. Although the Ghent records occasionally try to conceal uxoricide, fratricide was considered far more shameful. Philip's purchase of the Minnemersch property (*Map 1, I–J 7–8*) in 1374 or 1375, just as the de Meys were completing the atonement, may have been made with his share of the blood price.

The payment of the blood price ended the legal liability of the van Merlaers and de Meys for James the younger's death. This was a closed case by 1381, and Philip van Artevelde evidently accepted the fact. But no blood price was ever paid for James the elder. The deeds of violence involving the van Artevelde family always concerned the oldest male, as either perpetrator or victim. John van Artevelde may have thought that John de Scouteete was the only man directly responsible for his father's assassination. As the oldest son, he avenged his father's death. After John van Artevelde died, evidently in 1365, James the younger began taking the family's wrongs upon himself and was eventually murdered. We have no direct evidence between 1370 and 1381 that Philip van Artevelde, by then the sole surviving brother, was involved in city affairs or factional warfare; but indirect evidence shows that his sudden rise to prominence was not accidental. He was clearly a party leader, probably as the successor to his father and older brother. When he came to power, his patterns of violence show that the hostilities of the previous years had not been buried. Thus it is not accurate to say that only the memory of his father brought Philip to power in 1382. Many in the city—according to the chronicler, half—resisted his ascendancy, and some feared him personally, and obviously with good reason. He had been operating behind the scenes for some time before he finally struck in 1381. Philip van Artevelde was, in short, the archetypical godfather.

CHAPTER 6

"Vengeance Is Mine," Saith the Godfather: Philip van Artevelde's Reign of Terror, December 1381–February 1382

Although the chronology is somewhat confused, the municipal account of 1381–82 shows that captains were installed at the beginning of the fiscal year. Peace negotiations were in progress at Harelbeke, near Courtrai, by October (*Illust. 6*). Ghent sent twelve deputies, including the two first aldermen, Gilbert de Grutere and Simon Bette. On 27 December the aldermen or the captains named six commissioners to dispose of property confiscated from exiles who did not support the new regime. One of those named was Philip van Artevelde, who thus makes his first appearance in any context in the municipal accounts of Ghent. The six held office for four weeks; after van Artevelde became captain on 24 January 1382, the number of commissioners was reduced to four. Froissart asserts that the Harelbeke conference occurred after Philip van Artevelde became leader of the government of Ghent. This may be an error, since Philip is known to have become captain on 24 January. But since Froissart mentions the captaincy separately, it it is at least possible that van Artevelde was recognized as leader of the government by 27

6. Delegation from Ghent negotiates with Count Louis of Male, 1381.
Courtesy Bibliothèque Nationale, Paris, MS 2644, fol. 81v.

December because he was head of the board of confiscation commissioners.[1]

The occupational profile of the board of commissioners is quite revealing. The name of one, John Raes, was so common that it is not possible to identify him more exactly. Goessin Mulaert was a landowner, a member of the noble family who were lords of Eksaarde, north of Ghent. As early as 1361 he had unwittingly legitimized himself in the van Arteveldes' eyes by doing surety for Baldwin de Grutere against his kinsman Gilbert de Grutere, whose son would later be killed by Philip van Artevelde. On 17 March 1380 Beatrice de Winter of Bruges appointed Philip van Artevelde's younger sister, the wife of John de Scoteleere, her proxy to collect debts owed her by Mulaert, a fact suggesting that Mulaert and Philip were very close. Goessin Mulaert had succeeded John van Merlaer as captain, evidently on 7 November 1380, and served until 28 February 1381. He became first alderman in August 1382, confirming himself as a firm van Artevelde partisan.

Walter van den Vivere, the second commissioner, was a baker. The account of the count's bailiff of Oudenaarde for the term between 16 September 1381 and 13 January 1382 mentions the execution of two men whom Walter van den Vivere had hired to set fires in Oudenaarde when the militia of Ghent arrived, a piece of skulduggery indicating that the commissioners did not confine themselves to confiscating property. Walter van den Vivere, too, had been captain earlier in 1381. Giles Teys was a draper living before the Posterne gate (*Map 1, D 2*). He was dean of the fullers in 1380, but this does not necessarily mean that he was a fuller. He replaced the wine merchant Francis Augustins as alderman in 1382. Peter van den Brouke was either a dyer or a shipwright and was almost certainly a kinsman of Philip van Artevelde's future wife. After van Artevelde became captain, there were only four commissioners: Mulaert, Teys, and Raes were joined by John van der Bijle, who was probably a

---

1. *Rek. Gent 1376–1389*, 451–52; Froissart, *Chroniques*, vol. 10, chap. 228, 231, pp. 140, 145–47.

brewer. Mulaert and van den Vivere had thus been captains the previous year, and all of these men continued to serve the city during van Artevelde's captaincy. Yet the fact that van Artevelde took a leading role immediately suggests that he had actually been working behind the scenes earlier, and other evidence also lends credence to this supposition. The Mulaert, van den Vivere, and van den Brouke connections show that the appointments of December 1381 represent a movement of the more extreme party in the city, including but not limited to ancestral partisans of the van Arteveldes, utterly opposed to all compromise with the count.[2]

The elevation of Philip van Artevelde to the captaincy in January 1382 is described in graphic detail by the Ghent chronicler whose work is preserved in a Bruges manuscript. His account can be supplemented in some particulars by Froissart's chronicle.[3]

The alderman Simon van Vaernewijc had accused Francis Ackerman, dean of the weavers, one-time regent of the city, and eventual loyal colleague and successor of Philip van Artevelde, of failing to render accounts from the villages around Dendermonde, where he had been captain on behalf of Ghent. Ackerman tried to kill van Vaernewijc, but shippers shielded him and conducted him to his house, where he told his rescuers that he knew of one man who wanted to kill him and hinder the peace efforts with the count: the city attorney, Giles de Mulre. This clearly places Simon van Vaernewijc and at least some of the more moderate shippers in the peace party at the beginning of 1382. On 2 January 1382 the mob, with van Vaernewijc

2 Documents printed CA 345–47; *Rek. Gent 1376–1389*, 282–83. For Mulaert, see SAG, G 1, 4, fol. 38v; K 1, fol. 163r; Z 3, 2, fol. 2r; K 8, 1, fols. 6v, 24v; *Rek. Gent 1376–1389*, 240, 313. For Peter van den Brouke, SAG, K 7, fol. 5r, Z 6, 4, fol. 6r (the shipwright); and G 6, 3, fol. 19r; G 7, 3, fol. 16r; K 9, 1, fol. 16r (the dyer). For Giles Teys, G 6, 4, fol. 31v, *Rek. Gent 1376–1389*, 242. For Walter van den Vivere, *Rek. Gent 1376–1389*, 241; G 8, 2, fol. 21r. The brewer Lievin van der Bijle served as arbitrator for Philip van Artevelde's widow and her second husband in 1388 in their inheritance dispute with Philip's blood heirs, CA 397.

3. The Flemish account is printed in CA 350–53.

leading the way, found de Mulre at the town hall and killed him. Giles de Mulre or de Muelneere had been employed by the city during the fiscal year ending on 14 August 1381, but not thereafter; he was reimbursed in the next fiscal year for an embassy that had met Duke Albert of Holland and Hainaut when he came to Ghent the year before, and the eastern embassies were points of contention between van Vaernewijc and de Mulre and, later, Gilbert de Grutere.[4] If de Mulre was dismissed because he did not favor peace, the advent of van Artevelde and his fellow commissioners in December must be taken as a counterrevolutionary step against the government that had assumed power the previous August. The chronology given by the chronicler is almost certainly accurate, for Giles de Mulre's two legitimate daughters were given guardians on 20 January 1382 and were promptly sued by their father's angry mistress and her bastard.[5]

The mob took two prisoners in the fracas involving Giles de Mulre. Simon van Vaernewijc ordered the city clerk publicly to read their confessions, which had been given under torture. They claimed that not only Giles de Mulre, but also James de Rijke, Peter van den Bossche, and Francis Ackerman had hindered the peace, and the poor miscreants went to their deaths maintaining this. Ackerman succeeded van Artevelde as leader of Ghent, after serving him loyally. James de Rijke was dean of the landowners under van Artevelde's captaincy. He had succeeded John de Jonghe as captain on 18 June 1381 and served with James Diederic, who may be a kinsman of the second husband of Philip van Artevelde's wife. He probably died at Westrozebeke, for he was replaced at midyear 1382 as dean of the landowners by John van Merlaer, whose intermittent service to the van Artevelde regime is one of the more striking features of the situation. I shall discuss Peter van den Bossche separately, for he was or became a virtual alter ego to Philip van Artevelde. Given the subsequent careers of these men, it is unambiguously clear that Simon van Vaernewijc's maneuver, coming while van

---

4. *Rek. Gent 1376–1389*, 184–85, 266, 284.
5. SAG, G 7, 2, fol. 15v; K 9, 1, fol. 14v; K 8, 3, fol. 35v.

Artevelde was already a commissioner but not yet captain, was intended to forestall his accession by striking at people known to be his firm allies and opponents of the peace negotiations. This in turn means that the notion that power was virtually forced on a surprised van Artevelde is almost certainly errone-ous.[6]

The weavers denied that James de Rijke and Francis Acker-man had hindered the peace effort, "and they wanted James de Rijke and Francis Ackerman back and fetched them from their houses." The aldermen mediated peace between the factions. But the mob, which had now changed sides, demanded ven-geance for the death of Giles de Mulre. The weavers and ship-pers fought a battle over the issue in the Kammerstraat (*Map 1, F–G 7*), an aristocratic street near the Friday Market not gener-ally considered to be a seat of strength of either group (compare *Illust. 7*). No one was killed, but van Vaernewijc and several others were exiled. All of these events took place on 2 January 1382.

The van Vaernewijc family held a lordship northeast of Ghent that was outside the city's jurisdiction, but they were among the most prominent of the landowner families and were often in government. William van Vaernewijc had been captain during the regime of the first James van Artevelde. Simon van Vaer-newijc had not been exiled in 1349. He was a member of the delegations negotiating with the count in 1358. He joined Peter Mabenzoon, a later dean of the weavers, and William van Ar-tevelde in receiving money for the repatriated hostages in 1360, but had died by 6 June of that year. The man who was Estate Alderman in fiscal 1381 and was exiled the following January was his son.

The chronicler's version is almost certainly accurate, for Si-mon van Vaernewijc had definitely left the city by 14 February 1382, when his chattels were bought by Quintine, his daughter

---

6. *Rek. Gent 1376–1389*, 239, 339; SAG, K 8, 2, fol. 34v; K 8, 3, fol. 17r; G 7, 4, fol. 80r. This James de Rijke is probably not to be identified with the shipwright of that name, Z 6, 2, fols. 17v, 20r.

7. Civil war in Ghent. Miniature. Courtesy Microform Academic Publishers, Holkham Estate Office, and Lord Coke. Holkham MS 659 F.

by his first marriage and the wife of Simon van den Pitte. He had died by 28 June 1384.[7] Simon van Vaernewijc the elder had been a hosteler who posted bond to do brokerage at the cloth halls; and although his son evidently did not follow this profession, the fact that he continued to reside in his father's house in Onderbergen across from St. Michael's church (*Map 1, E 3–4*), near the docks and in an area frequented by the wealthier shippers, suggests that he may have continued in brokerage but not in textiles. These admittedly hypothetical considerations would certainly explain his alliance with the shippers and the fact that the weavers, who came to power in January 1382, wanted him exiled.

On 13 January 1382 the count's council sent a message brought by clergymen to Ghent that if the magistrates did not accede to the terms set by the conclave at Harelbeke and give hostages to insure compliance, all their efforts for peace thus far would be lost. From this point, the chronicler should be quoted directly:[8]

On Saint Paul's Eve [24 January] a letter was found and read at Ghent before the community, which stated that if they wanted success, they should choose for their captain and government [*sic*] Philip van Artevelde, and then they would be successful, just as they had been in the time of James, his father. Otherwise all would be lost. At this, half of the people, who wanted no part of it, left the marketplace [almost certainly the Friday Market (*Map 1, G–H 6–7*), the largest square in Ghent, which was used for most meetings and some pitched battles, such as on "Good Tuesday"]. But four or five banners [which suggests that on the important occasions when the general assembly met, the guild militias kept together in formation] also left the marketplace and went to look for Philip van Artevelde. They found him in a bathhouse and brought him to the town hall, and they received his oath. The following Friday four captains whom he chose swore with him, two from among the landowners, one weaver, and one shipper. And he chose people from all guilds to go with

7. CA 139; *Rek. Gent 1351–1364*, 340; SAG, G 2, 5, fol. 49r; K 1, fol. 60v; K 8, 3, fol. 14v; G 7, 4, fol. 70v; *Rek. Gent 1376–1389*, 262.
8. CA 351.

him, and he chose as his councillor a poor clerk named Henry. He told the people that he understood their wishes fully, and he did many things on Henry's advice.[9]

At this point Froissart's Chronicle adds material of considerable interest. As distress heightened in Ghent, there were increasing murmurs around town that things would be different if James van Artevelde were alive. Peter van den Bossche had been leader of the White Hoods since 1379, and the peace party blamed him specifically for the military emergency. He was also faulted for his role in the failure of a military expedition earlier that year. He was evidently imprisoned during the van Vaernewijc affair, as the account of the bailiff of Oudenaarde for the period from 13 January to 3 March 1382 mentions that "Philip van Artevelde was made chief captain of Ghent, and Peter van den Bossche was then fetched from the castle at Gavere and made dean of the small guilds." The language clearly shows that van Artevelde became leader of Ghent before Peter van den Bossche was released from prison. Yet both men began to receive wages as captain and dean, respectively, on 24 January 1382. This confirms the earlier suggestion that van Artevelde may in fact have been directing policy in the city since he took charge of the confiscations, evidently on 27 December 1381, just before the van Vaernewijc episode.

This, in turn, means that Froissart's famous story linking Peter van den Bossche with Van Artevelde's accession to the captaincy is probably erroneous. Van den Bossche's personal safety depended on the willingness of Ghent to keep up the war effort, and he thus allegedly fastened on Philip van Artevelde as a man who could unify the diverse elements of the city. Van Artevelde was a man "of whom the city of Ghent had no suspicions, [and] was of sufficient prudence, though his abilities were unknown, for until that day they had paid no attention to him." According to Froissart, however, van den Bossche went to van Artevelde's house and persuaded him to consider accepting the

9. The municipal accounts confirm the chronicler's statement that Philip's captaincy commenced on 24 January; *Rek. Gent 1376–1389*, 278.

captaincy. The next day van den Bossche proposed van Artevelde's election to an assembly. The citizens then went to van Artevelde's house, where he gave a hesitant speech, reminding them that they had rewarded his father's services by murdering him, but then accepted and was taken to the marketplace and sworn in. Froissart adds that in allowing van den Bossche to become in effect the kingmaker, Philip agreed always to act on his advice, and van den Bossche expressly urged him to act as cruelly as necessary to achieve his ends. Froissart's account portrays Philip van Artevelde as "arrived at manhood" and thus a young man, but in fact he was nearly forty-two when he assumed power. A central question in the ensuing discussion, and one to which no really satisfactory answer can be given, is whether Peter van den Bossche in fact was the real power behind Philip van Artevelde, at least in the early stages of his captaincy.[10]

Froissart's chronology for this episode is impossible to reconcile with the count's record if van Artevelde and van den Bossche assumed power together, but there is no reason to think that van den Bossche was not at liberty before 27 December. It is entirely possible that then he was still unacquainted with Philip but totally impossible as late as 24 January 1382. Thus we seem to be dealing with two separate episodes, one shortly before 27 December 1381 and the other around 24 January 1382, which the chronicler confused and merged into one story.

The Ghent chronicler goes on to report that Philip came on Saturday to the meeting of the aldermen, on 23 January (this is certainly an error for 25 January, the next day and a Saturday). Froissart adds that Peter van den Bossche had persuaded Philip to have an armed guard ready when the two of them entered the council chamber to hear the peace proposal read.[11] Philip asked why the city was at war; the attorney responded, "We do not

10. CA 356; *Rek. Gent 1376–1389*, 278; Froissart, *Chroniques*, vol. 10, chaps. 203, 207, pp. 82–83.
11. CA 351; Froissart, *Chroniques*, vol. 10, chap. 207, pp. 84–85.

know," to which Philip answered, "You know well enough," adding, "Tomorrow I will tell you." Then Peter van den Bossche stood up and reminded the aldermen that they had surrendered their own seals and that of the city into the count's hands on Christmas day. "And on Sunday [26 January], around eleven o'clock, Simon Bette, first Law Alderman, was killed."

This tale contains several important elements. Philip van Artevelde came to power as the leader of the weavers, but he maintained important links to the shippers, and at least one shipper joined him as captain. Second, someone carefully planned his elevation by planting the letter, but by implication he himself was not part of the plot and was caught by surprise. We are not told why the assembly was meeting on 24 January. Indeed, if a military assembly was being held on the Friday Market (*Map 1, G–H 6–7*), an event legally requiring the presence of all citizens, it would seem most improbable that the future captain, who already held an important post in the government, would have been taking his leisure in a public bath. Yet, as is true of so many stories about Philip van Artevelde, there is a plausible explanation of the literary tradition: there were numerous bathhouses in the side streets leading off the Friday Market and the Lange Munt (*Map 1, G 5*) toward the Leie river, and he could very well have been waiting in one of these establishments, very near the meeting place, until his elevation became official and he could make a triumphal entry. Even if the timing did surprise him, he had been in the government since at least 27 December 1381, and his behavior on assuming power was so calculatedly violent that it is hard to believe that he had not prepared his moves well in advance. It is thus probable that the surprise, if there was any, was over his appointment as confiscation commissioner rather than as captain.

The chronicler says that half the citizenry opposed Philip's elevation, but no one tried to prevent him from becoming captain. His statement to the aldermen the day after assuming the captaincy is internally inconsistent, a feature that would characterize the rest of his career. On the one hand he criticized the magistrates for capitulating to the count, but on the other he accused them of preventing peace. He killed or engineered the killing of Simon Bette, the first Law Alderman and thus the formal head of the government of the city. The chronicler was under the impression that the captains were chosen by member rather than by parish, and this is at least conceivable. In contrast to the accounts of the 1340s, those of the 1380s do not list the captains' parish affiliation, but the fact that once again there were five captains suggests that, just as in the 1340s, an attempt was being made to maintain occupational balance among the members while also making certain that one captain came from each parish.

Finally, the chronicler clearly states that van Artevelde was under the influence of a clerk. It is very tempting to identify "Henry" with Henry Colpaert, who came from a shipping family. He was reimbursed for many embassies undertaken during the two fiscal years beginning 15 August 1381. After 15 August 1382, most of them were to ecclesiastical establishments and to van Artevelde himself on the final campaign that led to his death. But, in contrast to most messengers, Colpaert was not paid a regular wage, a fact suggesting that he may have been Philip's retainer, although he did continue to perform duties for the city after Philip died. [12]

Van Artevelde proceeded to send troops to besiege the count's castles at Woestijne and Hansbeke. The latter was commanded for Count Louis of Male by Daniel van Haelwijn, the widower of Philip's niece, his brother John's daughter. Van Haelwijn retired to Bruges, and the van Haelwijns were excluded as enemies of the city from their share of Philip van Artevelde's estate when it was probated in 1385. [13] With enemy strongholds in the immediate environs thus neutralized, van Artevelde proceeded to eliminate his personal opponents nearer at hand. On Thursday 30 January he addressed the Collacie (see *Figure 1*), a body that normally met only during emergencies. [14] Philip had his clerk read aloud a letter to Gilbert de Grutere, accusing him of sending money to the

12. *Rek. Gent 1376–1389*, 273–76, 332–37; SAG, G 7, 3, fol. 43v.
13. CA 379–82.
14. On the Collacie, see Victor Fris, ed., *Dagboek van Gent*, 2 vols. (Ghent, 1901–04), I:18–21.

count that had been taken from the seven villages of the lordship of Dendermonde and of releasing hostages taken at Dendermonde. He also alleged that de Grutere had promised capitulation to the count in an assembly at Lille. De Grutere denied it, but van Artevelde went on to reproach him for having exiled John Parneele and William de Scepene. De Grutere responded that he had done this in his capacity as first alderman, but Philip responded, "You will never again banish my people," and ran him through on the spot in the hall of the Collacie.

Van Artevelde then took John de Ruemere, John Mayhuus, and John Sleepstaf, all of whom were confined in the prison on the Grain Market (*Map 1, F 4–5*), and summarily decapitated them. The chronicler's accuracy is confirmed by the account of the count's bailiff at Oudenaarde, dated 30 January 1382, which contains the report of a spy in Ghent that, after van Artevelde had been made chief captain and van den Bossche dean of the small guilds, van Artevelde had killed de Grutere at the town hall and two other men at an unstated place. A separate account from Oudenaarde also relates that twenty-five men had left that town on the evening of 21 February and ambushed seven persons who were bringing food to Ghent. The prisoners recounted that earlier that same day Philip van Artevelde had killed James Soyssone, the dean of the butchers.[15] It thus seems clear that van Artevelde came to power as a leader of the weavers, obviously due to the association with his father, and that while he was willing to work with the shippers up to a point, he faced serious opposition from them and from the victualling trades and inaugurated a violent proscription of his opponents.

No serious historian takes a chronicler's word unless it can be corroborated by other evidence, but the Flemish writer's veracity stands up extremely well under such scrutiny. Nevertheless, personal antagonisms were even more involved in the reign of terror that Philip van Artevelde inaugurated when he came to power than were political or ideological considerations. Our

15. Cited in CA 352–53, 356–57.

next task is thus to examine the careers, ideological backgrounds, and family ties of the men assassinated by Philip van
Artevelde in the weeks after he assumed power.

It has not been possible to ascertain John de Ruemere's profession, but by 12 June 1372 he owned half a house across from the
count's castle. This location makes virtually certain his kinship
with the pursemaker Nicholas de Roemere, who was the victim
of an assault in 1372 by John Beys and John van Merlaer. On 19
July 1380 he sublet from the widow of Francis van Hansbeke her
rights on the prison in the Burgstraat (*Map 1, G 3*), which was
near the castle and maintained for the count. It is easy to under-
stand how the count's jailor could offend the rebels, but the tie
to the van Merlaers is most suggestive. John de Ruemere was
evidently incarcerated in the municipal prison on the Grain
Market at the time of his execution. His estate was only settled
on 25 February 1383.[16]

John Sleepstaf is the only prominent weaver known to have
perished as an opponent of Philip van Artevelde. At least two
men of this name served in the magistracy on numerous occasions, the earliest in 1359. The Sleepstafs remained in the city
through the 1350s but are associated with the weaver restoration. John Sleepstaf represented the weavers when the city accounts of 1348–59 were audited. He acted as surety for the
weavers' guild in a quarrel with the fullers in 1379. He was city
receiver at some point between 1377 and 1380 and was alderman
in the year of his death. His revolutionary credentials would
thus seem beyond question.

But unimpeachable ideological purity afforded salvation for
no man who had given personal offense to any van Artevelde or
whose ancestors had done so. John Sleepstaf acted as guardian of
the children of John Beys or Beyaert in August 1376 and thus
was probably their uncle. John Beys had joined John van Merlaer in the assault on Nicholas de Roemere, almost certainly a
kinsman of the John de Ruemere who was executed with Sleep-

---

16. SAG, G 5, 2, fol. 57r; K 8, 1, fol. 28r; G 7, 3, fol. 45v; Z 6, 1, fol. 12r; Z
6, 2, fol. 10v.

staf. Another hint of a van Artevelde connection comes in May 1378, when Sleepstaf and John Borluut, whose family generally opposed the van Arteveldes, stood surety for the tailor Nicholas Ebbins, a relation of the linen merchant John Ebbins, who had killed Andrew van Merlaer in 1364. As John van Merlaer was serving in the government throughout the van Artevelde captaincy, it thus seems clear that the van Merlaer family was bitterly split, for Andrew van Merlaer was apparently killed by collateral relatives. Although the official records do not mention Sleepstaf's death explicitly, he was replaced as alderman at midyear. And since his heirs were already disputing his testament with the executors by 30 April 1382, the story of his murder in late January is surely accurate. John Sleepstaf thus clearly favored the rebellion against Count Louis of Male but was a personal enemy of Philip van Artevelde for reasons that are not told us. In view of the outcome, he may have had well-founded reservations about Philip's suitability for rule.[17] The only problem with this interpretation is that John de Ruemere and John Sleepstaf, the latter only indirectly as a kinsman of John Beys, were on opposite sides of the Beys/van Merlaer assault on Nicholas de Roemere in 1372.

James Soyssone, the dean of the butchers, may have had a tie through his mother with the van Arteveldes, for a Catherine de Coster, presumably the elder James van Artevelde's widow, and Lawrence de Sceppere were kindred of James Soys's children in 1351. The story of the circumstances of his death on 21 February is probably accurate, as his children were placed under wardship on 26 February, and their guardian renounced James's estate on 4 March 1382. He was a man of mature years, for he is mentioned as the adult son and namesake of another James Soyssone in 1361. There was clearly discord in this family; James Soyssone had been an alderman in the revolutionary magistracy of August 1379 but had been replaced by his uncle Lievin Soyssone in the government that took office in December.

17. SAG, Z 2, 4, fol. 15r; *Rek. Gent 1351–1364*, 422, 428; G 6, 1, fol. 48v; Z 6, 2, fol. 5r; K 6, 2, fol. 41r; K 7, fol. 52r; K 8, 3, fol. 4r; G 7, 2, fol. 28v.

The problems seem also to have been tied to internecine quarrels within the butchers' guild. On 20 January 1380 James Soyssone atoned the killing of John Neutman, who was evidently a member of the Meyeraert and Deynoot faction among the butchers, opposing the Soyssones. The two branches of the family were descended from the brothers John and the elder James Soyssone, who were bitter enemies; in 1373 John's two sons did pilgrimages for attacking James the younger, and one of James's sureties to keep the peace was his uncle Lievin. Lievin and the younger James were still friends as late as 26 February 1379, when Lievin stood surety for him. John's sons joined Henry Yoens and John Deynoot in doing surety in a homicide case, an alliance that would put them in the pro-shipper and extreme weaver faction, whereas by implication James the younger was not.[18] The John Soyssone branch was evidently acceptable to Philip van Artevelde, for his son Simon married Elizabeth de Wilde in late October 1382; he probably died at Westrozebeke a month later, as his estate was settled on 7 March 1383.[19] Elizabeth was the daughter of the wine merchant Arnold de Wilde and had been married previously to the younger John Houckin, a prominent miller. By the 1380s she was an independent businesswoman particularly active in peat speculation. She and Nicholas de Roemere, the pursemaker in the Lange-Munt (*Map 1, G 5*) whom we have discussed above, were owed joint debts in 1384.[20]

Lievin Soyssone is mentioned as surety in a homicide case in April 1380. He served as guardian of Giles Soyssone's children on 11 February 1382, but the next reference to him is on 14 March 1385. He may thus have left the city, although his property was not confiscated. By April 1388 he had married the widow of the tanner James Heinmans, who had been overseer

---

18. CA 257; SAG, G 1, 1, fol. 26v; G 7, 2, fols. 20r, 21v; G 3, 1, fol. 30v; Z 6, 5, fol. 1r; Z 3, 4, fol. 1r; G 7, 1, fol. 12r; Z 5, 3, fol. 11r; Z 5, 4, fol. 1v; G 6, 4, fol. 6r; Z 1, 3, fol. 10r.

19. SAG, K 9, 1, fol. 9r; G 7, 3, fol. 49r.

20. SAG, K 9, 2, fol. 35v; K 10, 2, fol. 54v; K 9, 1, fol. 25v; K 10, 1, fol. 39r; G 4, 2, fol. 8v.

of the property of James van Artevelde's grandchildren. In an agreement to accept arbitration in 1368, Lievin Soyssone stood surety for the butcher Lievin van Damiaet in an action against William van Artevelde and Henry Yoens. He was the brother of Francis Soyssone, who was definitely of the counterrevolutionary party, left Flanders during the rebellion, and served as alderman three times after 1385. Francis was an in-law of Lord Giles Leeuwerke, a shearer whose family was allied with the weavers. He was in the city government through 1378, and a John Leeuwerke was alderman in 1380, but thereafter all these men leave the written record until 1386.

It is thus clear that there was a personal as well as an ideological component to Philip van Artevelde's behavior, for numerous people who supported the rebellion in its early stages left Ghent at the first signs of a van Artevelde restoration in the person of Philip.[21]

The supposition of personal enmity is strengthened by the fact that the Soyssones had been opponents of the elder James van Artevelde. The priest John Soyssone served as city clerk during the 1350s. He eventually became a parish priest at St. Peter's and remained in the city during the 1380s.[22] In 1363 John, James, and Lievin Soyssone and the younger James van Overdwater were called kinsmen from the maternal side of the children of James Borluut; the Borluuts and van Overdwaters were clearly identified as van Artevelde opponents.[23] Giles Soyssone was alderman in 1350. He was obviously considered reliable by the counterrevolutionary regime of the 1350s, for he replaced Lambert van Tideghem as dean of the small guilds in 1353, after van Tideghem had been compromised by involvement in the miscarried rebellion of that year. Yet in November 1356 he stood surety for John de Scoteleere, who would later

21. SAG, Z 6, 5, fol. 5v; K 10, 1, fol. 42r; G 6, 1, fol. 32v; BB 68, fol. 1r; G 8, 1, fol. 43v; G 9, 1, fol. 17v, which mentions Francis having received financial assistance from his mother while he was outside Flanders; G 7, 2, fol. 17v; G 8, 3, fol. 76 bis r; *Rek. Gent 1376–1389*, 353.
22. SAG, Z 1, 3, fol. 10r; G 2, 2, fol. 2r; K 8, 3, fol. 22v; K 11, 1, fol. 92v.
23. On the Borluut tie, see SAG, G 3, 3, fol. 38v; G 5, 4, fol. 22v.

marry James van Artevelde's youngest daughter.[24] Curiously, he was not disgraced in the revolution of 1359–61, for he was a guild councillor of the butchers in 1361–62, although he was never again alderman. He may have been a victim of van Artevelde's hostility even before James Soyssone, for his children were placed under wardship on 11 February 1382, two weeks before James was killed. But he had an adult son, Giles, who was not included in this wardship, and Giles the younger was still living in the family home in March 1384. Although some Soyssones remained in the city during the 1380s, notably James Soyssone Before the Count's Castle,[25] the family as a whole had been political enemies of the van Arteveldes since at least the 1340s and had compounded the political tie by intermarrying with other lineages inimical to the van Arteveldes. Such people did not live long in Ghent in 1382.

The most prominent men killed at Philip van Artevelde's instigation were Simon Bette, first Law Alderman, and Gilbert de Grutere, dean of the small guilds. The Bette assassination seems to have been motivated by personal antagonism, for the Bette and van Artevelde families had long been enemies, but there was a policy consideration as well, dating to the period in 1379 when Bette and de Grutere were first aldermen of the two benches of the city council. The Flemish chronicler does not attribute Bette's assassination to Philip van Artevelde personally, but rather describes a mob scene in which van Artevelde deliberately fomented passions. Froissart claims that Peter van den Bossche killed Bette while van Artevelde dispatched de Grutere at the same assembly. Like the de Gruteres, the Bettes were an ancient landowner family with several branches that did not always follow the same line in city politics. Several texts

24. Cornelius de Scoteleere is mentioned in Ghent on 3 December 1380 but not again until 12 March 1386, when Francis Soyssone agreed to terms of repayment for a loan; SAG, K 8, 1, fol. 8v; K 10, 2, fol. 34v. Although the two families were clearly in close contact, Cornelius was the son of a Giles de Scoteleere, not of John; G 3, 1, fol. 64r.

25. SAG, G 1a, fol. 33r; Z 2, 2, fol. 15r; Z 3, 2, fol. 12v; G 7, 2, fol. 17v; K 9, 2, fol. 35v; G 8, 4, fol. 21r; *Rek. Gent 1351–1364*, 51, 229.

mention Bettes and de Gruteres as kinsmen, but in contexts suggesting in-laws.

The man killed in 1382 was known variously as Simon Bette in the Koestraat (*Map 1, C 6*) and Simon Bette in the Ameede, the name of his residence in that street, which is just across the Kalandenberg from the Paddenhoek. The Bettes had clearly been close neighbors of James van Artevelde, though not of Philip, and we have seen that physical proximity did not endear the van Arteveldes to anyone, either in Ghent or in rural Flanders. Bette was alderman in 1371 and was first Estate Alderman in the first magistracy of 1379, which would place him in the shipper faction. Gilbert de Grutere was then the official head of the city government as first Law Alderman, and it is likely that van Artevelde's hostility over the banishments of John Parneele and William de Scepene extended to both, for we shall see that he was clearly enraged with de Grutere over the matter. Bette then returned as first Law Alderman in August 1381. His minor children were placed under wardship on 10 June 1382, nearly six months after his assassination.[26]

Some members of the Bette family had served the rebel regime of the 1340s. Thomas Bette was castellan of Rupelmonde, while John Bette at different times was receiver and captain of the parish of St. John in the last stages of the revolt.[27] The personal enmity of the Bettes toward the van Arteveldes probably dated from the time of Gerolf Bette, a weaver and lord of the cloth hall who was alderman at various times between 1320 and 1336, then returned in January 1349, 1351, 1355, and 1360. The chronology of his service clearly establishes him as a partisan of the count.[28]

In addition to being landowners, the Bettes practiced various professions, notably in textiles, a fact that makes Simon's association with the shippers somewhat surprising. Several Bettes remained in the city after he was assassinated. With rare exceptions, they had not been aldermen or tax farmers in the years of

26. SAG, G 7, 2, fol. 29v.
27. *Rek. Gent 1336–1349*, 2:198, 258; 3:148, 198.
28. Ibid., 3:327; *Rek. Gent 1351–1364*, 430.

James van Artevelde's ascendancy, but most do not seem to
have left the city, and William Bette in the Koestraat (*Map 1, C
6*), who was probably the father of the man killed by Philip van
Artevelde, loaned money to the city in 1342 and 1347.[29] Although Jordan Bette was active in Ghent during the 1350s, he
was acceptable to the restored weaver regime, for he was alderman in 1361 and 1364 and a lord of the Cloth Hall.[30]

Clearer suggestions of hostility to the van Arteveldes are provided by William Bette, Anthony's son. He paid a fine to the
city in 1338 for leaving and then returning. Although he loaned
money to the city in 1342, he served in the magistracy during
the 1350s and was related by marriage to John de Grutere of
Botelaer and to various Borluuts, all of them van Artevelde
enemies.[31] But, in contrast, William Bette the son of Lord As-
scheric, although a fiefholder of the count, seems to have been
loyal to the rebel regime of the 1340s both before and after the
killing of James van Artevelde. He was not exiled, however,
and joined Gilbert de Grutere in representing the landowners in
the negotiations with the count in 1358.[32]

None of this, except the fateful tie with the magistracy of
1379, should have been enough to qualify Simon Bette for Philip van Artevelde's hit list in 1382. But the accusation against
Gilbert de Grutere does take on overtones of policy. According
to the chronicler, van Artevelde summoned the Collacie in
effect to "set him up" on 30 January 1382. Although de Grutere
was not generally used on expeditions outside the city during
this year, he was sent to Hansbeke on 28 January, returning the
next day just in time for a carefully orchestrated greeting.[33] We

---

29. *Rek. Gent 1336–1349*, 2:165; 3:168.

30. *Rek. Gent 1351–1364*, 28; SAG, K 2, 2, fol. 13r; K 5, 1, fol. 25r.

31. *Rek. Gent 1336–1349*, 1:261; 2:106; *Rek. Gent 1351–1364*, 84; Z 3, 5, fol.
9v; G 6, 1, fol. 6v.

32. *Rek. Gent 1336–1349*, 1:119, 155, 270, 384; 2:93, 102, 166; 3:354; *Rek.
Gent 1351–1364*, 393.

33. *Rek. Gent 1376–1389*, 298. The account for this year is a rough draft, and
this paragraph is crossed out, suggesting that the authorities wanted to conceal
the truth but did not get around to having the accounts recopied into final
form. Gilbert de Grutere is not mentioned again in the expeditions for this year,
further confirmation of the chronicler's date for his murder.

have seen that Philip's clerk read a statement accusing de Grutere of various treasonable acts, but what most enraged Philip
was Gilbert's role as alderman in 1379 in the exile of William de
Scepene and John Parneele. We must thus reconstruct the
careers of these men to ascertain their ties to Philip van Artevelde.

William de Scepene appears in October 1371 as damaged
surety for John van den Brouke, who may have been related to
the lady who later married Philip van Artevelde. He is last
mentioned as alive in the official records in July 1379 in another
surety case. The next reference to him, on 10 August 1386,
involves his widow. The family name, which means "alderman," is quite unusual, and he was probably related to James de
Scepene, dean of the bakers in 1386 and alderman in 1387. We
have seen that bakers were involved in the van Artevelde story
during the 1360s; and a source of 1369, shortly after John de
Grave murdered the younger James van Overdwater, van Artevelde's enemy, gives James de Scepene the nickname James de
Grave.[34]

Our information for William de Scepene is thus circumstantial; but John Parneele was evidently a tailor who quarreled with
his own guild, and he had no position in the government of the
city before 1379. He and William de Scepene may have been
relatives, for John Parneele and a William de Grave were joint
guardians of an orphan in 1374. At some point during the fiscal
year 1378–79, a truce was declared between two groups of persons who agreed to accept the aldermen's judgment for their
unspecified misdeeds against Arnold van der Varent, a carpenter
who was a long-term dean of the small guilds, and his deputies.
The involvement of the overdean suggests that the matter was a
quarrel among various small guilds. Of the persons and their
sureties in the first group who can be identified by profession,
all were smiths except one kettlemaker and a saddler who lived
in a concentration of smiths on the Kalandenberg (*Map 1, D–E
6*). The second group consisted of tailors except for one embroi-

---

34. SAG, WD fol. 36r; Z 5, 2, fol. 1v; G 6, 4, fol. 32v; G 4, 5, fol. 9 bis r; G
8, 1, fol. 78r.

derer. Neither a William de Scepene nor a William de Grave appears on either list, but the tailor group includes John Parneele. Evidently in connection with this affair, two men in the second list, Parneele and Bartholomew van Meesine, were ordered on 31 March 1379 to pay substantial fines to the tailors' guild. Van Meesine remained in the city during Philip van Artevelde's captaincy, although he held no offices until he became dean of the tailors in 1386. The account of the count's bailiff for 20 September 1378 through 11 January 1379 mentions a fine levied on one Betsy Clapal "for having been the informant of a deed that occurred in the Houtbriel [*Map 1, F 8*] at Ghent for which seven people were banished." While the surviving records do not mention the banishments, the chronology and the large number of persons involved in the action between the smiths and the tailors suggest that this may be the same episode.[35]

Froissart informs us, however, that Jan Parneele became "principal leader and master of the White Hoods" after John Yoens's death in October 1379.[36] When he heard that the kindred of the count's assassinated bailiff had avenged his death by ambushing a convoy of grain boats and blinding their pilots, Parneele assembled the White Hoods without telling the aldermen of his intentions, marched quickly on Oudenaarde, and seized it. He stayed for a month, destroying the fortifications of Oudenaarde on the side toward Ghent. The city magistrates, whose leaders were the first aldermen Gilbert de Grutere and Simon Bette, were trying to negotiate a peace with the count's men and accordingly protested that they were innocent of complicity in the deed. The count's men responded that as the alder-

35. SAG, G 5, 5, fol. 1r; truce recorded BB 78, fol. 59r; SAG, WD fol. 36r.; K 7, fol. 31b v; G 6, 5, fol. 18r; G 7, 1, fol. 9r; G 7, 2, fol. 5v. For the bailiff's case, see ARA, RR 1384.

36. The later *Notae Gandavenses* list Parneele as one of the five parish captains of 1379, but the city accounts name John de Drussate; cited in de Muynck, "Gentse Oorlog," 314. Parneele was evidently a tailor, and John de Drussate was a weaver-draper, facts that strengthen the case for the chronicler's statement that the captains were chosen for occupational balance as well as for parish affiliation. SAG, K 11, 2, fol. 71v.

men had left Parneele there for a month without trying to halt his activity, they must have approved of it. Fearing the worst, the government recalled Parneele from Oudenaarde. In a sentence indicating that he had acted without their knowledge or approval, they banished him from Flanders for life. Their anger may have been the more intense since he was a member on behalf of the city of the electoral board (*figure 1*) that chose the new benches of aldermen to take office on 21 December, including Gilbert the son of Baldwin de Grutere, his kinsman's bitter rival. The first set of aldermen of the year, who served between 15 August and 21 December, had thus banished Parneele after their successors had been chosen but before they took office. Parneele went to Ath, in Hainaut, but the authorities delivered him to the Flemish Count Louis of Male, who had him executed. The records of Ghent show him dead by 27 June 1380.[37]

No formal municipal account survives from 1379–80, but a list of miscellaneous expenditures incurred between 1377 and 1380 includes a payment that "John Parneele and William de Scepene incurred on the catapult at Oudenaarde."[38] Nothing else associates William de Scepene with either the White Hoods or John Parneele, but this passage proves conclusively that the city government had countenanced the seizure of Oudenaarde, if only after the fact. The aldermen's cowardly act of exiling Parneele can be explained only as a deliberate decision to sacrifice one man for the safety of many.

That Gilbert de Grutere and Simon Bette set up Parneele and William de Scepene as sacrifices is shown clearly by the fact that the shipper John Boele, who was with Parneele at Oudenaarde and was his colleague as elector of the second group of aldermen in December, remained as dean of the small guilds through this fiscal year, although he eventually yielded to the more radical Peter van den Bossche. An undated fragment inserted at the end of the aldermen's register for 1379–80 is usually dated early

---

37. *Rek. Gent 1376–1389*, 447; see also Froissart, *Chroniques*, vol. 10, chap. 116–17, 122, 130–33, pp. 191–95, 217–26; SAG, G 6, 5, fol. 18v.
38. *Rek. Gent 1376–1389*, 129.

1380, after the new board had taken office, but in fact it seems to refer to the autumn of 1379. In it, John Boele informs the general assembly of Ghent that he and other good people had come into Oudenaarde and had torn down some of the walls and wanted further instructions. The assembly ordered them to destroy the walls on the side toward Ghent but then to return home as soon as the job was done.[39] The text does not mention Parneele, and the technicality may be raised that the assembly and not the aldermen gave the order. What is clear, however, is that the White Hoods had begun the action on their own initiative but evidently were given some sort of authorization later.

John Parneele and William de Scepene were thus linked, perhaps by blood and definitely by participating at the siege of Oudenaarde and being exiled. Philip van Artevelde took their banishment as a personal affront. Not a shred of evidence ties van Artevelde personally to the White Hoods, who would continue to function into the fifteenth century. But the fact that they simply drop out of Froissart's Chronicle after van Artevelde became the leader of Ghent suggests that their members were among the guards paid regularly by the city after January. Peter van den Bossche, whom Froissart identifies as Philip's mentor, was Parneele's colleague as chief of the White Hoods in 1379. Philip's speech at the de Grutere killing thus lends verisimilitude, as the chronology does not, to the notion that he was the creature of Peter van den Bossche at that stage, as does Froissart's claim that van den Bossche killed de Grutere while van Artevelde murdered Bette in the same meeting of the Collacie; the Ghent chronicler places Bette's death six days before de Grutere's, implicating van Artevelde, and accuses van Artevelde of killing de Grutere.[40] Whatever van den Bossche's role may have been in van Artevelde's rise to power, the captain remained psychologically dependent upon Peter in the early days of his rule, although he assumed a more independent posture after the conquest of Bruges on 3 May 1382.

39. Printed in *Rek. Gent 1376–1389*, 448.
40. Froissart, *Chroniques*, vol. 10, chap. 207, 232–33, pp. 82, 147–49.

A central question of our inquiry is the extent to which Peter van den Bossche was the real power behind Philip van Artevelde's throne, as Froissart thought. Van den Bossche is one of the more mysterious figures of the history of Ghent. Although van Artevelde came to power as a leader of the weavers, van den Bossche was a small guildsman, serving as their overdean after having been captain and leader of the White Hoods in the early stages of the Ghent rebellion. But his origins are obscure. He did not participate in the battle at Westrozebeke in which van Artevelde lost his life; for the week before, as leader of a separate force, he had tried and failed to prevent the invading French army from crossing the Leie River into Flanders and had retreated, seriously wounded, to Bruges, where Philip had installed him as captain. Van den Bossche quickly withdrew to Ghent, where he continued to be a leader of the resistance to the count until the peace in 1385. He was clearly a violent man. Even if Froissart's stories of his influence on Philip van Artevelde are exaggerated, he was responsible for killing at least one man and seriously injuring another during a military campaign in the summer of 1381. He had led the militia but had been held under guard for three extra days, probably in connection with the violence. The blood price was only fixed on 26 August 1382, however, in a special action by the aldermen of both benches, the two other deans, and Philip van Artevelde as captain. Given amnesty after the war, van den Bossche declined to remain in Ghent, according to Froissart, mentioning his own humble origins and his fear of the vengeance of the powerful de Grutere and Bette families. He went to England and entered royal service.[41]

Peter van den Bossche bore an extremely common name, and three men who may be he are mentioned in the sources. The name is found in a list of carpenters of 1352–67, but this man cannot be proven still to have been alive in the 1380s. The homicide atonement of 1382 mentions the dean's father as Baldwin van den Bossche, and no person of this name appears in the

---

41. CA 359–60; *Rek. Gent 1376–1389*, 202, 268; Froissart, *Chroniques* vol. 10, chap. 207, p. 83; vol. 11, chap. 500–501, pp. 310–12.

carpenters' register.[42] A wine merchant who was admitted to that guild in 1368 was still alive as late as 1383,[43] but that the political leader's father was still alive in 1382 suggests that he was rather young. Thus the most likely candidate for the political Peter van den Bossche is a baker of that name. This man lived at Tussen Walle (*Map 1, B 6*), in the weaver quarter and near the van Arteveldes' ancestral home on the Kalandenberg (*Map 1, D–E 6*). The baker was still in the city as late as March 1385, owing a debt to Peter van Beerevelt, a painter who had decorated the banners for the city militia earlier in the war. The next reference to the baker is in a text of December 1387, when he sold a bread rent secured on his residence. He was still alive in 1390.[44]

Froissart claims that although van den Bossche began as an humble man, he accumulated considerable property while in public life and was permitted to take it with him to England. Although several van den Bossches in 1386–87 paid the "issue" fine that Ghent levied on property taken outside the city, Peter was not among them. But in 1389 a Peter van den Bossche whose profession is not given was suing the collectors of issue.[45] Two other considerations make this professional identification more probable. William de Scepene was evidently a baker, and since we know nothing of other professional involvements, van den Bossche may have associated a man of his own guild with him at Oudenaarde. Froissart also speaks of him as a protégé of John Yoens, with van den Bossche referring to Yoens as his late "master." There is no record of a shipper named Peter van den Bossche, but the boat captains had personal and professional ties with the grain measurers and bakers whom they served,[46] and Yoens would naturally look for hatchet men among his personal

---

42. SAG, ser. 190–1 fol. 4v.
43. SAG, ser. 176, no. 1, fol. 1r; K 9, 1, fol. 17r.
44. SAG, K 10, 1, fol. 59v; K 11, 1, fol. 40v; Z 9, 1, fol. 17r.
45. SAG, K 11, 2, fol. 76r.
46. Froissart, *Chroniques*, vol. 10, chap. 207, p. 82, and passim. On the ties between the shippers and the grain and bread guilds, see Nicholas, *Metamorphosis*, chap. 9.

friends. It is thus likely that the captain was a baker who had left Ghent for two years but then had thought it safe to return. If so, he found safety from his blood enemies but not from the tax collectors.

But although Peter van den Bossche was obviously very influential, there was more to Philip van Artevelde's hostility toward Gilbert de Grutere than the exile of Parneele and de Scepene. Three Gilbert de Gruteres figure in our account. The de Gruteres were brewers and landowners. They held the hereditary right to a tax on grout, the coarse herbs used for brewing beer until hops were introduced, and were among the most ancient lineages of Ghent. Some de Gruteres seem to have been loyal to James van Artevelde's regime. Henry de Grutere, a fiefholder of the count, was alderman in 1337 and performed various functions for the city, including trying to get the unfortunate militia leader Zeger de Kortrijzaan released in 1338. Because he was the count's man, the city used him in early 1345 to "represent" the count at Oudenaarde.[47] Everdey de Grutere was alderman in 1336 and loaned money to the city in 1342. He sold rents at Brussels on behalf of Ghent in December 1346 and so was willing, as most were, to serve the post-1345 regime as well as that of van Artevelde.[48]

But other de Gruteres were openly hostile to the revolutionary regime. Even Henry de Grutere, who had served James van Artevelde as late as 26 February 1345, became first Law Alderman in January 1349. Gilbert de Grutere had been first Law Alderman in 1341 but evidently died in midyear, for he was replaced by John van Ghelre, and his widow loaned money to the city in 1342. His son and namesake, however, may have left the city, for he is not mentioned in the records of the later 1340s, and he became alderman in 1353, following the weaver conspiracy of the previous year and clearly in reaction against it. The younger Gilbert stood surety in 1355 for Simon de Grutere, son of the Henry who had become alderman in January 1349.

---

47. *Rek. Gent 1336–1349*, 1:107, 172; 2:385.
48. Ibid., 1:60; 2:168; 3:64.

He or his son continued to serve on the town council after 1361, however, and he thus must have been at least minimally acceptable to the weavers.[49]

As we have seen with the Yoens and Soyssone families, the de Gruteres were split into antagonistic factions. Gilbert the younger was alderman for the term beginning 15 August 1379, but the account of the city debt compiled in 1380 says that his regime led the city only three weeks, until 5 September. Expenses were then rendered by the "leaders" John Yoens and his colleagues, as power fell into the hands of the shippers. It is not clear whether the de Grutere magistracy was deposed or simply subordinated to the captains, but on 21 December two new boards of aldermen, led by Gilbert the son of Baldwin de Grutere and Henry Yoens, took control.[50] By this time power was definitely in the weavers' hands. Our entire chronology of events thus hinges on the question of which Gilbert de Grutere—the son of Gilbert or the son of Baldwin—was assassinated by Philip van Artevelde.

Philip's victim was overdean of the small guilds during the fiscal year 1381. Gilbert de Grutere the younger paid 20 lb. to the city in 1380. While this heading in the accounts includes both loans and confiscations from fugitives, the fact that the aldermen never resold his property suggests a loan. He leased the tax farm on paving stones from the city in 1380. He was at all events identified with the shipper faction rather than the weavers. The affair of Simon van Vaernewijc suggests that the shippers may have had the upper hand when the magistracy was rotated in August 1381, but that the weaver party had begun to assume some offices in December, when Philip van Artevelde became commissioner of confiscations. The story of Gilbert de Grutere's assassination is lent credence by the fact that a wardship was established for his three daughters on 18 April 1382. He also left an adult son, but no blood price was ever paid.[51]

49. Ibid., 2:168; 3:327; SAG, G 1, 5, fol. 26v.
50. *Rek. Gent 1376–1389*, 115.
51. Ibid., 177, 277; SAG, G 7, 2, fol. 27r.

It is possible that van Artevelde's hostility to Gilbert de Grutere was attributable solely to his being allied with the shippers
and to his having exiled two of van den Bossche's colleagues
among the White Hoods; but there were personal aggravations
as well. It is possible but unlikely that the two families were
rivals within the brewers' guild. John den Amman of Dendermonde, who had held the younger James van Artevelde in prison in 1350, had used Henry de Grutere to collect James's debts
from his relatives.[52] Most de Gruteres were brewers, and John
de Grutere was clerk of the guild in 1386.[53] Gilbert and Oste
were the sons of Baldwin, who died in 1353.[54] A text of 1389
shows that Baldwin's son Gilbert was dead by that time and that
Celie van Vaernewijc was the widow of John de Grutere of
Botelaer, but there is no indication that John and Oste or Baldwin were siblings.[55]

The two branches of the de Grutere family, descended from
Gilbert the elder and Baldwin, were bitterly divided. The split
probably originated during the 1340s. Baldwin de Grutere had
been alderman in 1324 and 1333. He is then mentioned in a text
of 20 May 1339 in a quarrel with the brewers of light beer, but
he does not appear thereafter in the registers of the aldermen
until 1350, although he did loan money to the city in 1342. On
28 October 1361, Gilbert and Oste, Baldwin's two sons, were
sent on pilgrimages for having untruthfully accused the younger
Gilbert of being false to them and threatening him. The arbitrators included John Parijs, and the sureties for Baldwin's sons
included the fateful name of William Bette, son of Lord Anthony. The hard feelings evidently continued for at least a dec-
ade and a half, for the case was only crossed out as quit on 20
July 1376.[56] And we have seen that Gilbert de Grutere the younger, who was associated with the shipper party, was alderman at

52. CA 288.
53. SAG, ser. 160, no. 6, fol. 22r.
54. SAG, G 1, 4, fols. 14v–15r; G 3, 2, fol. 47r.
55. SAG, K 12, fol. 36r.
56. SAG, K 1, fols. 1r, 72 r–v; Rek. Gent 1336–1349 2:168; Z 3, 2, fols. 1r,
2r.

the beginning of the fiscal year 1379 but was succeeded by Gilbert the son of Baldwin, who leaned toward the weaver party.

The areas of antagonism with the van Arteveldes also include a tie of the Baldwin de Grutere branch to the van Merlaer assassins of James van Artevelde the younger. We have seen that a John de Grutere was a maternal half brother of John son of Walter van Merlaer. Their common mother was Catherine Parijs, probably a member of the dyer family that had been such bitter enemies of James the elder. A text of 22 November 1363 shows that John de Grutere, father and son, were related to the family of Gilbert son of Baldwin, but Gilbert the younger is not mentioned. However, on 6 October 1377 Gilbert de Grutere the son of Baldwin willed a substantial sum to a second John de Grutere, this one his adult bastard.[57]

It is impossible to determine absolutely whether the half brother of John van Merlaer was the bastard or the younger and legitimate John de Grutere, but it is likely that he was the bastard. The elder John de Grutere survived his wife and was acquitted by his evidently legitimate son of the maternal estate on 10 September 1365. Bastards could inherit from their mothers in Ghent during the fourteenth century, but not from the father unless he willed them something. The fact that the father of John de Grutere is never named by a man in a genealogy-conscious family that had several branches, when Lievin de Beere and John van Merlaer acquitted Catherine Parijs' estate, and that she is never called the wife of any de Grutere but simply Catherine Parijs, suggests that John may have had some reason not to advertise his paternity. Catherine Parijs was already the widow of Walter van Merlaer by August 1355, and at that time John van Merlaer was called by a diminutive name, suggesting that he was almost certainly younger and perhaps considerably younger than John de Grutere. Baldwin de Grutere had been alderman in 1324 and 1333 and thus could easily have had a son of sufficient age to father a child by a prominent woman who

57. SAG, G 5, 2, fol. 57v; G 4, 5, fol. 50r; G 3, 4, 12r; K 6, 2, fol. 8r.

later, as a shunned castoff, married a man of undistinguished parentage. Baldwin's son Gilbert was already a mature man by 1351, and he was exiled to Pisa for a homicidal attack on his brother-in-law, Anthony Melaus, on 11 December 1353, in what was evidently a quarrel over the inheritance of Baldwin de Grutere.[58] It is virtually certain, therefore, that the half brother of John van Merlaer was the bastard son of Gilbert son of Baldwin de Grutere, who became alderman in 1375 and in the second magistracy of 1379–80 but evidently retired thereafter from public life. The fact that the van Merlaers were in good standing with the van Artevelde regime in the 1380s despite their role in the killing of the younger James may reflect the fact that they were kinsmen of the branch of the de Grutere family hostile to Philip's enemy, Gilbert the son of Gilbert.

The de Gruteres were thus generally of the party inclined toward the Flemish counts and as such would have had problems with the van Arteveldes. Both branches, those descended from Gilbert the elder and from Baldwin, had been in the city during the 1350s; but while the Gilbert de Grutere branch was in the city government, that of Baldwin was not, and some of its most important males were exiled. Both branches, therefore, had reasons to fear a van Artevelde captaincy, but particularly that of the younger Gilbert. By 1379 they were allied with different factions in the city, those of the weavers and of the shippers, both of which supported the rebellion but one of which wanted van Artevelde—the weavers and Gilbert the son of Baldwin de Grutere—while the other did not—the shippers and Gilbert de Grutere the younger. The narrative dealing with van Artevelde's ascent to power shows that the shippers wanted peace with the count by the beginning of 1382, whereas the weavers did not, and Philip van Artevelde claimed in the meeting of the Collacie that not only had Gilbert de Grutere exiled his men, but he had also been negotiating independently with the count against the interests of the city. We have seen that the

58. SAG, G 4, 1, fol. 2r; Nicholas, *Domestic Life*, 154; SAG, G 2, 1, fol. 1v; Z 1, 1, fol. 7v; Z 1, 4, fol. 2v; G 1, 4, fols. 14v–15r.

family background and alliances of Gilbert de Grutere the younger were enough to excite Philip's wrath and that he had indeed
betrayed John Parneele. Our next question is thus whether there
was any truth to the charges of treason.

There are suggestions in the municipal accounts of 1381–82
even before van Artevelde formally entered the government
that Gilbert de Grutere, although dean of the small guilds, was
considered unreliable and was not to be sent outside the city.
Alone of the three deans, he was replaced by substitutes on
expeditions to Overmere on 7 September, and to Aalst on 28
August and 4, 24, and 28 September. The Aalst expeditions
were to obtain grain or to bring it back to Ghent. He was
replaced on an expedition to Ninove for food on 13 September,
to Deinze on 24 October, and to Aksel on 7 November, although on 19 November he did accompany the other deans and
a delegation of aldermen to Hulst to requisition grain. Perhaps
most telling is the evidence of the account that the count's bailiff
of Oudenaarde rendered on 12 January 1382, before Philip van
Artevelde became captain but while he was confiscation commissioner. The bailiff informed the count that on 13 October
the militia of three parishes left Ghent to accompany merchants
of Brussels, but Gilbert de Grutere's retainers had said, "We
want peace, for we intend to act within the peace; we cannot
function outside it." They apparently said this in Ghent and
were not negotiating directly with the count's men, for the
bailiff paid the messenger who brought him the news of this
development from Ghent. The municipal account confirms that
all three deans were replaced at this time by deputies on a mission eastward to accompany merchants of Brabant who were
bringing food to Ghent.[59] There was clearly serious disaffection
at Ghent that had come to the attention of the count's men,
although only the chronicler's evidence suggests that Gilbert de
Grutere himself negotiated directly with Louis of Male.

59. *Rek. Gent 1376–1389*, 284–94; CA 345. Curiously, the account claims
that the dean of the weavers was replaced by Walter van den Vivere, who was a
baker, and that de Grutere was replaced by Giles van den Westvelde, a draper.

On balance, we cannot maintain that Philip van Artevelde had no cause to suspect the loyalty of Gilbert de Grutere. But there was also clearly an element of settling old scores with a personal opponent, and it is likely that had de Grutere and the shippers prevailed in January 1382, the greatest disasters of the "Ghent War" would have been averted.

The "atonement books" kept by the aldermen are not complete records of homicides but contain only those that the parties concerned wished to have recorded. Their form changes in 1380. While the book of that year lists a few homicide atonements, it is essentially a record of parties agreeing to accept arbitration, and the books of 1381 and 1382 contain no homicide records at all except for one unusual case arbitrated by Philip van Artevelde himself. The records suggest a considerably heightened level of violence during the 1380s, for the truces are far more numerous than before the war. Still, it is curious that there is no record of a blood price ever having been paid for de Mulre, Bette, Soyssone, Sleepstaf, de Ruemere, or de Grutere. Philip van Artevelde was not involved in de Mulre's death, and the chronicler's description of Bette's end suggests a riot that van Artevelde had instigated but in which he may not have struck the final blow. Nonetheless, his personal responsibility for the deaths of the other four cannot be denied. Most homicides seem to have been atoned rather quickly, but the families of the dead men would have had no reason to shy away from making claims on van Artevelde's estate after his death. Under the custom of Ghent, the widows and blood heirs of dead murderers were each liable for half of the blood price. Since Yolante van den Brouke delayed for almost a year in offering a division of assets to Philip's heirs, it is possible that there were negotiations about blood prices. There can be no question, in my opinion, of the written record having been altered to delete reference to these deeds, for the manuscript "atonement books" of the 1380s are in a very rough state and lack the finished precision that one would expect of a coverup. It is possible that deeds of violence committed while one was captain, an office endowed with emergency military powers, were immune from prosecution, but there is no evidence that any of the other captains shared Philip's proclivity to murder personal rivals against whom they must, as human beings, have borne grudges.[60] That no blood vengeance was exacted in retribution after November is almost certainly due to the fact that van Artevelde's only surviving male kinsmen were in the female line and were thus considered innocent parties.

But whether begun at van den Bossche's inspiration or not, the homicidal fury of Philip van Artevelde did not end with the men against whom he had both policy quarrels and personal grudges. Our sources suggest that he set out deliberately to avenge his father's death. Nothing would have prevented him from doing so before he assumed power in late 1381, for blood vengeance was an inalienable right, and indeed was a positive obligation of the eldest male of the family. The fact that twenty years elapsed between the killing of John de Scouteete by John van Artevelde and Philip van Artevelde's murders suggest that the van Artevelde family did not know who else had been involved in the events leading to James the elder's death in 1345 until Philip entered the city government in late December 1381. From that time, Philip had at his disposal not only the summary city accounts that we can use now, but other written information not later entered in registers and now lost. Despite his tender years when his father died, Philip van Artevelde had much more complete information by 1382 about his father's assassination than we do.

Froissart claims that Philip had twelve persons beheaded in his presence during his first days in power because "some said" that they had been implicated in his father's death.[61] Froissart seems diffident about his sources, and it is not likely that that many people old enough to participate in James van Artevelde's murder in 1345 would still have been alive thirty-seven years later. But Philip's documented behavior makes me reluctant to

60. This question cannot be considered in the case of James van Artevelde the elder, for the first surviving atonement book is from the fiscal year 1349–50, five years after his death.
61. Froissart, *Chroniques*, vol. 10, chap. 228, p. 140.

dismiss out of hand the tale of twelve killings. Indeed, during his period in power he had his own private executioner, whom the city paid for amputating the ears of unnamed miscreants.[62] It is possible that the origin of the story tying Philip's murders to his father's death is the fact that James de Rijke and James Diederic presided over the beheading of seven unnamed Germans shortly after van Artevelde took power, and it is highly improbable that they would have done anything this drastic without Philip's express authorization. But the count's German mercenaries were mentioned in the peace of 1 December 1379 as an abuse to be corrected, and thus they, rather than persons connected to James van Artevelde, may have been the victims.

Another possible tie to the death of James van Artevelde is the fact that one Dennis de Scoemakere [Shoemaker] was brought into Philip's presence at some point during his ascendancy. We are not told that Dennis was executed, but the Flemish chronicler claimed that a shoe restorer had given James the death stroke. This passage has given rise to controversy. Froissart used the word *teliers* (weaver) for "Thomas" Denijs, James's assassin, and scholars have maintained that later copyists and borrowers misread this as *seliers* (cobbler). But the Flemish chronicler distinguished between Gerard Denijs, the dean of the weavers who led the mob to van Artevelde's house, and the "old shoemaker" who actually dispatched him. Furthermore, "old shoemaker" did not mean an elderly cobbler but a restorer of old shoes; the two groups had separate guilds in Ghent at this time.[63] Personal names were frequently conflated with place of origin or profession, and the same person may be called by several different names. The connections are fragmentary, but together they suggest that the Flemish literary tradition was probably accurate and that both a shoe restorer and the weaver

62. *Rek. Gent 1376–1389*, 343.
63. Ibid., 280, 344, 445; Froissart, *Chroniques* vol. 3, chap. 237, p. 103; for the Flemish chronicler, see CA 248. For the argument of textual corruption, see CA 246, and Napoléon de Pauw, "L'Assassinat d'Artevelde et l'Instruction de ce Crime," *Cour d'Appel de Gand* 4 (Ghent, 1905). On the distinction between the cobblers and the shoe restorers, see Nicholas, *Metamorphosis*, chap. 10.

Gerard Denijs had been involved in the assassination of James van Artevelde.

The records of property confiscations in late 1381 and early 1382 likewise point to Philip van Artevelde's obsession with avenging his father's murder on the senior surviving male descendants of the men he held responsible. Some families who felt themselves in danger evidently took the precaution of leaving Ghent as early as the spring of 1381, a fact that confirms other suggestions that van Artevelde's assumption of power was not as unexpected as most have assumed. Francis Sloeve had been an ally of James van Artevelde initially but later turned against him, became alderman in 1345, and survived the change of regime in 1349. In May 1381 an enormous amount of money and a house were confiscated from John Sloeve, his younger son. John is only attested in Ghent again in December 1386, and in early 1387 he was settling the estate of his older brother Francis, who had either been exiled or conceivably had died in the tumult of 1381.[64] John Stocman, the goldsmith son of the Peter Stocman who may have been involved in the van Steenbeke conspiracy in 1343 and the assassination of James van Artevelde the elder, was dead by 15 January 1386; but since his wife paid the "issue" tax on property taken out of the city in 1380–81, he had probably died then, and she was simply leaving Ghent with her half of their common funds.[65]

These families left Ghent before Philip van Artevelde assumed power, but the linkage of 1345 with 1382 becomes clearer with the uten Dale family, an ancient landowner lineage who had been enemies of the van Arteveldes, although matters evidently did not come to violence until 1382. Zeger uten Dale apparently sympathized with the rebellion in 1338 but not with James van Artevelde personally. He was alderman in 1334 and 1338. The city accounts do not show him involved on any of the

64. For the Sloeves, see CA 275; SAG, K 1, fol. 26v–27r; SAG, Wenemaers, charter March 1354; G 2, 3, fol. 32v; *Rek. 1376–1389*, 176; K 8, 1, fol. 28r; K 10, 2, fol. 69r; G 8, 2, fol. 25v.

65. For John Stocman, see above and *Rek. Gent 1376–1389*, 173; SAG, G 8, 1, fol. 24r.

embassies to James at Sluis in July, but he was first Estate Alderman in 1344, the year of Jacob's assassination, and this alone may have been enough to qualify his descendants in Philip's eyes. Zeger uten Dale was again first alderman in 1347 and in 1357, showing that he mended his political fences very quickly. He was related to the de Gruteres.[66] We are not told his relationship to Nicholas uten Dale, for whose debt to Thierry van Lens William van Artevelde was damaged surety in 1339, but he bought grazing land in 1349 from William van Artevelde the younger and his wife, Zwane van Mirabello. It was evidently his son whom Philip van Artevelde held responsible for the family's position in 1344. Nicholas the younger's ties with Gilbert de Grutere may have played a role as well. He was dead by 23 February 1382, near the end of the period of Philip van Artevelde's assassinations, and his confiscated chattels were sold by the city three days later.[67] Although we are not told explicitly that he was murdered, the circumstances are most suspicious.

No vengeance was exacted from the heirs of three men whose conduct in 1345 would have aroused Philip's suspicion. The fuller Joseph Aper died in defense of the city in 1349, whereas the city clerk James van Loevelde died in 1358 and left a son who became a monk. Van Loevelde had met James van Artevelde on his way back from Sluis on 11 July 1345 and thus would have been a prime target.[68] Clerical status also seems to have protected the sons of the city clerk Augustine van Zinghem. He had died by 16 December 1360. Of his two sons, who took Augustijns as their family name, Francis became a wine merchant who supplied the troops at Edelare, while John became a priest who was actually appointed clerk of the Estate Aldermen on 20 Feb-

66. For Zeger uten Dale, see Rogghé, "Stadsbestuur," 149; *Rek. Gent 1336–1349*, 2:345; SAG, K 1, fol. 38r; G 1, 1, fol. 13r; G 3, 4, fol. 12r.

67. For Nicholas uten Dale, see SAG, K 1, fols. 4v, 10v, 41r; G 3, 2, fol. 47v; K 8, 3, fol. 16r; G 7, 2, fol. 20r. His son and namesake returned to Ghent after the war, K 11, 1, fol. 67r.

68. For Joseph Aper, see SAG, G 1a, fol. 11r; for James van Loevelde, see *Rek. Gent 1336–1349*, 2:392; *Rek. Gent 1351–1364*, 328, 331; SAG, K 3, 2, fol. 3r.

ruary 1382. That John de Scoteleere, Philip van Artevelde's brother-in-law, stood surety for him doubtless was a factor in his rise. Both men apparently perished at the battle of Westrozebeke.[69]

Philip van Artevelde confiscated property from other persons who had family ties with aldermen of 1344. John van Bost was Estate Alderman in 1344, and on 27 December 1381, the very day when Philip became commissioner of confiscated property, another Philip van Bost bought a house confiscated from Daniel van Bost. Three John van Bosts—a shearer, a cardmaker, and a baker—lived in Ghent during the 1350s, suggesting that if one of them had been the alderman, he not been seriously compromised in the count's eyes. It has not been possible to connect either Philip or Daniel to one of them, but the coincidence of confiscation makes it probable.[70] The first Law Alderman in 1344 was the weaver John van der Vloet, who participated in the embassy to Sluis on 11 July 1345. Although he was not exiled during the 1350s, he took no further part in political life. He had died by March 1375, and there is no mention of male heirs. If Philip van Artevelde exacted vengeance against his descendants in the female line, the women's changes of name has made this impossible to trace.[71]

The clearest evidence of van Artevelde's attempt to wreak vengeance on those involved in his father's death concerns Lievin van Waes, a weaver-draper who was Law Alderman in 1344 and had died by 1369. He too was sent on negotiations to Sluis, although it is not clear that he was involved directly with James van Artevelde there. He apparently remained in Ghent during the 1350s, although only in 1358, as the weavers were beginning their ascent to power, did he again sell cloth to the city government. He left two sons, Lievin and Peter. Lievin the

69. On the Augustijns, see *Rek. Gent 1336–1349*, 2:392; SAG, K 1, fol. 224v; G 3, 1, fol. 48r; K 8, 3, fol. 15r; G 7, 3, fol. 25v; K 9, 2, fol. 9v.

70. On the van Bosts, see *Rek. Gent 1336–1349*, 2:345; SAG, K 8, 3, fol. 8v; G 1, 2, fol. 28r; G 2, 1, fol. 37r; Z 1, 2, fol. 9r; RAG, SN 118, fol. 60v.

71. On John van der Vloet, see *Rek. Gent 1336–1349*, 2:345; SAG, G 1, 2, fol. 39r; G 1, 3, fol. 19r; K 5, 1, fol. 24r.

younger was still in Ghent in May 1380. He was owed a debt on 24 March 1382, but the private document recording this was only registered by the aldermen in 1388. Three weeks later, on 16 April 1382, his brother, Peter, who was Estate Alderman this year, bought his confiscated chattels from the government. Yet Lievin van Waes was back in Ghent by August 1383 at the latest. He eventually served as provisor of the Weavers' Hall, and he did surety in 1386 in connection with the death of John de Mey, the jerkin maker of Antwerp whose relatives had killed James van Artevelde the younger. His case can only be explained by two circumstances: as his father's namesake he was probably the older son, and Philip van Artevelde thus would hold him, but not his younger brother, responsible for James's death; and he left the city when Philip van Artevelde took power in early 1382 and returned after his death but before the rebellion was over. He clearly fled to avoid Philip, not because he sympathized with the Flemish count.[72]

The registers of the two boards of aldermen and the city accounts contain references to numerous confiscations of property. These are insignificant before 14 August 1381, but the city seized the property of more than two hundred persons between that date and July 1382. The figures are probably lower than the actual situation, for the accounts record no confiscations after the seventh month of the fiscal year, which ended 19 February 1382, about the time the van Artevelde murders had run their course.[73] Philip van Artevelde had been both confiscation commissioner and captain during these months, and it is simply inconceivable that his presence, the homicides, and the large number of confiscations could be coincidental. Officially, the government of Ghent was fighting a war against the count of

72. On Lievin van Waes, father and son, see *Rek. Gent 1336–1349*, 2:345, 392; *Rek. Gent 1351–1364*, 387; *Rek. Gent 1376–1389*, 251; SAG, G 4, 4, fol. 36v; G 4, 5, fol. 26b r; K 8, 2, fol. 6r; K 8, 3, fol. 25r; K 11, 1, fols. 10b r, 62v; G 8, 1, fol. 74r; G 7, 3, fol. 69r.

73. *Rek. Gent 1376–1389*, 262; for a general discussion of the confiscations, see Nicholas, *Metamorphosis*, chap. 1.

Flanders that had begun in 1379. Unofficially, it was consummating a van Artevelde vendetta that had begun in 1345.

Thus it is simply inaccurate to say that only the memory of his father brought Philip van Artevelde to power in 1382. For all the edifying tales about how the masses loved him, as much as half the population of the city opposed his elevation, and some feared him personally and obviously with good reason. Indeed, he does not seem to have concerned himself with any broader questions of policy, and least of all the plight of the workers, until a month into his captaincy, by which time he had finished paying off old scores. He had been operating behind the scenes for some time before he struck in 1382. The Parneele and de Scepene cases suggest that Peter van den Bossche may have inspired him to seize control as captain. But he was already in the government, probably as its recognized leader, confiscating the property of his personal enemies and of opponents of the revolutionary regime, for a month before his elevation to the captaincy gave him the means and the license to murder with impunity. Whereas the de Grutere and Bette assassinations at the beginning of Philip's regime bear the mark of van den Bossche as well as of van Artevelde, the later killings are tied exclusively to Philip van Artevelde's family involvements rather than to the policy concerns of van den Bossche. Indeed, had Peter van den Bossche been directly implicated in all of the van Artevelde assassinations, it is most unlikely that he could have survived the war in Ghent, let alone come back after a brief exile, as the sources suggest.

Philip van Artevelde was a landowner who held little property in the city and derived most of his income from rural estates. By the end of February 1382, the godfather had quenched his thirst for blood. We now turn to the domestic and foreign concerns of the last nine months of Philip van Artevelde's life.

CHAPTER 7

The Hero Repugnant: The Road to Westrozebeke, March–November 1382

We are now in a position to examine the career of Philip van Artevelde during the turbulent period between late February 1382, when his vengeance had apparently been accomplished, and his death on 27 November on the battlefield of Westrozebeke. Indeed, we may not be finished with the homicides, at least those of the nonpolitical variety. Van Artevelde showed no mercy toward those who violated his orders, even members of his own family. A chronicler of Courtrai claims that while van Artevelde was at Bruges in May, his own second cousin once removed, who has proven impossible to identify, violated Philip's order that there be no pillaging. Summoned into the captain's presence, the youth protested that he had not known of the prohibition, since it had not been proclaimed publicly, and pledged to atone his misdeed and not to sin again. Rejecting all pleas for clemency, Philip ordered his guards to seize his kinsman and throw him out the window onto the market square, where he was impaled on pikes. He evidently hoped to convince

convince the Brugeois of his impartiality by this act, but seems only to have terrified them.[1]

Philip van Artevelde's behavior in his first two months had left him badly in need of allies outside the textile trades. If, as seems probable, the initiative for van Artevelde's marriage after he became captain came from him, we must try to assess what made Yolante van den Brouke so desirable, and on this subject we are reduced to pure conjecture. Unmarried politicians in more recent times have contracted late and hasty marriages to avoid the imputation of homosexuality, and that possibility cannot be excluded in the case of Philip van Artevelde. On the other hand, perhaps he was simply a middle-aged bachelor smitten by a pretty face. His other behavior in the months of his ascendancy reveal him as an man whose emotions were close to the surface. I have been utterly unable to find evidence about any of the van den Broukes that would establish grounds for a firm conclusion that he married Yolante to cement a political alliance. Even her exact ancestry raises questions. She had at least two brothers. She may have been the sister of Peter van den Brouke, one of van Artevelde's colleagues as receiver of confiscations in December 1382 and alderman in 1382. Another Peter van den Brouke was the captain installed at Ypres by van Artevelde's regime and was beheaded there in December 1382.[2]

But the profession of Peter van den Brouke causes problems. Yolante may have been related to the Peter van den Brouke who was the son of a carpenter named John van den Brouke of Cruushoutem, who held a tenement not far from Philip van

---

1. Document quoted in CA 749–50. On 4 May 1382 a messenger came from Bruges with news of the fighting there, but van Artevelde is not mentioned personally; *Rek. Gent 1376–1389*, 305. Froissart, *Chroniques*, vol. 10, chap. 279, p. 235, mentions the proclamation against pillaging but says nothing about the death of van Artevelde's cousin. He obviously had sources close to the scene of the action and was usually not reticent about telling stories that reflected badly on van Artevelde, and it may thus be an invention of the Courtrai chronicler, whose work survives only in a fifteenth-century manuscript.

2. CA 387; *Rek. Gent 1376–1389*, 382.

Artevelde's in 1375.[3] Another Peter van den Brouke was a dyer. Marriage of a man associated with the weavers to the sister of a dyer would have been a logical consolidation of power, and the dyer is generally assumed to have been Philip van Artevelde's brother-in-law. The fact that the dyer was definitely dead by 9 June 1383 lends some credence to this hypothesis. But though five Estate Aldermen who took service in August 1382 died in office, the composition of the board of Law Aldermen remained unchanged. Thus, while the dyer may have been captain at Ypres, it is unlikely that he was also alderman.[4]

But other considerations suggest that more than one Peter van den Brouke was in the government of Ghent during 1381 and 1382 and that Yolante was related to a shipwright of that name rather than the dyer. The dyer is first mentioned in a text of 1378, but the shipwright was much older. The son of Zeger van den Brouke, he is mentioned as an adult in a street fight in 1364, which would make him roughly the age of Philip van Artevelde. He lived in the Kalverstraat behind the Oudburg (*H–I 5–6*) and had a son named Peter who was a minor in 1368, and the son is identified in 1378 as a shipwright whose debts were not to be honored. This Peter van den Brouke had another son named John who was old enough to be involved in a brawl in 1378.[5] John and Peter van den Brouke the younger could thus qualify as Yolante's two brothers, while the dyer is known to have had only two children: a son, inconveniently for our purposes named Peter, and a daughter, Marie. The alderman was sent on a mission on 23 October 1382 to Philip van Artevelde in the militia at Edelare "because of the shippers."[6] Although this may be coincidental, magistrates sometimes handled the affairs

3. SAG, ser. 152, no. 4, fols. 4r, 5v.
4. SAG, G 6, 3, fol. 19r.
5. SAG, Z 3, 4, fol. 12v; WD fol. 37r; K 4, 1, fol. 10r; G 4, 4, fol. 6r; G 5, 4, fol. 11r; K 7, fol. 5r; G 6, 3, fol. 1r; Z 6, 3, fol. 17v.
6. SAG, K 9, 1, fol. 26r; G 8, 1, fol. 76r; *Rek. Gent 1376–1389*, 330. The business of the shippers was probably connected with their loss of boats at Deinze in that year, for which they were compensated in 1382, ibid., 325.

of their own guilds with the city administration, and this fact strengthens the case for van Artevelde's ally being a shipwright.

Since no property was given to minors when the shipwright died in 1387, his children were evidently of mature years. Yolante almost certainly was a kinswoman of the man associated with Philip van Artevelde in December 1381, but it is curious that she is mentioned in no act before her husband's death. Her given name is most unusual at Ghent and suggests a French tie. The shippers and shipwrights of Ghent had extremely close ties with French merchants, from whom they obtained their grain, and some even maintained houses in northern France. Yolante's anonymity suggests that she may have been the shipwright's illegitimate daughter by a French mother. That Yolante was the daughter of the shipwright rather than the dyer is made more likely by the virtual certainty that her second husband, Peter Diederic, was a shipwright, as we have seen.

But if Philip van Artevelde's marriage was political, why would he marry into a shipping family? His family was far more prominent than that of his wife or her second husband.[7] An obvious reason is that as the champion of the textile trades he had no need to repair his relations with them. Of the various persons whom he is known to have attacked in his first weeks in power, only John Sleepstaf was a weaver. All the others were landowners or members of the trades making up the small guilds, and the shippers were his particular enemies. But whereas there was considerable overlap in membership between the shippers and shipwrights, the two guilds were separate and at times hostile because the shipwrights resented the shippers' practice of buying their boats in France. The small guilds were divided among themselves, with factions within each trade. Yet van Artevelde desperately needed allies in the small guilds if his regime were to have any chance of success, for although no individual small guild was as large as the weavers, by the 1380s

7. See de Pauw's comment, CA 397, on the fact that the estate arbitrators on Philip's heirs' side were far more eminent than those named by Diederic and his wife.

the small guilds as a group were probably a larger element in the work force of the city than the textile artisans.[8]

The evidence of the municipal accounts also suggests that the small guilds as a group were so out of favor with van Artevelde's regime that they were dismissed from the government for the fiscal year 1382–83. The thoroughly reliable Peter van den Bossche succeeded the murdered Gilbert de Grutere as their dean in early 1382, but the military expeditions of that year involve only the weavers and landowners in a corporate capacity, although in general levies all segments of the population served. The landowners, the group to which van Artevelde himself belonged, assumed an increasingly independent posture, evidently at the expense of the small guilds. John uten Hove in the Scelstraat had represented the small guilds at a meeting in 1377, but he represented the landowners in August 1380.[9] Peter van den Brouke may simply have been of a faction among the shipwrights who favored the extreme position of the weavers, for no guild, not even the weavers, presented a totally united front.

In all probability, therefore, the van den Brouke marriage either resulted from personal attraction, at least on Philip's side, or represented van Artevelde's attempt to mend his political fences after the bloodbath of his first two months. Given the violence of his behavior when he assumed power, such a reconciliation would not have been possible until some time had elapsed, and thus the marriage to Yolante, which Froissart did not know had even taken place, probably occurred in the summer or early autumn of 1382.

The captaincy of Philip van Artevelde began on 24 January 1382. The fifteenth-century *Cronyke Van Vlaenderen* (*Chronicle of Flanders*) and the later narratives based on it, those of Meyerus in 1561 and Nicolaes Despars in 1562, mention a set of statutes that

8. On the rivalry between shippers and shipwrights, and on the decline of the textile trades and rise of the shippers, see Nicholas, *Metamorphosis*, chaps. 6, 9.

9. *Rek. Gent 1376–1389*, 86–87, 184, 311, 339, 350.

Philip issued, allegedly on Peter van den Bossche's instigation, as his first official act after the Bette and de Grutere killings. His father had done the same thing two days into his captaincy. In view of his means of seizing power, there is an almost ironic ring to these laws, if in fact they are genuine. Homicide became a capital offense, and feuds were to be at truce until two weeks after peace was made between the count and Ghent. Persons who fought without drawing blood, patronized taverns, gambled, swore falsely, or held unauthorized public meetings were to be imprisoned for forty days on bread and water. Meetings of the Collacie (*figure 1*) were compulsory for all, "the poor as well as the rich." Only one moneychanging establishment was to be kept, and the moneychangers were to be honest.[10] The city accounts were to be audited monthly, and false imprisonment was forbidden. All residents were to wear clothing with a white left sleeve on which van Artevelde's motto, "God Help Us," would be emblazoned in red letters.[11]

No strictly contemporary source mentions these statutes, but they have the ring of truth. Although the chronicler places them at the beginning of van Artevelde's captaincy, they were probably issued at the end of February, when Philip had avenged all his family's injuries and thus, in the mode of more recent and better documented dictators, was in a position to become self-righteous about other people's antisocial behavior. He knew that there had been bitter opposition to him, and the sleeve emblem would have been the sort of psychological device that would reassure him and could conceivably have served to make conspiracies more difficult. Given the fact that his elevation was bitterly opposed by the shippers and their allies and by all who had reason to fear his private vengeance, and that his first weeks in power had been marked by an officially inspired massacre unparalleled in the city's history, it is astounding that there is not a trace of evidence that he faced opposition during the last

10. This may indeed have been a confirmation of established practice. See Nicholas, *Metamorphosis*, chap. 5.
11. Selections printed in de Pauw, *Voorgeboden*, 158–161.

nine months of his life. Whatever he did, it worked, and the statutes may have been part of his attempt to impose a draconian standard on the behavior of others.

Philip van Artevelde received a substantial wage of 12 lb. gr. per month and had a guard of sixteen men, while the other captains received 4 lb. gr. and had six guards. On an annual basis, this is roughly five times what his father had been paid, although the severe debasements of the Flemish coin by Count Louis of Male account for part of the difference. The accounts mention no other reimbursement to him, although messengers to him were paid, and it thus seems evident that he was using his wages and his private resources to pay his own expenses during his lengthy sojourns outside the city with the militia, just as his father had done. As had also been true of his father, Philip and John van Bracht, who was probably a city attorney, received the same uniforms as the aldermen, while the other four captains wore a different outfit. The three deans—James de Rijke of the landowners, Lawrence de Maech of the weavers, and Peter van den Bossche of the small guilds—each received 4 lb. gr. per month but had eight bodyguards. The four captains other than Philip van Artevelde were clearly subordinate figures.[12]

The other four captains who took office on 24 January 1382 with Philip van Artevelde were Alexander van Vaernewijc, who was clearly distancing himself from his kinsman Simon, Raes van den Voerde, John de Hert, and John Herman. Herman was a weaver who served as their dean later in 1382. Curiously, he

12. *Rek. Gent 1376–1389*, 278; CA 353, 355–56. Curiously, a text of the aldermen of 1 March 1382 refers to James de Rijke and James Diederic as captains; SAG, K 8, 3, fol. 17r. The city paid no attorney in this year, contrary to its usual practice, but the omission is probably due to the state of emergency. On grounds of payments made by Philip's widow and heirs to John van Bracht and John de Wulslaghere in the estate settlement in 1385, de Pauw (CA 355, 404) concluded that John van Bracht was Philip's squire. But for his profession, see SAG, G 6, 1, fol. 21r; G 6, 4, fol. 8v. John de Wulslaghere was amman, a jailor, in the Burgstraat in 1384 and confiscated the residence there of Martin van Erpe, the son of Philip van Artevelde's half sister, for an unpaid debt; see CA 388–89; G 8, 2, fol. 25v and G 9, 1, fol. 65v. The widow was to pay all of John de Wulslaghere's costs and two-thirds of van Bracht's, suggesting that they had been collecting debts owed to her late husband's estate.

was sent on a pilgrimage in 1376 for assaulting James and John van den Brouke, who may have been related to Philip van Artevelde's future wife. He evidently lived across from St. Peter's abbey.[13] Raes van den Voerde was a knight and landowner. He was alderman in 1384 and one of the few persons close to the van Artevelde regime who lived to prosper after 1385. He may have lived in the aristocratic Kammerstraat (*Map 1, G 7*), in the parish of St. James, in a house formerly owned by Thomas van Vaernewijc. Like the van Arteveldes, he owned property in northeastern Flanders, and he was connected by marriage to the nobleman Bernard van Belle.[14] Alexander van Vaernewijc was also a landowner living in the Veldstraat (*Map 1, D–E 4*), in the parish of St. Nicholas.[15] The captain John de Hert was probably a shipper, but in late 1385 a weaver of this name was guardian of the son of John Diederic, who was almost certainly a shipper.[16] If John de Hert was a shipper, therefore, he had close ties to the weavers.

Except for van den Voerde and van Artevelde, both of whom lived in the parish of St. James, the captains came from different parishes. Whether van Artevelde was still a landholder in the city is doubtful, but he was from a landowner family allied with the weavers. The small guilds played little role in this regime, and the fullers, the proletarians of the textile industry, had been excluded from the government since the 1360s. Although there is no evidence that the fullers of Ghent took advantage of the distress of their city to revolt, some definitely left Ghent when the rebellion against the count persisted. Fullers of Ghent aided in the defense of Dendermonde in 1380. After the battle of Westrozebeke, six exiled fullers of Ghent were quickly recruited by the city government of Bruges to guard the gates as the occupying forces retreated toward Ghent. There was clearly an

---

13. *Rek. Gent 1376–1389*, 453; SAG, Z 6, 2, fol. 3r; G 7, 4, fol. 70v.
14. SAG, K 10, 1, fols. 13v, 37v; K 10, 2, fol. 108r; K 11, 1, fol. 60v.
15. SAG, K 2, 2, fol. 21r; K 3, 1, fol. 28 bis.
16. SAG, G 8, 1, fol. 19v; Z 4, 3, fol. 11r; BB 71, fol. 7r; Z 6, 1, fols. 1v, 5r. De Muynck, "Gentse Oorlog," 317, calls de Hert a shipper, but the possibility that he was a weaver cannot be excluded.

element of revenge in this, as they were hired "because they knew the people of Ghent who were leaving better than the others did."[17]

Philip van Artevelde's regime was thus, on the one hand, more aristocratic than his father's had been; but, on the other, it represented a naked alliance between the old aristocracy of the city and the revolutionary element of the economically depressed textile industry at the expense of the food merchants and importers. It is thus likely that the opinion of the Bruges chronicler that the basis for choice of captains was occupational is correct, even if the formality of parish affiliation was maintained.

The three deans were also close personal allies and friends of van Artevelde. We have discussed Peter van den Bossche, who surrendered his captaincy to become dean of the small guilds, the group in which most of the opposition to van Artevelde was concentrated. The weaver Lawrence de Maech was to stand surety for Philip's heirs against his widow in 1384. He surrendered the deanship to become alderman in August 1382. The de Maechs were one of the most prominent weaver families. They had been allies of the van Arteveldes as long ago as 1333, when Thierry de Maech had been sent on a pilgrimage to Scotland for aiding the weavers who helped William van Artevelde. Zeger de Maech was arbitrator for Jan de Scoteleere and his wife, Philip van Artevelde's sister, in their conflict with St. Bavo's abbey over land at Weert.[18] James de Rijke, the dean of the landowners, surrendered the captaincy to become dean. He probably died at Westrozebeke, for he was replaced as dean at midyear 1382 by John van Merlaer.[19]

After he had settled old scores and eliminated his most prominent potential foes, the major task confronting Philip van Artevelde was the city's grain supply. The count's blockade had

---

17. Cited de Muynck, "Gentse Oorlog," 309–10; City Archive of Bruges, Stadsrekeningen 1382–83, fol. 32r.
18. CA 124, 388, 328, 353; *Rek. Gent 1376–1389*, 240.
19. CA 355; *Rek. Gent 1376–1389*, 239, 339; SAG, G 7, 4, fol. 80r.

been disastrously effective, but the abbeys and citizens who owned rural land had grain in their storehouses. Van Artevelde ordered these stores to be opened and sold at a fixed price to the populace. Under the circumstances, it is not surprising that he was evidently idolized by the poor in the spring of 1382. But this could only be a temporary measure, for the city soon exhausted these supplies.[20]

The other Low Country princes had an interest in ending the conflict in Flanders and thus arranged a peace conference at Tournai for Easter week (31 March–6 April) 1382. Philip van Artevelde personally led the Ghent delegation, leaving Peter van den Bossche behind in Ghent, perhaps a sign of his growing independence. Louis of Male refused to attend and sent word through envoys that he would accept no terms except the unconditional surrender of Ghent. All Gentenars between the ages of fifteen and sixty were to present themselves before him, bareheaded and with a halter around the neck, in a pose of total submission. Although Froissart claims that Philip personally was willing to endure exile, he refused the count's demand on grounds that the envoys of Ghent had no power to agree to anything involving bloodshed. He did agree to put the question to the assembly of Ghent when he returned; but after laying out the count's terms, he personally recommended that they be rejected and that the militia of Ghent instead march on Bruges, where the count was staying.[21]

That nearly a month elapsed between the peace conference and the assault on Bruges suggests that the decision to attack was not taken as soon as van Artevelde returned. In fact, the count's intransigence left Philip little choice. The month of April, however, seems to have been used for diplomatic initiatives with England. Most have accepted Froissart's claim that Philip van Artevelde hoped to obtain the mediation of King Charles VI of France in the Flemings' quarrel with Louis of Male and that

20. Froissart, *Chroniques*, vol. 10, chap. 228, p. 140.
21. Ibid., vol. 10, chaps. 266–70, pp. 208–14; Quicke, *Pays-Bas*, 319. The Ghent accounts do not mention the March conclave.

he turned toward England only after Charles had contemptu-
ously rejected Philip's overture and briefly imprisoned his envoy.[22] But no unclouded mind in early 1382 could have thought
that the French would side with the unruly Flemish cities against
the count, who was the father-in-law of the king's uncle, and it
is extremely likely that Philip van Artevelde was chosen captain
in January, not only because of the weavers' emotional association with his father's name, but also because James had fash-
ioned an open English alliance.

The English, in turn, clearly hoped to further the discomfi-
ture of Louis of Male at minimal cost to themselves. On 8
November 1381, seven weeks before van Artevelde came to
power at Ghent, the regents controlling the government of the
young King Richard II authorized the export of three hundred
quarters of wheat to Flanders, probably to foster the hope in
Ghent that the English would help. Louis of Male, of course,
maintained correct relations with the English and tried only to
hinder English grain and wool from reaching places in Flanders
in rebellion against him.[23] Negotiations between England and
Ghent cannot be proven to have taken place until after the Easter
negotiations at Tournai collapsed, but van Artevelde must have
sent agents to England almost immediately thereafter, for Louis
of Male's spies in London reported to him on 22 April 1382 that
van Artevelde's direct appeal to Richard II's government posed
a real threat of English intervention in Flanders. The English
regency, the council, and the Lords promised assistance by summer, but in May the Commons refused to appropriate the necessary subsidy. Before van Artevelde learned of this, however,
the Ghent militia had taken Bruges. It is thus conceivable that
the attack on Bruges was not only a desperate measure—it
could hardly have been other—but also an attempt to show the
English that Ghent still had military power and conceivably to
secure the coast at nearby Sluis for an English landing.

22. Quicke, *Pays-Bas*, 330–31; on the count's confiscations, see Nicholas,
"Scheldt Trade."

23. Froissart, *Chroniques*, vol. 10, chaps. 293–94, pp. 260–63; van Herwaarden, "War," 110.

But Philip van Artevelde ultimately failed to obtain English backing and was left out on the proverbial limb, and he probably knew that he was doomed from that moment. The fact that two Englishmen went to Flanders in July 1382 "to obtain a safe-conduct for Philip van Artevelde and others" suggests that Philip, like his father before him, may have hoped eventually to escape into an English exile. Still, van Artevelde continued to negotiate with the English for military aid through the summer and openly recognized Richard II as king of France and lord of Flanders. But by the time the English finally did send a force to Flanders, in early 1383, van Artevelde had perished.[24]

The English mission in July is connected with an episode about which Flemish historians have been understandably reticent. We shall see that Ghent sent emissaries to the English court on 17 October 1382. As these men were returning to Flanders, the English Issue Rolls record under the date of 14 November that they were given the sum of 66 lb. 13s. 4d. sterling, or 100 marks, as arrears and final payment through 14 November 1382 on a pension of 12s. per day owed by the English crown to "Philip van Artevelde, knight, son of James van Artevelde, of Flanders." Since there is no reason to think that Philip was ever formally dubbed a knight, the English court evidently used the title as a term of respect, as it had for his father during his lifetime.[25]

The amount of money would represent one hundred and eleven days of service at this rate. Philip van Artevelde thus had not been paid since 26 July, and the English mission to give him a safe-conduct may have been a vain attempt to ensure his safety by cutting off his funds and giving him passage to England. But the Issue Roll also states unambiguously that the daily pension

24. On the extremely important point of the timing of van Artevelde's negotiations with the English, see J. J. N. Palmer, *England, France and Christendom, 1377–99* (Chapel Hill, N.C., 1972), 22–23, 45, and especially 228 and 245.
25. An anonymous and nearly contemporary life of Richard II referred to Philip van Artevelde as "a certain squire," not even mentioning his father. George B. Stow, Jr., ed., *Historia vitae et regni Ricardi Secundi* (Philadelphia, 1977), 76.

had been granted to Philip van Artevelde for the latter's lifetime by Richard's grandfather, King Edward III, who had died on 21 June 1377 and who in his youth had been the friend of Philip's father. The version of this text contained in the Patent Rolls simply calls it a grant by Richard II to van Artevelde and does not mention Edward III.[26]

The Patent and Close Rolls contain no mention of a pension granted to Philip van Artevelde by King Edward III. The text of 14 November may refer to obligations still owed on the pension that Edward had granted to James van Artevelde the elder, but that money had been granted to James personally, not to his sons. The English had granted only protection, not a pension as far as is known, to the younger van Arteveldes during their exile. Thus it seems likely that at some point before war broke out between Ghent and the Flemish count in 1379, Philip van Artevelde was in fact an English agent. During the war Philip doubtless paid many of his troops' expenses from this source; but if he held it during the peaceful period before 1379, it may help to explain two troubling mysteries: why there is so little evidence of him at Ghent, where he lived inconspicuously in an undistinguished part of town; and how he managed to live as a landowner with what seems to have been a minimal inheritance from his parents. Philip van Artevelde was a hero with feet of clay and a heart of gold.

For whatever reason, the militia of Ghent marched on Bruges on 2 May 1382, as Bruges, with the count in attendance, celebrated the Procession of the Holy Blood. On the very day of the march on Bruges, the aldermen of Ghent sent to the rulers of Louvain in Brabant, with whom they were allied, a copy of the humiliating demands that Louis of Male had made at the peace conference the month before.[27] On 3 May the two armies met outside the walls of Bruges at the Beverhoutsveld, and the Ghent forces won a complete victory. Louis of Male escaped

26. Document printed CA 373, from the Issue Roll of 1382. The version from the *Calendars of the Patent Rolls* is cited in Quicke, *Pays-Bas*, 335.
27. Quicke, *Pays-Bas*, 319 n. 99.

from Bruges to Lille after many picturesque adventures, and van Artevelde and Peter van den Bossche were masters of the second largest city and major port of Flanders.

The records are not completely consistent about what the troops of Ghent did in Bruges, but apparently there was no indiscriminate butchery. The Gentenars massacred numerous butchers and fishmongers, both large guilds that had given the weaver-dominated regime trouble at Ghent, and glaziers and jerkin makers, who had been involved in the resistance of Oudenaarde to Ghent. Eager to restore Flanders' damaged overseas trade, however, van Artevelde promptly placed all foreigners under special protection, and the chronicle of the Englishman Thomas Walsingham confirms the success of these measures. Van Artevelde and van den Bossche went to Sluis and Damme immediately to get food from the ports to send to Ghent. After Bruges had been secured, van Artevelde ordered Francis Ackerman to prevent looting.[28] Although he permitted the militia to wreck the count's favorite castle at Male, near Bruges, the prohibition against looting in the city was enforced, although there is evidence that the Brugeois had to pay for their own protection. The accounts of the church fabric of St. Donatian record a payment to "Daniel [probably Peter] de Winter and other retainers of Philip van Artevelde for ejecting numerous mad and meretricious fellows from the houses of the provost and the dean."[29]

Peter de Winter, like his colleague Peter van den Bossche, had obscure origins, but he was definitely from the small guilds and was probably a dyer. A "Peter de Wint" and the weaver Giles Rijpegherste led militia contingents to the coast on 23 May 1378 at a time when the landowners were evidently not considered a separate political member of the city. Since he was stationed at Bruges with van den Bossche, he was not engaged at West-

---

28. Ibid., 331; Froissart, *Chroniques*, vol. 10, chaps. 279–82, pp. 235–41. Yet Froissart in the same breath claims that two hundred cartloads of booty were being sent daily to Ghent from Bruges.

29. Episcopal Archive of Bruges, Sint-Donaas, G 1, fol. 7r.

rozebeke, survived the war, and remained in Ghent after the peace in 1385. He eventually married the widow of the bastard of the shipper Peter Mayhuus, whose family had been bitter enemies of the Yoens and thus implicitly allies of the van Arteveldes.[30]

Ackerman and Peter de Winter then took numerous prominent citizens of Bruges to Ghent as hostages.[31] The rest of Flanders except for the towns of Oudenaarde and Dendermonde, south and east of Ghent respectively on the Scheldt, sent their submissions to van Artevelde at Bruges. Van Artevelde is alleged to have lived magnificently in the count's apartments in the city. He not only collected all revenues ordinarily owed to the count but also demanded new taxes of his own. On 2 September 1382, when van Artevelde was at the siege of Oudenaarde, a conclave of representatives of several churches in and near Bruges referred to the "subsidy that Philip van Artevelde demanded from them, [and] which they had given under duress, contrary to their own will, for they only wanted to give money or subvention for expenses incurred in making peace between our venerable prince and the fatherland, his county. Otherwise it cannot be acceded to, and they may refuse to pay anything except under threat and danger of death."[32] Van Artevelde ordered that the walls of Bruges be destroyed and the moat filled up, and van den Bossche evidently accompanied this with an "economic recovery program," for the church of St. Donatian later sent a messenger "to Philip van Artevelde at Ypres to petition him that we should not be compelled to con-

30. *Rek. Gent 1376–1389*, 104; SAG, K 11, 1, fols. 20r, 105r; K 9, 2, fol. 48v; G 8, 1, fol. 31r. There was also a shipper named Peter de Winter, and he may have been a kinsman of the dyer. He was alderman four times between 1368 and 1376 and dean of the shipwrights in 1366. But his house was confiscated and sold by the city on 30 May 1382, at a time when the other Peter de Winter was rendering service, and he is next mentioned in Ghent in April 1386; WD fol. 29v; K 8, 3, fol. 29r; G 8, 1, fol. 51r.

31. Froissart, *Chroniques*, vol. 10, chap. 283, p. 241, alleges five hundred, but his tendency to inflate figures is notorious. This would have been about eight percent of the male heads of household in Bruges at this time, which is most improbable.

32. Episcopal Archive of Bruges, Sint-Donaas, A 48, fol. 99r.

struct a mill," presumably on the outskirts where the wall had been.[33] This text has the incidental effect of showing that the Brugeois believed appeal from van den Bossche to van Artevelde was possible.

Leaving Peter van den Bossche and Peter de Winter at Bruges as governors, Philip van Artevelde proceeded to Ypres on 24 or 25 May. There the representatives of the city and the various rural governments of the region received him "as though he were their natural lord" and did homage to him. He issued new laws and renewed the powers of the local magistrates. After a stay of eight days at Ypres, he went to Courtrai for five days. As he was leaving to return to Ghent, he again sent a message to Oudenaarde demanding its submission, but its governors retorted "that they had nothing to fear from the son of a mead brewer."[34] He evidently got back to Ghent on 9 June.

Froissart reports that between 9 June and 12 July, by which time he was besieging Oudenaarde, Philip van Artevelde was living in luxury in Ghent. His delights included banquets with the local ladies, and romantics may wish to assume that Lente van den Brouke caught his eye at one of these soirées. He maintained his own chamber of accounts, and he received money from the other Flemish communities. Although van Artevelde was clearly popular with the masses between March and May 1382, Froissart says nothing about this after he returned from Bruges, and his behavior reverted to the quixotically violent pattern of the early stages of his rule. His success at the Bev-

33. Ibid., G1, fol. 7r. I owe all references from the Bruges archives, here and in notes 17, 29, 31, and 32 above, to the courtesy of Professor James Murray of the University of Cincinnati. This material has given us a much fuller picture than was previously possible of van Artevelde's activity at Bruges.

34. This chronological progression is derived from Froissart, *Chroniques*, vol. 10, chaps. 283–84, pp. 241–43, but is confirmed by the Ghent accounts, which show that a messenger was sent to Bruges and then on to Ypres on 25 May, suggesting that van Artevelde had left by the time he arrived. Another messenger went to Courtrai on 6 June, thirteen days after van Artevelde presumably left Bruges. On 7 June an envoy went "toward" Ypres, but the text does not say that he got there. No embassies left Ghent between 10 and 24 June, suggesting that van Artevelde was in the city during those two weeks. *Rek. Gent 1376–1389*, 305.

erhoutsveld seems to have emboldened him to the point of overconfidence. In June 1382 the count was in flight and van Artevelde controlled a line of fortified towns along the Leie river. He needed Oudenaarde and Dendermonde to control the Scheldt. He styled himself "regent of Flanders" and in so doing went further than his father had done: James at least had had Simon van Mirabello stand in for him.[35]

Philip van Artevelde began to demonstrate a more active interest in the governance of his city during the summer months. We have seen him up to this point chiefly as a military leader. At least twice he served as an arbitrator in homicide cases. There was nothing in itself extralegal in this. Homicide actions rarely came to formal trial in Ghent at this time because, as the penalty for conviction was death, families normally asked prominent persons to arbitrate.[36] We have seen that on 20 August 1382 Philip van Artevelde and the other two deans set the blood price due from Peter van den Bossche for a homicide committed while on campaign the previous year. Since all parties were in the militia, they evidently turned to the city's chief officers rather than to their relatives, for no family tie can be proven between Philip van Artevelde and the victims. The blood price, however, was extraordinarily low for a homicide atonement at this time, and it seems probable that Peter van den Bossche had simply killed some local peasants.

The second case contains more peculiar features. Given at Edelare in the army on 15 October and recorded by the aldermen of Ghent the following day, the judgment was written in the first person by Philip van Artevelde himself. He informed the magistrates of Ghent that he and the two commanders of the militia of Bruges had rendered judgment concerning the death of John Kerstiaenszoon. He asked them to record the ruling in their book, give final judgment in their own name, and give the parties a copy of the record. The phraseology and orthography are rather ornate in Philip's version, suggesting an educated,

---

35. Froissart, *Chroniques*, vol. 10, chap. 284, p. 243.
36. Nicholas, "Crime and Punishment," part 2.

even pedantic man. The aldermen confirmed Philip's ruling but simplified his language. He clearly took some pride, perhaps misplaced, in his prose style. The involvement of the Bruges captains in the case almost certainly means that the parties were citizens of Bruges, but van Artevelde's judgment as supreme captain would be desirable or perhaps even necessary for a homicide committed while the troops were under arms. The case was recorded at Ghent simply because of van Artevelde's authority and because communications with Ghent were more secure than those with Bruges.[37]

Philip van Artevelde was determined to destroy Oudenaarde. Its strategic importance—for Ghent could not control the Scheldt grain trade from the south unless it had been secured—was now linked to a personal vendetta because the place had defied him. By 24 June summonses had gone out to all Flemish communities to have their contingents in battle array before Oudenaarde, and van Artevelde evidently levied a hearth tax throughout Flanders to pay for the siege.[38] He must have been directing operations at Oudenaarde personally by late June, for envoys were sent to him there from Louvain on 3 July, and it would have taken the magistrates some time to know that he was there.[39]

The troops of Ghent were concentrated at Oudenaarde and made little effort at this time to take Dendermonde, which controlled access eastward. Ghent did not lack allies to the east. Although Antwerp was loyal to Louis of Male, Mechelen and Louvain, both closely linked to the commercial network centered on Ghent, supported van Artevelde.[40] Van Artevelde also sought support from the towns of Hainaut, notably Mons, but they gave him only moral, not material assistance. The Flemish

---

37. CA 366–68.
38. *Rek. Gent 1376–1389*, 305–6. Froissart, *Chroniques*, vol. 10, chap. 287, p. 246, has the siege of Oudenaarde beginning 9 June; cf. also Quicke, *Pays-Bas*, 326. But since van Artevelde could not have arrived in Ghent until 9 June and then took time to socialize, Froissart evidently wrote down the wrong month.
39. Quicke, *Pays-Bas*, 327.
40. Ibid., 322–25.

count had retreated to Lille after the battle at the Beverhoutsveld. He immediately asked the young French king for
aid, and conditions in France played into his hands. "Long live
Ghent!" had become a rallying cry in the summer of 1382 in
Paris, Amiens, and Rouen, where revolts broke out against the
reimposition of the royal hearth tax. Despite the evident reluc-
tance of some at the royal court to do something that would so
obviously promote the interests of the duke of Burgundy, by
August the government of Charles VI had agreed in principle to
invade Flanders.

The van Artevelde regime had been in contact with London
since at least April. Particularly since Louis of Male was even
less able after 3 May than before to guarantee English shipping
against piracy, the English government was more increasingly
inclined to deal with Ghent on matters relating to the wool
staple. On 28 May 1382, while van Artevelde was at Ypres, two
English merchants were sent to the regent. Shortly after they
had returned to England for new instructions, they were sent
back to Flanders between 24 June and 20 July, this time accompanied by royal officials on "secret business." On 11 July the
English sent the herald Richard Hereford to Oudenaarde to deal
directly with van Artevelde, and on 15 July they paid the expenses of "a certain envoy coming from Flanders from Philip
van Artevelde, knight." Perhaps hoping to convince the English
of their seriousness, the aldermen of Ghent, Bruges, and Ypres,
apparently under van Artevelde's direction, equipped a fleet in
August to deal with piracy along the coast.[41]

Philip van Artevelde himself accompanied three aldermen to
Bruges between 4 and 8 September, a mission probably connected to troubles that erupted at Ypres between the weavers
and fullers. He seems to have been accompanied by officials of
Bruges when he returned to Ghent. On 12 September the magistrates of Bruges and Ypres, including not only the normally
chosen aldermen but also the regents appointed by van Artevelde, confirmed an arbitral judgment between the drapers

41. Ibid., 331–32.

and fullers of Ypres given by van Artevelde, the other captains, and the deans of the three members of Ghent. The language of the text claims that the litigants had asked for their arbitration. While only terminal naiveté would cause anyone to believe that they did this willingly, the judgment is absolutely explicit on the point that the captains and deans of Ghent had given judgment. The sentence was rendered in the presence of both benches of aldermen of Ghent, the dean of the weavers and two deputies of Bruges, and the regent and two deputies from Ypres. It was then confirmed by the magistrates of the three cities. The "drapers and weavers" were cloth merchants, some of them enrolled formally as weavers, as well as those who still made cloth. The two trades are hard to distinguish in most Flemish cities, and it is clear that the fullers, who were the "blue-collar" part of the textile industry, were suing for higher wages from those who hired and paid them, as they had been doing periodically since the 1340s.

In early 1383 the count's bailiff at Ypres fined nine men, eight of them drapers but only one a representative of the fullers, who had "been sent to Philip" in connection with the wage dispute. The fines were substantial but were justified instead of execution "because the trip cannot have affected my lord's interests much." Yet the composition of the Ypres delegation was reflected in the settlement, for the fullers' wage was confirmed at its customary level. The fullers apparently had also tried to prevent the drapers from using workers from outside Ypres whenever there was too much business for the local fullers to handle, but the ruling allowed them to do this.[42] There is thus even less evidence for Philip van Artevelde than for James as a promotor of "economic democracy."

Philip van Artevelde apparently remained in Ghent for much of September 1382. The city sent messengers specifically to the lord of Herzele and Raes van den Voerde at Oudenaarde on 20 September, which suggests that Philip was not there at that time. He was definitely back with the army at Edelare, how-

42. Documents printed CA 361–64; cf. *Rek. Gent 1376–1389*, 328.

ever, by 23 September. At some point in August or September, Philip van Artevelde sent an envoy to Charles VI's court asking for his arbitration, as we have seen; but this came to naught. Van Artevelde was clearly playing a double game, but the treatment of his messenger undeniably pushed him further toward an open English alliance. Yet a messenger from the French king came to Ghent on 13 September 1382, when van Artevelde was probably still in the city, and it is possible that negotiations were not completely stalled.

Embassies continued to cross the channel to and from the English court between August and October. Two aldermen of Ghent and a clerk went to England on 13 September, and on 29 September the alderman William de Otter went to Bruges "to examine the agreement between the king of England and the land of Flanders," a clear suggestion that some kind of provisional treaty had already been sealed. Philip van Artevelde did not go to Bruges personally, for on 30 September a separate delegation of magistrates went to the siege at Edelare "to speak to Philip van Artevelde and the good people generally."[43] The negotiations were sometimes conducted by delegations from Ghent alone, but the English understandably preferred to deal with representatives of all the Flemish cities.[44] On 14 October the three cities gave plenipotentiary powers to a delegation comprised of five men from Ghent, four from Bruges, and three from Ypres to negotiate on behalf of the three cities and the "common land" of Flanders. The embassy did not leave Ghent until 17 October, however, and the negotiators were accompanied by three other persons. On 16 October, between the appointment of the ambassadors and their departure, the French court, rather than the Flemings, offered new negotiations, evidently fearing both a winter campaign in marshy Flanders and the still present danger of an Anglo-Flemish alliance.[45] Although Philip van Artevelde was clearly informed of these de-

43. *Rek. Gent 1376–1389*, 329–30.
44. Ibid., 330; CA 365.
45. *Rek. Gent 1376–1389*, 330.

velopments, he was evidently not in Ghent at the time. Couriers seem to have gone regularly between Oudenaarde and Ghent, which are only twenty-five kilometers apart; on 15 October he rendered an arbitral judgment at Oudenaarde that was confirmed, at his request, by the aldermen of Ghent the next day.[46]

The decision to break relations with France in mid-October had been signaled by another of van Artevelde's peculiar moves. Peter van den Bossche and Peter de Winter had imprisoned several diplomats of Tournai at Bruges. In retaliation the aldermen of Tournai imprisoned some Courtraisiens but sent emissaries to van Artevelde to arrange an exchange. Van Artevelde received them civilly, but then he harangued them about Charles VI's seizure of his own envoy. When the Tournaisiens protested that this was a dead issue since the man was already back in Flanders, van Artevelde responded that Charles had released him only because he feared the Flemings. He gave a safe-conduct to these men but warned that until Oudenaarde and Dendermonde were surrendered to him, all French subjects who entered Flanders would be arrested.

On 20 October van Artevelde insisted again in a particularly arrogant response to Charles VI, written from Oudenaarde, that both Oudenaarde and Dendermonde be handed over to him as a condition for a settlement. He admitted negotiating with the English but placed the blame on Charles VI for having imprisoned his envoy. It was still not too late, but peace was possible only if Oudenaarde and Dendermonde were surrendered. He added in his letter to the king that no Tournaisiens might come to Flanders in the future save under safe-conduct; for "we know that you promote treason, especially against me, Philip, whom God preserve, and also make discord in the land." Curiously, on 22 October he wrote a more conciliatory letter to the city government of Tournai.[47]

If van Artevelde had a coherent plan in any of this, it escapes

---

46. CA 366–67.
47. Letter printed in *Rek. Gent 1376–1389*, 461–63. See also Froissart, *Chroniques*, vol. 10, chaps. 298–306, pp. 269–82.

our analysis. While he was doubtless in grave personal danger, the letter to Charles VI is the work of a paranoiac. Although he did not formally break off negotiations at this point, he informed the king that the imprisonment of his own envoy had caused him to open discussions with the English, although we have seen that he had been in contact with them since April. He seems to have decided to offer terms that he knew Charles VI could not accept. Under the circumstances, van Artevelde may have hoped to frighten the French by raising the specter of an English alliance for which he obviously still hoped but had thus far failed to materialize. It is hard to fault Fritz Quicke's assessment that "this tribune did not double as a diplomat."[48]

There now opens one of the more remarkable chapters in the history of Philip van Artevelde's diplomacy, one that symbolically brings his family saga full circle and suggests a touch of megalomania. On 17 October, three days before his arrogant letter to the French, he sent envoys with plenipotentiary powers to England. The instructions given to the envoys on 14 October have been preserved in the copy given to the English court, where the heading was appended "These are the points and articles of intent of Philip van Artevelde, the three good cities, and the entire county of Flanders." This language reveals clearly that the English thought of van Artevelde as the prince of Flanders, in a position to speak for all political units of the county. The envoys were to offer Richard II's government a military alliance, joint action against pirates, and access to the Flemish ports, with free traffic for merchants on both sides of the Channel. They also asked the English to transfer to them all exiles who had crossed to England from Flanders since 13 May (almost certainly an error in the transcription for 3 May) and pledged to hand over English exiles in Flanders. The envoys were also to ask the English for repayment of 140,000 pounds sterling that the Flemings had loaned them. Van Artevelde was apparently referring to funds that the Flemings and his father had given to Edward III in the 1340s. The Flemings also wanted

48. Quicke, *Pays-Bas*, 327–28.

the English wool staple moved from Calais to a place to be chosen by Ghent "and their [sic] successors," but for the first three years to Bruges. The English rejected these terms, evidently because of the two latter demands, and it is hard to believe that even Philip van Artevelde could have believed that Richard II's regents would take seriously such an arrogant demand from a man whose very life depended on English help. Still, the English sent a plenipotentiary at the beginning of November to negotiate further with the Flemings. But the French were able to prevent him from landing at Calais, and the only assistance that Philip van Artevelde ever received from the English was the pension of 100 marks that we discussed earlier and the dispatch of two hundred English archers from Calais to help at the siege of Oudenaarde.[49]

The last month of Philip van Artevelde's life requires little elaboration. He continued to display an interest in governance. He had been at Edelare on 24 October, when he received Peter van den Brouke "on account of the shippers." On 28 October he joined the aldermen in arbitrating a quarrel between the free shippers, whose privileges on the Leie and Scheldt had led to the outbreak of the war in 1379, and the "unfree shippers," who were confined to small boats in the Lieve canal that linked Ghent and Damme. Although he had taken the side of the wealthy weavers and drapers against the fullers at Ypres, he had no political motive for favoring the free shippers. Thus he issued regulations binding on both groups and postponed the settlement of contested fines, which had evidently been levied by the free shippers, until the armies returned.[50]

Van Artevelde realized that the French army was about to invade, and he went briefly to Bruges shortly after the settlement with the shippers, evidently around 29 October. He instructed Peter van den Bossche to guard the Leie river at Comines and Peter de Winter to proceed to nearby Warneton. Van

49. Froissart, *Chroniques*, vol. 10, chap. 297, pp. 267–69; Quicke, 333–35, for a thorough analysis of the English diplomatic documents; CA 368–70, for the instructions given to the envoys.
50. CA 371–72.

Artevelde himself went to Ypres on 30 or 31 October, where he
spent five days "haranguing the people in the open marketplace"
and holding out hope for English aid that he must have known
by now could not come in time. He then spent two days at
Courtrai and returned to Edelare, perhaps going to Ghent first,
arriving before 9 November. He apparently returned to Ghent
for final preparations the following week.[51]

The French army moved rapidly toward Flanders and crossed
the Leie river at Comines, probably on Monday 18 November.
Peter van den Bossche was seriously wounded in this engage-
ment and was taken back to Bruges. Van Artevelde heard the
news the next day and apparently got the impression that van
den Bossche was dead. On the advice of the lord of Herzele,
who had commanded the army during van Artevelde's trip
to Bruges the previous month, he made a quick trip to Ghent to
raise a larger force. On 20 November he returned from Ghent to
the army and the same day continued on toward Courtrai and
Diksmuide. He was at Courtrai on 21 November and at Wervik
on 22 November, showing clearly that he was chasing the
French army westward, not waiting for it to attack him. On 23
November the French took Ypres in a single assault and killed
the Ghent captains there, including van Artevelde's brother-in-
law, Peter van den Brouke.[52]

Despite the French invasion, it is likely that, if Philip van
Artevelde had stayed at Oudenaarde instead of going to meet
the French, he could at least have held out for the winter and
perhaps received English aid for the next campaigning season.

51. Froissart, *Chroniques*, vol. 10, chaps. 310–12, pp. 286–93, seems to have
an accurate relative chronology of Philip's movements. The Ghent accounts
suggest that he was with the army until at least 26 October. As some aldermen
were at Edelare with the army, he may have handled the arbitration there
without returning to Ghent. He was definitely back at Edelare by 9 November,
when he accompanied a delegation of magistrates to the siege; *Rek. Gent 1376–
1389*, 330–31.

52. Quicke, *Pays-Bas*, 337; *Rek. Gent 1376–1389*, 331, 335–36; Froissart,
Chroniques, vol. 11, chap. 325, p. 27, adds the detail that as he left Oudenaarde
he met the English herald John Chandos, who told him that English aid would
be coming as soon as Chandos and his companion got back to England.
Froissart evidently confused this embassy with the one in July.

The west Flemish terrain was marshy, and 1382 had been an especially rainy year. It was very late in the season for a campaign involving the heavy French horses and artillery, but van Artevelde, whose victory at the Beverhoutsveld in May had seemingly convinced him that he was a military genius, decided that he had to force a battle. This time he apparently did not even order prayers, contenting himself with giving a dinner for his captains the night before the battle and ordering them to take no one alive except the French king. Van Artevelde's decision to move is all the more curious in that the French were marching west, away from his army and toward Bruges, which suggests that they had only limited military objectives for this season. Van Artevelde proceeded from Courtrai toward Diksmuide but encountered the French at the village of Westrozebeke, just southwest of Roeselare and about halfway between Courtrai and Diksmuide. On Thursday, 27 November, the morning of the battle, he abandoned a strong position on a hill to try to attack the French, who trapped his soldiers in the morass between them (*Illust. 8*).

The Flemish defeat was total. Froissart claims that van Artevelde's body, found in a ditch by the French after a considerable search, bore no trace of a mortal wound and suggests that he may have been crushed to death in the stampede of his troops. The French hanged the corpse symbolically anyway, and the bailiff of Ypres put it on the wheel a week later. Bruges surrendered to the French two days later. But although the duke of Burgundy urged an assault on Ghent, the other French leaders preferred to go home on grounds that it was too late in the season, a decision that astonished even contemporaries. Peter van den Bossche and Peter de Winter escaped from Bruges, abandoning their chaplain and valet, who were decapitated by the French. With Francis Ackerman, who was returning from England at the time of the battle, they continued to direct the resistance of Ghent for another three years. Louis of Male knew from his spies that the surviving inhabitants of Ghent were totally demoralized and ready to submit in the aftermath of Westrozebeke, but he apparently had minimal influence on

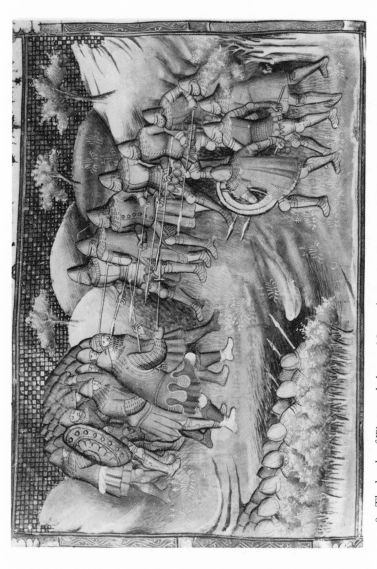

8. The battle of Westrozebeke, 27 November 1382. Courtesy Bibliothèque Municipale de Besançon, MS 865, fol. 135v.

French policy toward his own county.[53] As soon as the English received word of the Flemish defeat, they considered all agreements broken and ended negotiations.

An undercurrent to the hostilities in Flanders after 1379 had been the schism in the papacy. While the cities supported Pope Urban VI in Rome, their count and the French favored the Avignon papacy of Clement VII. In view of the obvious piety of Philip van Artevelde, it is curious that we have no direct indication of his stance, although he could hardly have had the stature at Ghent that he did had he favored Clement. It is thus particularly ironic that when significant English aid for Flanders finally did arrive, in the spring of 1383, it came not from the royal government but from the bishop of Norwich, who hoped to drive schismatics from Flanders. His "crusade" was a dismal failure. Ghent managed to hold out until peace was made at Tournai on 18 December 1385 and to obtain a general amnesty from the duke of Burgundy, who had succeeded his father-in-law, Louis of Male, as count of Flanders in 1384.

The meteoric public career of the van Artevelde family was extinguished with Philip. He died childless, the last male of his line. Of his nephews, the van Erpes had supported the count during the war, while the de Scoteleeres became tanners and played no political role. His widow married into a shipping family and also died without issue. The van Arteveldes left a legend, but no legacy.

53. CA 375–76, citing Flemish bailiffs' accounts; Quicke, *Pays-Bas*, 327; Froissart, *Chroniques*, vol. 11, chaps. 335–43, pp. 43–61; Stow, *Historia Ricardi Secundi*, 76.

CHAPTER 8

The Mirror or the Image?

No single individual before James van Artevelde had ever dominated Ghent to the extent that he did, bypassing the normal institutional structure of the city. After Philip van Artevelde, none would do so again. Both men were colossi, isolated and meteoric in their ascent and in their ephemerality.

There are obvious parallels between the two van Arteveldes, but also important differences. Our evaluation is clouded by the fact that scarcely anything is known of James before he took power at Ghent in early 1338. The city accounts enable us to reconstruct his activities as captain rather well, but few transactions of the aldermen survive from his period. Most of our information about his family connections is in sources written after his death. We know something of Philip's early years, and notably about his property and family alliances, most of it from charter evidence and the aldermen's registers. Philip's public career was much shorter and ended with a defeat more total than anything that James had ever suffered.

James died as a result of personal feuds in Ghent. The refusal to recognize the Prince of Wales as count of Flanders was simply a pretext to cloak the enmities that his personal conduct, some of which must be difficult for the most persistent of van Artevelde partisans to excuse, had aroused in his city. But his defeat did not mean the end of two essential aspects of his policy: alliance with England and control of Flanders by the three largest cities, which in turn were dominated by Ghent. A third line of policy that James had followed was a casualty of the conflicts after his death: reconciliation of the diverse elements of the citizenry and the participation of all groups recognized as corporations in the magistracy. It is most unlikely that anything he could have done would have tempered the hostility between weavers and fullers, although a firm alliance with the weavers in the spring of 1345 might have preserved his life for a few more years. But the textile industry of Ghent entered a severe decline with the suppression of the weavers in 1349, and it is unlikely that any government could have included both weavers and fullers after the 1350s.

Both van Arteveldes came to power in periods of turmoil as allies of the weavers, and in Philip's case this ascent was prompted at least in part by his father's memory. Both were violent, quixotic men. They were literate in both French and Flemish and pursued an active diplomacy. There is no direct evidence that either knew Latin, although if Philip was destined for holy orders at one time he would have been at least conversant with it. The surviving documentation permits us to determine the personal hostilities as well as the political issues involved in the assassinations attributable to Philip, whereas the reasons that drove James to murder are murkier. But while James had arisen as a conciliator whose task was to mediate between the counts' foreign policy and the cities' dependence on English wool, as well as between the weavers and the fullers, Philip was an overt party leader, or conceivably a party figurehead, whose major opponents were the shippers rather than the fullers.

For the great growth of the power of the shipping in Ghent is perhaps the most striking difference in the political and economic configuration of the city in 1381 from that in 1338. When James became captain, Ghent was not yet fighting the count. And when it became clear that van Artevelde could not survive a restoration of Louis of Nevers, the overly sanguine loyalties of much of the citizenry were offended. Philip van Artevelde rose and died as an opponent of the count, but by that time there was little serious sentiment in Ghent favoring Louis of Male except among the landowners.

Although James van Artevelde was not universally beloved, he seems to have worn his mantle of authority with more aplomb than his son, who did not really survive long enough to become accustomed to the graceful use of power. James's rule was at least accepted, however grudgingly, by most residents of the larger cities, and substantial parties favoring him emerged in Bruges and Ypres. But Philip was able to control the other cities only by force, and the domination of Bruges and Ypres by Ghent became intolerable during his brief period of supremacy. Both van Arteveldes relentlessly sacrificed the interests of the smaller cities and the rural areas to the policy imperatives of Ghent. Above all, the defeat of Philip van Artevelde meant the defeat of the Flemish cities' pretensions to independence. Count Louis of Male died before the war against Ghent was over, and the succession as count of his son-in-law, Duke Philip of Burgundy, meant the incorporation of the Flemings into a larger state that revolved in a French rather than an English orbit.

The van Arteveldes' desire to limit French influence in Flanders, an aspect of policy that was much stronger with Philip than with James, and their evident belief that the proper form of government for Flanders was for the count to act as a figurehead for the aspirations of the three great cities, certainly qualify them as heroic figures in the history of Flemish nationalism. But the claim so often made for them as democratic reformers is utterly groundless. Though James seems to have met with little opposition when he assumed power, he was in serious trouble by 1342 at the latest and had to protect himself with an enormous bodyguard. The chroniclers tell us unambiguously that half the population resisted Philip's captaincy in the beginning. While dissident elements in all occupations favored him, he had the virtually united support of only the weavers. Similarly, neither James nor Philip favored the economic aspirations of the lower classes. Although James was not opposed to political rights for the fullers, he consistently opposed their demands for higher wages. Neither man ever sided with the journeymen of any guild against the aristocratic masters, and Philip's hearth tax weighed more heavily on the poor than on the rich, a fact that did not escape contemporaries such as Froissart. That both James and Philip van Artevelde tried to assure supplies of grain and wool for Ghent says nothing other than that they wanted to prevent starvation, violent revolution, or both.

It is extremely significant that no strictly contemporary writer thought of James van Artevelde's rebellion as an uprising of the masses. Hostile though they were to him, these chroniclers portrayed him as an insolent parvenu who revolted against his legitimate lord, not as a champion of the lower orders. His fall and death in Ghent were due in large measure to personal hostilities kindled by his arrogant behavior.

In obvious contrast, the Flemish rebellion of the 1380s was one of several outbreaks against princely authority that struck fear into the hearts of society's rulers. There were revolts at Montpellier in 1379 and at Paris and Rouen in 1382, and the latter two were evidently inspired directly by the rebellion of Ghent against Count Louis of Male.[1] The disorders in his own cities reinforced the young king Charles VI's resolve to intervene in Flanders. The capital of the English king, Philip van Artevelde's would-be ally, was terrorized for three days in June 1381 by mobs of peasants and townsmen inflamed by the egalitarian doctrines of Lollard preachers, and other English cities experienced serious riots. Princes and prelates everywhere saw the established order in danger of collapsing through the misbehavior of the misbegotten masses. It is indicative of the existing climate of opinion that Froissart reports some English aristocrats expressing relief at the failure of the uprising in Flanders, even though their government had hoped to exploit the situation there to discomfit the French.[2]

1. Léon Mirot, *Les Insurrections urbaines au début du règne de Charles VI (1380–1383): Leurs causes, leurs conséquences* (Paris, 1905), pp. 84, 144–45, 159–64.
2. Froissart, *Chroniques*, vol. 11, chap. 348, p. 68.

In stark contrast to Edward III's reaction to James' death in 1345, there was no regret in London at the passing of Philip van Artevelde, who seems to have become a monumental embarrassment to the English. Philip's personality inspired a visceral loathing in his opponents that far exceeded the essentially political hostility directed by persons outside Ghent toward his father. He symbolized an age, an outlook, and a menace. Within weeks of his death, the commissioners in charge of the massive confiscations of his adherents' property were commonly referring to 1382 as "Phil's time." Thus, although the Flemish revolt was essentially a political struggle among privileged groups and had a much less clearly "social" character than did the other outbreaks of the 1380s, the timing of the rebellion of Ghent and Philip van Artevelde's association with it were instrumental in the subsequent association of the van Artevelde name with the lower classes. Although posterity's legend of the van Arteveldes as democrats has been focused largely on James, Philip's career actually seems to have loomed larger in such perceptions among their contemporaries.

Both van Arteveldes may have played the prince during their ascendancy, but the evidence for this is much clearer with James than with Philip, for whom we have only the testimony of Froissart and the fact that he, like his father, had a larger bodyguard than the other captains and was furnished a more luxurious uniform. There is no evidence that James van Artevelde ever leaned on any ally, even Gelnoot van Lens, to the extent that Philip probably depended on Peter van den Bossche. Yet our only evidence on this point is Froissart's Chronicle, and the facts that the two men had little contact after 25 May 1382 and that van Artevelde modified some of van den Bossche's orders for Bruges, evidently without consulting him, suggest that even if he had assumed power as van den Bossche's creature in December or January, he quickly asserted his own independence. The most conspicuous, if hitherto least understood, motive for the deeds of Philip van Artevelde was his consciousness of his family responsibilities and his solemn duty to avenge all unatoned wrongs done to the van Arteveldes, most specifically his father's murder. Whether family concerns may have been behind any of James's violent deeds must remain an unanswered question, for the records of the aldermen, which are our major source in reconstructing Philip van Artevelde's family concerns and feuds, do not survive for the period preceding James's public career. Yet James's murder of Fulk uten Rosen does seem to have been motivated by the grievance that his brother William bore against the victim and suggests a consciousness of family responsibilities that is more clearly provable for his son.

No institutional innovation can be attributed clearly to either van Artevelde, although both seem to have had some talent for administration. James was extremely conservative and retained the count's governing institutions, making only changes in personnel. He preferred to work behind the scenes and usually stayed in Ghent, whereas Philip acted more openly and was more often away from the city. Philip, indeed, cannot be proved to have been in Ghent for more than a few days at any one time after 3 July 1382, a fact suggesting that he may have been surer of his position at home than his father had been. But although his tenure of power was much briefer than James's, Philip may have been more interested in the mechanics of governance, and there are suggestions that he may have thought not only of collecting revenues owed to the count—which his father had also done—but also of establishing new sources of income. James definitely set overall lines of policy that were implemented by others, but we have more evidence of Philip intervening directly in matters of administration, justice, and governance.

We cannot be certain of the basis upon which aldermen were chosen in the period of James van Artevelde. The small guilds assumed a position of great power early in the 1330s, but evidently before James van Artevelde became captain and as a consequence of the growing importance of the local market. The "quarter" concept seems to have been formulated in James's period, although as a natural outgrowth of the "five-mile" monopoly privileges that the great cities had enjoyed for their textile industries for some years. The tone of lèse majesté that

Philip van Artevelde adopted in demanding the surrender of Oudenaarde and Dendermonde shows that he considered east Flanders the domain of Ghent and himself its prince. The landowners became the third member of the urban body politic during Philip's ascendancy, after having functioned intermittently in that capacity earlier. Both "tribunes" placed revolutionary captains or regents, most of them citizens of Ghent, in charge of all local governments, rural and urban, large and small, but aside from this they did not alter local governing structures. On balance, we are left more curious about what turn Flemish policy might have taken if Philip van Artevelde had won the battle of Westrozebeke than if James had escaped the assassin's axe.

The case of the van Arteveldes of Ghent and Baasrode is an object lesson illustrating man's eternal quest for a glory transcending his own mundane, terrestrial reality. Heroes are made in the future but must live in the past. For, unlike a condition admitted as future, heroism must be seen as fact. It cannot be speculative. Heroes must thus be situated in past time to serve the inspirational imperatives of a transcendent world beyond the present. The present does not exist for the hero or his creator.

The biases of posterity create and sustain the myth of the hero. No public figure becomes a hero in history unless he foreshadowed or can be seen dimly to anticipate the guiding prejudices of later generations. Charlemagne is a hero because he conquered, governed effectively in the context of his time, seems to have had an embryonic world vision; and above all because he patronized the church and the clergy. This guaranteed him the accolades of contemporary writers of history, most of whom were in holy orders, and struck a sympathetic chord among most later scholars who have studied his period. Giangaleazzo Visconti of Milan is not a hero because the bias of most historians is, with a disconcertingly typical inconsistency, toward both democracy and Florence. We honor Pericles, who subverted democratic institutions but did so with oratorical flourishes as he paid conspicuous court to "the people."

Heroes are rarely leaders of small groups. Some—the tragic heroes such as Joan of Arc or Thomas More, whose careers ended in failure but who seem grander to posterity—expounded or seemed to embody notions that transcended the bounds of their own times. Most who did enjoy success, such as Charlemagne and perhaps Richard the Lion Hearted, incarnated the values of their contemporaries, or at least of their own social order, but did so in a way that made possible the distortion of the posthumous folk memory of their deeds to make them appear prescient. Their fellow-citizens thought of them as leaders, as men of power, not as visionaries heralding a new age.

The urban revolution of the central Middle Ages and the accompanying population increase together constitute one of the great turning points of European history. Since then, scarcely ever has a figure attained heroic dimensions who did not show mass appeal at some point in his career, either by manipulating the public or by inspiring it to deeds thought great by contemporaries or particularly by posterity. The involvement of such figures with "the people," generally leading a public if not a popular movement against considerable odds, thus facilitates the mythmakers' task of apotheosizing them as "democrats." Heroes die well. Some, like Philip van Artevelde, perish before the shortcomings of their policies get them into difficulties with their constituencies. The reputations of others, such as the otherwise totally dissimilar James van Artevelde and Abraham Lincoln, may owe as much to their martyrdom as to their deeds, abilities, or ideals.

The growth of nationalism and ethnic consciousness has fostered the cult of heroes from the pasts of groups that eventually became, or attempted to become, the nucleus of states. The stark violence of the medieval period spawned a peculiarly rich plethora of national heroes. Clovis, Charlemagne, Alfred the Great, and Frederick Barbarossa are only a few who spring immediately to mind. Closer to the van Arteveldes' period, we have the religious reformer John Hus, whose career inspired a nationalist movement in Bohemia, and King Henry V of England, a conqueror with a sense of divine mission. Nationalism and military victory have enshrined some improbable personalities in the pantheon of heroes, such as the cowardly, treacherous, neurotic, and extremely lucky King Philip Augustus of France.

The Flemish national movement affords us a peculiarly instructive example of the need of nationalism to create heroes, perhaps because it ultimately failed to produce a nation. Nationalist sentiment is fostered by community of language. Yet the county of Flanders was not the only part of the Low Countries where Flemish was spoken in the Middle Ages, and except between 1305 and 1369 it also had a substantial French-speaking minority population. There is evidence of ethnic hostility between the French and Flemings in Flanders as early as the tenth century, and Flemish resentment of the French was extremely strong long before the van Arteveldes' time.

The borders of most modern states have been drawn more to accommodate political expediency than to recognize ethnic imperatives, but the Belgium established in 1830 was an extreme case. It was a fatherland embracing two mutually antagonistic language groups of nearly equal strength, under a king who belonged to neither, and subordinating the larger population to the smaller on grounds of alleged cultural inferiority and backwardness. The shabby treatment that the Flemings received in Belgium during the nineteenth century makes perfectly understandable the attractive power of a pair of men who had died fighting French influence in Flanders in a distant past.

Yet the reputations of most heroes do not stand up well under close scrutiny of their deeds on earth; for heroism is mythology, a considerably more selective art than history. Although there are some exceptions, most men are not enshrined as heroes until many years and sometimes centuries after their deaths, when their conspicuous deeds have entered the folk memory for timely evocation, but when their faults can be resurrected only by careful detective work in incomplete historical records. No one can deny the van Arteveldes the distinction of having defended Flanders against the French and led Ghent to dominate Bruges, Ypres, and rural Flanders. Yet our investigation has shown that while James came to power to meet a public emergency, he used his office for personal aggrandizement, although apparently not for pecuniary gain, and took whatever measures, including homicide, he considered necessary to maintain his position. Philip van Artevelde, too, assumed power during a crisis, but he took steps to resolve it only after he had used the resources of the city government to avenge his family's honor on the eldest male descendants of those whom he held responsible for his father's murder.

The fact that Charlemagne's court historian claimed proudly that his hero had slaughtered 4,500 Saxons who had resisted his authority has been known to historians since 782. The figure is probably exaggerated, but the error comes from the inadequacy of the means at Charlemagne's disposal, not impurity of intent. The royal hero wanted posterity to believe that he had committed mass murder. Yet the incident has not diminished Charlemagne's posthumously heroic stature in the least. What the Saxons who escaped him may have thought of their resplendent conquerer is not recounted to us in the surviving sources, all of which come from the Christian side. Even if Saxon sources had been preserved, most medieval historians would dismiss them as anachronistic lamentations against the inexorable march of the Christian God in history. A millennium later, Charlemagne is even revered in Saxony. Yet in the context of his time this horrendous massacre makes him no less a butcher than more recent figures whose blood lust has not yet faded from the public consciousness. Will these men, now conceded even by their own peoples to have been monstrous villains, be honored as heroes at some time in the future, when those who sympathized with their victims have been silenced by death and the selectivity of the records kept by history's victors?

This book has been a work of history, necessarily based on a combination of records that the van Arteveldes wanted to survive, others to which they were indifferent, and still others whose composition and preservation were beyond their control. It has discussed the achievements of the van Arteveldes, but it has emphasized them as men, creatures of their time, who shared with their contemporaries an exaggerated consciousness of their own blood as reality and symbol and an evidently unquenchable thirst for that of others. But exposure of the personal flaws of the van Arteveldes will not tarnish them in the eyes of folk ideologues anywhere. For objective existence in history is reserved to mortal men. The hero exists in the mind, outside history.

Bibliography

Documents

MANUSCRIPT SOURCES

Algemeen Rijksarchief (General Archives of the Realm), Brussels
  Roll Accounts 1367, 1384: Bailiffs of Ghent
  2407: Bailiff of Bornem
Archive of Church of St. James, Ghent
  Charters
  647: Rent book, 1370
Rijksarchief te Gent (State Archive of Ghent)
  Church of St. Michael
    Charters
  Church of St. Nicholas
    SN 118: Cartulary
    SN rollen 122, 128, 131: Holy Ghost Accounts
  Bishopric
    K 2533: Ledger of leaseholders at Weert, 1395
  St. Veerle Chapter
    Charters
  Abbey Groenen Briel
    Charters

Stadsarchief te Gent (Municipal Archive of Ghent)
  [ser.] 152, nos. 2–5: Rent books, ca. 1360–1404
  156, no. 1: Wijsdommen der dekenen
  160, no. 6: Guild book of brewers
  190–1: Guild book of carpenters
  301, nos. 1–12: Registers of aldermen of the *Keure*
  330, nos. 1–9: Registers of aldermen of *gedele*, with *Zoendincboeken*
(Atonement Books)
  400, nos. 9–10: Municipal Accounts, 1365–76
  Wenemaers hospital
    Charters
    Wool weavers' almshouse and chapel
      268: Rent book, 1390s
Episcopal Archive, Bruges
  Sint-Donaas, A 48, Acta Capituli
  G 1, Accounts
Municipal Archive, Bruges
  Municipal Account 1382–83

PUBLISHED SOURCES

Calendar of the Close Rolls, Preserved in the Public Record Office. Edward III. 14 vols. London: HMSO, 1896–1913.
Calendar of the Close Rolls, Preserved in the Public Record Office. Richard II. 6 vols. London: HMSO, 1914–27.
Calendar of the Patent Rolls, Preserved in the Public Record Office. Edward III. 16 vols. London: HMSO, 1891–1916.
Calendar of the Patent Rolls, Preserved in the Public Record Office. Richard II. 6 vols. London: HMSO, 1895–1909.
de Pauw, Napoléon, ed. *Cartulaire historique et généalogique des Artevelde.* Brussels: Kiessling, 1920.
———, ed. *De Voorgeboden der stad Gent in de XIVe eeuw (1337–1382).* Ghent: C. Annoet-Braeckman, 1885.
———, and Julius Vuylsteke, eds., *De Rekeningen der stad Gent. Tijdvak van Jacob van Artevelde, 1336–1349.* 3 vols. Ghent: H. Hoste, 1874–85.
Espinas, Georges, and Henri Pirenne, eds. *Recueil de documents relatifs à l'histoire de l'industrie drapière en Flandre.* 4 vols. Brussels: Commission Royale d'Histoire, 1906–24.
Fris, Victor, ed. *Dagboek van Gent.* 2 vols. Ghent: C. Annoet-Braeckman, 1901–04.

Froissart, Jean. *Chroniques.* Publiées pour la Société de l'Histoire de France. 15 vols. Paris: Jules Renouard and successors, 1869–1975.
Limburg-Stirum, Thierry, Comte de, ed. *Cartulaire de Louis de Male, comte de Flandre, 1348 à 1358.* 2 vols. Bruges: Louis de Plancke, 1898–1901.
Lyon, Mary, Bryce Lyon, and Henry S. Lucas, eds., with the collaboration of Jean de Sturler. *The Wardrobe Book of William de Norwell 12 July 1338 to 27 May 1340.* Brussels: Commission Royale d'Histoire, 1983.
Pirenne, Henri, ed. *Chronique rimée des troubles de Flandre en 1379–1380.* Ghent: A. Siffer, 1902.
Stow, George B., Jr., ed. *Historia Vitae Et Regni Ricardi Secundi.* Philadelphia: University of Pennsylvania Press, 1977.
van der Meersch, P., ed. *Memorieboek der stad Gent.* 4 vols. Ghent: C. Annoet-Braeckman, 1852–61.
van Werveke, Alfons, ed. *Gentse Stads- en Baljuwsrekeningen (1351–1364).* Brussels: Commission Royale d'Histoire, 1970.
Vuylsteke, Julius, ed. *Gentsche Stads- en Baljuwsrekeningen, 1280–1336.* Ghent: F. Meyer-Van Loo, 1900.
———, ed. *De Rekeningen der stad Gent. Tijdvak van Philips van Artevelde, 1376–1389.* Ghent: A. Hoste, 1893.

PUBLISHED INVENTORY

Nélis, Hubert. *Chambre des Comptes de Flandre et de Brabant. Inventaire des Comptes en Rouleaux.* Brussels: Goemaere, 1914.

LITERATURE

Barel, Yves. *La Ville médiévale. Système social. Système urbain.* Grenoble: Presses Universitaires de Grenoble, 1977.
Blockmans, W. P. *De Volksvertegenwoordiging in Vlaanderen in de Overgang van Middeleeuwen naar Nieuwe Tijden (1384–1506).* Verhandelingen van de Koninklijke Academie voor Wetenschappen, Letteren en Schone Kunsten van België, Klasse der Letteren, jaargang 40, no. 90. Brussels: Paleis der Academiën, 1978.
Carson, Patricia. *James van Artevelde. The Man from Ghent.* Ghent: E. Story-Scientia, 1980.
de Muynck, R. "De Gentse Oorlog (1379–1385). Oorzaken en karakter." *HMGOG,* n.s. 5 (1951): 305–18.
de Pauw, Napoléon. "L'Assassinat d'Artevelde et l'instruction de ce crime." *Cour d'Appel de Gand,* 4. Ghent: A. Hoste, 1905.

de Pauw, Napoléon. *Audenarde sous Artevelde.* Oudenaarde: Bever-
naege, 1916.

――――. *Conspiration d'Audenarde sous Jacques van Artevelde (1342). Critique historique.* Ghent: Hoste, 1878.

――――."L'Enquête sur les capitaines de Courtrai sous Artevelde (1338–
1340)." *Bulletin de la Commission Royale d'Histoire* 79 (1910): 219–91.

de Potter, Frans. *Gent van den oudsten tijd tot heden.* 8 vols. Ghent: 1883–
1901.

Laslett, Peter. *The World We Have Lost. England before the Industrial Age.*
3d ed. New York: Charles Scribner's Sons, 1984.

Lucas, Henry S. *The Low Countries and the Hundred Years War, 1326–
1347.* Ann Arbor: University of Michigan Press, 1929.

――――. "The Sources and Literature on Jacob Van Artevelde." *Speculum* 8 (1933): 125–49.

Mirot, Léon. *Les Insurrections urbaines au début du règne de Charles VI
(1380–1383). Leurs causes, leurs conséquences.* Paris: Albert Fonte-
moing, 1905.

Mollat, Michel, and Philippe Wolff. *The Popular Revolutions of the Late
Middle Ages.* Translated by A. L. Lytton-Sells. London: Allen &
Unwin, 1973.

Nicholas, David. "Artevelde, Jacob van, kapitein van Gent." In *Nationaal Biografisch Woordenboek* 5 (1971): cols. 21–36.

――――. "Crime and Punishment in Fourteenth-Century Ghent." *Revue
Belge de Philologie et d'Histoire* 48 (1970): 289–334, 1141–76.

――――. *The Domestic Life of a Medieval City: Women, Children, and the
Family in Fourteenth-Century Ghent.* Lincoln: University of Nebraska
Press, 1985.

――――. *The Metamorphosis of a Medieval City: Ghent in the Age of the
Arteveldes, 1302–1390.* Lincoln: University of Nebraska Press; Leiden: E. J. Brill, 1987.

――――. "The Scheldt Trade and the 'Ghent War' of 1379–1385," *Bulletin de la Commission Royale d'Histoire* 144 (1978): 189–359.

――――. *Town and Countryside: Social, Economic, and Political Tensions in
Fourteenth-Century Flanders.* Bruges: De Tempel, 1971.

――――. "Weert: A Scheldt Polder Village in the Fourteenth Century."
Journal of Medieval History 2(1976):239–68.

Packe, Michael. *King Edward III.* London: Routledge & Kegan Paul,
1983.

Palmer, J. J. N. *England, France and Christendom, 1377–99.* Chapel Hill:
University of North Carolina Press, 1972.

Pirenne, Henri. *Histoire de Belgique.* Vol. 1, *Des origines au commencement du XIVe siècle,* 5th ed. Brussels: M. Lamertin, 1929. Vol. 2, *Du*

Commencement du XIVe siècle à la mort de Charles le Témeraire. 3d ed. Brussels: M. Lamertin, 1922.

Quicke, Fritz. *Les Pays-Bas à la veille de la période Bourguignonne (1356–1384).* Brussels: Editions Universitaires, 1947.

Rogghé, Paul. "De Democraat Jacob Van Artevelde. Pionier van het Vlaamsnationaal bewustzijn." *Appeltjes van het Meetjesland* 14 (1963): 56–68.

———. "Het eerste bewind der Gentse Hoofdmannen (1319–1329)." *Appeltjes van het Meetjesland* 12 (1961): 1–47.

———. "Gemeente ende Vrient. Nationale Omwentelingen in de XIVe eeuw." *Annales de la Société d'Emulation de Bruges* 89 (1952): 101–35.

———. "Het Gentsche Stadsbestuur van 1302 tot 1345. En een en ander betreffende het Gentsche Stadspatriciaat." *HMGOG*, n.s. 1 (1944): 135–63.

———. "De Gentse Klerken in de XIVe en XV eeuw. Trouw en Verraad." *Appeltjes van het Meetjesland* 11 (1960): 5–142.

———. "De Samenstelling der Gentse Schepenbanken in de 2e helft der 14e eeuw. En een en ander over de Gentse poorterie." *HMGOG*, n.s. 4 (1950): 22–31.

———. *Vlaanderen en het zevenjarig beleid van Jacob van Artevelde. Een critische-historische studie.* 2 vols. Brussels: A. Manteau, 1942.

Vanderkindere, Léon. *Le Siècle des Artevelde: Etudes sur la civilisation morale & politique de la Flandre & du Brabant.* Brussels: A.-N. Lebègue, 1879.

Vander Maesen, M. "Vlaanderen en Henegouwen onder het Huis van Dampierre." In *Algemene Geschiedenis der Nederlanden*, 2:399–440. 2d ed. Haarlem: Fibula-Van Dishoeck, 1982.

———, and D. Nicholas. "Lodewijk van Male." In *Nationaal Biografisch Woordenboek* 6 (Brussels: Paleis der Academiën, 1974): cols. 575–85.

van Herwaarden, Jan. "The War in the Low Countries." In J. J. N. Palmer, ed., *Froissart: Historian*, pp. 101–17. Totowa, N.J.: Rowman & Littlefield, 1981.

van Oost, Angeline. "Sociale Stratifikatie van de Gentse Opstandelingen van 1379–1385. Een kritische benadering van konfiskatiedokumenten." *HMGOG*, n.s. 29 (1975): 59–92.

van Werveke, Hans. *Ambachten en Erfelijkheid.* Mededelingen der Koninklijke Vlaamse Academie, Klasse der Letteren, 4, no. 1. Brussels: Paleis der Academiën, 1942.

———. *De Gentsche Stadsfinanciën in de Middeleeuwen.* Brussels: Paleis der Academiën, 1934.

————. *Jacques Van Artevelde*. Brussels: La Renaissance du Livre, 1942. Dutch translation *Jacob Van Artevelde*. The Hague: Kruseman, 1963.

————. *De Koopman-ondernemer en de ondernemer in de Vlaamsche laken-nijverheid van de Middeleeuwen*. Mededelingen van de Koninklijke Vlaamse Academie, 8, no. 4. Antwerp: Vlaamse Academie, 1946.

Vermeulen, J. "De groei en de bloei van de Arteveldefiguur in de Vlaamsche Volksziel," *Oostvlaamsche Zanten* 13 (1938): 101–208.

Vuylsteke, Julius. "De goede Disendach. 13 Januari 1349." *HMGOG* 1 (1895): 9–47.

INDEX

All personal names refer to citizens of Ghent unless otherwise indicated.